Cambodia's Neoliberal Order

Neoliberal economics have emerged in the post-Cold War era as the predominant ideological tenet applied to the development of countries in the Global South. For much of the Global South, however, the promise that markets will bring increased standards of living and emancipation from tyranny has been an empty one. Instead, neoliberalisation has increased the gap between rich and poor and unleashed a firestorm of social ills.

This book addresses the relationship between 'post-conflict' geographies of violence, authoritarianism, and neoliberalisation in Cambodia. Applying a geographical analysis to contemporary Cambodian politics, the author employs notions of public space and radical democracy as the most substantive components of its theoretical edifice. He argues that the promotion of unfettered marketization is the foremost causal factor in the country's inability to consolidate democracy following a United Nations-sponsored transition. The book demonstrates Cambodian perspectives on the role of public space in Cambodia's process of democratic development and explains the implications of violence and its relationship with neoliberalism.

Taking into account the transition from war to peace, authoritarianism to democracy, and command economy to a free market, this book offers a critical appraisal of the political economy in Cambodia.

Simon Springer is Assistant Professor in the Department of Geography at the National University of Singapore. His ongoing research focuses on the intersections between neoliberalism and violence.

Routledge Pacific Rim geographies

Series Editors: John Connell, Lily Kong and John Lea

Cambodia's Neoliberal Order

Violence, authoritarianism, and the contestation of public space

Simon Springer

LONDON AND NEW YORK

First published 2010
by Routledge
2 Park Square, Milton Park, Abingdon, Oxon OX14 4RN

Simultaneously published in the USA and Canada
by Routledge
711 Third Avenue, New York, NY 10017

*Routledge is an imprint of the Taylor & Francis Group,
an informa business*

First issued in paperback 2012

© 2010 Simon Springer

Typeset in Times by
RefineCatch Limited, Bungay, Suffolk

British Library Cataloguing in Publication Data
A catalogue record for this book is available from the British Library

Library of Congress Cataloging-in-Publication Data
Springer, Simon.
    Cambodia's neoliberal order : violence, authoritarianism, and the
    contestation of public space / Simon Springer.
        p. cm.—(Routledge Pacific Rim geographies ; 8)
    Includes bibliographical references and index.
    1. Cambodia—Politics and government.   2. Cambodia—Social
    conditions.   3. Cambodia—Economic conditions.
    4. Neoliberalism—Cambodia.   5. Democracy—Cambodia.
    6. Social conflict—Cambodia.   I. Title.
    JQ935.S67 2010
    306.209596—dc22   2009052576

ISBN 978–0–415–56819–7 (hbk)
ISBN 978-0-415-62753-5 (pbk)
ISBN 978–0–203–84896–8 (ebk)

For Om Savee

Contents

Tables

Acknowledgments

Barry Riddell at Queen's University showed remarkable faith in my abilities and his marvellous humor and careful guidance throughout the early stages of this process have been invaluable. My time at Queen's was further enriched by many individuals, where John Holmes, Anne Godlewska, Audrey Kobayashi, Peter Goheen, Villia Jefremovas, Bruce Berman, Brendan Sweeney, and Sarah de Leeuw all stand out as having been instrumental in the conception and implementation of this project. Joan Knox, Kathy Hoover, Sharon Mohammed, and Sheila MacDonald all deserve recognition, not only for making me feel welcome in the department, but also for their help in cutting through all the red tape while I was overseas. My experience at Queen's University would never have occurred if not for the fantastic people in the Geography department at UNBC. Gail Fondahl, Neil Hanlon, and Wim Kok provided much motivation and encouragement, while Catherine Nolin in particular has inspired me through her commitments to social justice in Central America and a genuine enthusiasm for learning.

Judy Ledgerwood and Steve Heder both offered invaluable input on this project at an early stage. I am grateful to both of them for sharing their experiences in Cambodia with the ethics committee and myself so that this project could take flight. Sorpong Peou and Caroline Hughes have also provided valuable comments and criticisms on my work over the last few years, and both are inspirational in their passion for Cambodian studies. In the later stages of this project, Philippe Le Billon, Jamie Peck, Jim Glassman, and Derek Gregory provided much encouragement, support, and critical feedback during my time at the University of British Columbia.

Thank you to Vladimir Bessarabov and the Cartographic Section at the United Nations for allowing me to reproduce their map of Cambodia. Many thanks to Suzanne Richardson, Jillian Morrison, Sue Dickenson and Dorothea Schaefter for their editorial assistance and enthusiasm for this project. I am similarly grateful to the editors of the Routledge Pacific Rim Geographies series, John Connell, Lily Kong, and John Lea, for agreeing to publish my book alongside such a great body of scholarship. I also extend my appreciation to the anonymous referees who offered insightful comments and challenged me to rise to their critiques.

In Cambodia, Oun Rithy, Sopheak Seang, Kong Sopeak, and Phon Navin all displayed remarkable dedication to this project, and without their assistance, this research could not have been completed. I am also indebted to the many friends I have made in Cambodia over the years. There are far too many of you to name, but it is your gracious hospitality that has made Cambodia my second home. Back in Canada, Matthew Redekop from HOPE International is responsible for first introducing me to Cambodia through my participation in their UNION program. Former Canadian Ambassador to Cambodia, Gordon Longmuir, who shows a remarkable continuing dedication to the country, has been most willing to share his perspectives and listen to mine, even if we agree only sometimes. And Phangsy Nou has been a wonderful teacher of the Khmer language and a very dear friend.

I thank my mother-in-law Brenda for accepting me into her family and continuing to support me through my scholarly pursuits. My father-in-law Garry has shown a keen interest in my work, for which I am grateful. I have endlessly competed with my brother since the moment I first joined this world. However, Stevan has always been two steps ahead, and has unknowingly been my idol throughout my entire life. My Mom and Dad have given me a wonderful life of opportunity, and for this, I love you both very much. My Mom has always encouraged me to "follow my bliss", wherever it should take me, even if it regrettably means I might not make it home for Christmas some years. My Dad is the original geographer in my life, and his homemade "what's the capital of" game fired my imagination as a child and ultimately steered me down this path.

My daughter Solina and my son Odin are the two greatest joys my life has ever known. Each child has taken a hold of my soul in ways that I could never have possibly imagined prior to becoming a father. I wouldn't trade all the diaper changes, sleepless nights, and crying fits for anything, because every single moment spent with each of you is a blessing. You make me proud to be your father each and every day, and your wide-eyed innocence fills my heart with elation and renews my faith in humanity. I love you both with every ounce of my being.

Finally, and most importantly, I would like to thank my best friend and the love of my life, Marni. Without you, the flowers would not bloom, the birds would not sing, and the sun would never rise. Your support and assistance in every aspect of this project has made it infinitely better than it otherwise would have been, and your adoration, devotion, and patience is responsible for my courage to begin this research in the first place. You are the light at the end of the tunnel, the beacon fire in the dark, the glimmer of hope, and truly the meaning of my life. I will love you until the end of time.

Abbreviations

ADB	Asian Development Bank
ADHOC	Cambodian Human Rights and Development Association
ASEAN	Association of Southeast Asian Nations
BLDP	Buddhist Liberal Democratic Party
CFF	Cambodian Freedom Fighters
CGDK	Coalition Government of Democratic Kampuchea
CGM	Consultative Group Meeting
CPK	Communist Party of Kampuchea
CPP	Cambodian People's Party
DK	Democratic Kampuchea
ESAFs	enhanced structural adjustment facilities
FBI	Federal Bureau of Investigation
FTU	Free Trade Union of Workers of the Kingdom of Cambodia
FUNCINPEC	National United Front for an Independent, Neutral, Peaceful, and Cooperative Cambodia
IFIs	international financial institutions
IMF	International Monetary Fund
KNP	Khmer Nation Party
NEC	National Election Committee
NGOs	nongovernmental organizations
NICs	newly industrialized countries
PDK	Party of Democratic Kampuchea
PPA	Paris Peace Agreements
PRGFs	poverty reduction and growth facilities
PRK	People's Republic of Kampuchea
RGC	Royal Government of Cambodia
SACs	structural adjustment credits
SAPs	structural adjustment programs
SOC	State of Cambodia
SRP	Sam Rainsy Party
UN	United Nations
UNTAC	United Nations Transitional Authority in Cambodia
US	United States of America
WTO	World Trade Organization

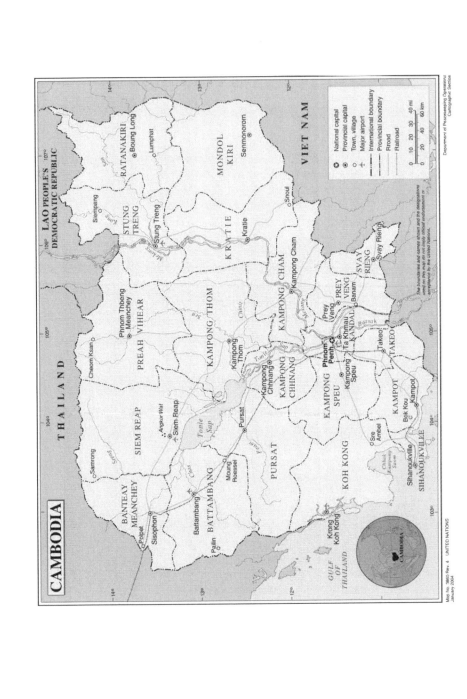

CAMBODIA

THAILAND

LAO PEOPLE'S DEMOCRATIC REPUBLIC

VIET NAM

RATANAKIRI
Boung Long
Lumphat

MONDOL KIRI
Senmonorom

STUNG TRENG
Siempang
Stung Treng

KRATIE
Kratie
Snoul

Cheom Ksan

PREAH VIHEAR
Phnom Tbeng Meanchey

KAMPONG THOM
Kampong Thom

KAMPONG CHAM
Kampong Cham

SIEM REAP
Angkor Wat
Siem Reap

BANTEAY MEANCHEY
Sisophon
Poipet

BATTAMBANG
Battambang
Pailin
Moung Roessei

PURSAT
Pursat

Tonle Sap

Samrong

KAMPONG CHHNANG
Kampong Chhnang

Phnom Penh

PREY VENG
Prey Veng
Banam

SVAY RIENG
Svay Rieng

KANDAL
Ta Khmau

KAMPONG SPEU
Kampong Speu

TAKEO
Takeo

KAMPOT
Kampot
Bok Kou

KOH KONG
Krong Koh Kong

Sre Ambel

SIHANOUKVILLE
Sihanoukville

GULF OF THAILAND

CAMBODIA

National capital
Provincial capital
Town, village
Major airport
International boundary
Provincial boundary
Road
Railroad

0 10 20 30 40 mi
0   20   40   60 km

The boundaries and names shown and the designations used on this map do not imply official endorsement or acceptance by the United Nations.

Map No. 3860 Rev. 4   UNITED NATIONS
January 2004

Department of Peacekeeping Operations
Cartographic Section

1   Introduction

Setting the stage for neoliberalization

> You want others to become petrified from fear of your power, to be apprehensive of and praise your courage; but your status will not be as you assume, what you will have is only self-destruction.
>
> – Cambodian Proverb.

The small Southeast Asian country of Cambodia (formerly known as Kampuchea) has suffered tremendously in recent years. Cambodia's 30-year civil war during the latter part of the twentieth century has had an enduring effect on the collective memory of the Cambodian people. Indeed, the psychological scarring and unspeakable suffering caused by the infamous Khmer Rouge and their four-year reign of terror in the late 1970s is a national commonality. In a population of seven million at the time, over one and a half million people died as a direct result of Khmer Rouge policy and administration (Banister and Johnson 1993; Chandler 1996; Heuveline 2001; Kiernan 1996). Less well known to most of the world is that this atrocity was preceded by another of comparable magnitude. From 1969 to 1973 the United States (US) reprehensibly and mercilessly bombed the neutral country in an effort to flush out Viet Cong forces thought to be operating from within Cambodia, leaving an estimated 600,000 Cambodians dead (Herman 1997; Kiljunen 1984). Thus, the Cambodian holocaust had two distinct stages in what a Finnish government report refers to as "the decade of the genocide" (Kiljunen 1984). The Cambodian genocide was followed by ten long years of silence at the international level, as it was Vietnamese communist forces that had brought down the Khmer Rouge regime (Chandler 1991; 1996; Kiernan 1996). Throughout the 1980s Cambodia was governed as Hanoi's client state, and accordingly, with Cold War geopolitics continuing to command the foreign policy agendas of Global North governments, Cambodia and its recent holocaust were largely ignored. As the Iron Curtain fell in 1989, the global political climate shifted. Accordingly, the Cambodian question that had been allowed to fester for a decade could finally be answered. Democracy came to Cambodia in 1991 under a United Nations (UN) sponsored transition that was intended to provide a final solution to the country's ongoing civil war.

However, peace remains a relative term as politically motivated killings are frequent during election times and often go unpunished. Amnesty International (1997: np) calls Cambodia's pervasive impunity "a cancer at the heart of national life," while political violence has disgraced every single election the country has held since Vietnam's occupation of Cambodia ended in 1989. Inducing sentiments of intense fear and vehement loathing, state-sponsored violence has fostered a political atmosphere in Cambodia that is non-conducive to public life and individual representation in both civic and national affairs.

The recent unfolding of events in Cambodia took place during a time of monumental change at the global level. The Cold War, a war that Cambodia by way of proxy was all too familiar with, ended following the collapse of the Soviet Union. The breakdown of the Soviet Union was itself precipitated by a massive upheaval of global economics during the 1970s. Between 1973 and 1979 world oil prices rose dramatically, and the impact on the First World was a severe economic recession, the Second World went into an economic tailspin that eventually led to its disappearance, and the Third World fell into a "debt crisis" that would give rise to a condition of aid dependency that continues to this day. This unprecedented and unforeseen disruption of the world economy marked the beginning of an economic paradigm shift, as profound disillusionment with the record of state involvement in social and economic life swept over the Global North, leading to an unsophisticated and naïve belief that the most efficient economic regulator would be to "leave things to the market." The involvement of the state in the economy was deemed overly bureaucratic and thus an inefficient and unnecessary drain on public coffers. Hence, in spite of variance in doses among regions, states, and cities, the basic neoliberal policy treatment is underpinned by a vision of naturalized market relations that seeks to: eradicate obstacles to the operation of free markets; hold back all forms of collective initiative and public expenditure primarily via the privatization of common assets and the imposition of user fees; advocate individualism, competitiveness, and economic self-sufficiency as fundamental virtues; attenuate or nullify social protections and transfer programs; and actively "recruit" the poor and marginalized into a flexible labor market regime of precarious work and low-wage employment (Peck 2001; Peck and Tickell 2002). This is the essence of neoliberalism, or what has been identified by economist John Williamson (1990) as the "Washington Consensus," an economic ideology that is fundamentalist in its execution, and seeks to deregulate markets as much as possible to promote "free" trade. It traces its roots back to the neoclassical economics of Adam Smith and David Ricardo – hence neo (new) liberalism (Simon 2002).

Conceptualizing neoliberalism requires an understanding of the complex interplay of local and extralocal forces acting within the global political economy (Brenner and Theodore 2002; Peck 2001). Jim Glassman (1999) alerts us to this notion in his analysis of the Thai state as a concurrently internationalized and internationalizing agent. In focusing exclusively on external forces we risk producing over-generalized accounts of a monolithic and ubiquitous neoliberalism, which insufficiently accounts for local variability and internal constitution. On the other hand, overly concrete or introspective analyses of the local are inadequately attentive to the significant connections and necessary features of neoliberalism as a global project (Brenner and Theodore 2002; Peck and Tickell 2002). Accordingly, Jamie Peck and Adam Tickell (2002, 383) propose "a processual conception of neoliberalization as both an 'out there' and 'in here' phenomenon whose effects are necessarily variegated and uneven, but the incidence and diffusion of which may present clues to a pervasive 'metalogic'. Like globalization, neoliberalization should be understood as a process, not an end-state." In other words, rather than a singular and fully actualized policy regime, ideological form, or regulatory framework, we need to think in terms of "actually existing neoliberalisms" (Brenner and Theodore 2002), where, as protean outcomes of historical specificity, internal contradiction, and contextual embeddedness within national, regional, and local processes of market-driven sociospatial transformation, neoliberalism is continually redefined by the consequences of inherited institutional frameworks, policy regimes, regulatory practices, and ongoing political struggles.

The emerging neoliberal doctrine quickly became the economic orthodoxy in the Global North and was exported to the Global South via measures to address the debt crisis in the form of development aid, primarily though the auspices of the International Monetary Fund (IMF) and the World Bank (WB). "Market fundamentalism," as George Soros (1998) calls neoliberal economics, predicts that free-market forces will lead to a prosperous future for the Global South, where all of the world's peoples will come to live in a unified and harmonious global village. While the globalization of the economy is not a new experience for the Global South, and has deep historical roots in both Southeast Asia and Cambodia, the intensification of this process is new. Economic globalization has heightened over the last 25 years under the programs of the International Financial Institutions (IFIs). These structural adjustment programs (SAPs) have facilitated the spread of a neoliberal, global, economic system dominated by multinational corporations and the governments of the Global North, and enforced by the World Trade Organization (WTO). Yet in spite of such "top-down" measures, the willingness of local elites to adopt and internalize such policies should not be underestimated.

Barry Riddell (2003a: 659) warns that such intensified process of economic globalization in the Global South is "especially disturbing to many citizens and most states because there has been a marked decline in their ability to control, plan, and regulate the commanding heights, or revenue generating sectors, of their economies." The reality of a constricted ability to control economics has very often also translated into a contemporaneous condition of declining local control over social and political conditions. As the Cambodian state is increasingly both neoliberalized and undergoing internationalization

(Glassman 1999) in its developmental agenda, planning agencies, decision-making powers, and economic orientation as each becomes increasingly integrated into transnational circuits of capital and expertise (Sneddon 2007), democratic control wanes further. Indeed, what makes "actually existing" neoliberalism in Cambodia distinctly Cambodian is how local elites co-opted, transformed, and rearticulated neoliberal reforms. This has been done in such a way that it reinforces existing patron–client relations through a framework which "asset stripped" foreign resources brought in to support the building of the liberal peace (Richmond and Franks 2007), thus increasing the exposure of the average citizen to corruption, coercion, and violence.

In the Cambodian context, such lack of democratic accountability has meant that the poor have had to contend with recurrent economic crises. Private firms have plundered Cambodia's forests along with numerous public assets. This situation of privatization has served to consolidate the wealth and privilege of the elite while simultaneously placing even more pressure on the limited economic means of the poor. The underprivileged are now forced to purchase goods they were previously able to collect from communally held forests, and pay user fees for services that were formerly provided for "free" by the state. There have been extensive cuts to public health care and education, and while many private companies have stepped in to fill this lacuna, the poor cannot afford to pay for such services and are accordingly condemned to a life of sickness and ignorance. Civil service downsizing and salary slashing have resulted in both high levels of unemployment and pervasive rent seeking. Footloose capital has caused numerous factory closures, which has translated into severe job insecurity and union-breaking tactics by the state. The cost of living has risen at an astronomical rate due to IFI economic policies that promote inflation and currency devaluation. Rampant land speculation has forced many of the rural poor off their land and into an urban life of squatterdom, where begging for food often provides the only opportunity to keep fed because the job prospects are so bleak. Finally, as the economic situation for the poor has continued to worsen, many Cambodians have looked to the "informal" economy as the only possible way to make a living, a condition that has promoted a human trafficking epidemic across Southeast Asia as young women are forced into prostitution to supplement the incomes of their families. In short, the world has effectively been turned upside-down for the Cambodian poor.

This marked lack of control stands in stark contrast to the language of empowerment that accompanies the neoliberal doctrine. The agenda of "governance" stands at the forefront of the neoliberal canon, under which democratic empowerment is linked to economic liberalization, and a positive outcome, that is, "good governance," is only possible if the state adheres to the ideology of the free market. Contradiction runs deep in neoliberal thinking, as a predetermined economic model removes the very element that defines democracy, that is, the freedom to choose. A manifestly democratic economic strategy is one that places people in a position of power, allowing them to participate in decisions that affect their economic lives so that neither the state *nor* the market is allowed to dominate (MacEwan 1999). Cambodia's transition to democracy marks an early example of the implementation of the "good governance" agenda at the global level. The furtherance of free-market reforms, which Cambodia had been experimenting with in the late 1980s, was a project simultaneous with the United Nations Transitional Authority in Cambodia's (UNTAC) peacekeeping efforts, and alongside a democratic constitution, a liberalized economy was a mandated outcome of the UN operation.

Despite the fact that over a decade has now passed since the promulgation of a new constitution which marked the beginning of the country's new life as a democratic and free-market state, conditions of repression, surveillance, intimidation, vote buying, and other behaviors commonly defined as "undemocratic" continue as the prevalent modes of governance in Cambodia. The realities of Cambodian political life are far from democratic, open, fair, and just. Not only has neoliberalization done little to change this situation, but such political economic reform has actually exacerbated conditions of authoritarianism in Cambodia. Accordingly, neoliberalization is conceived as effectively acting to suffocate an indigenous burgeoning of democratic politics. Such asphyxiation is brought to bear under the neoliberal rhetoric of "order" and "stability," which can be read through Cambodia's geography, and specifically through the production of the country's public space. Public space is the product of two competing ideologies (Mitchell 2003b). On the one hand, the "ordered" view constitutes public space as the site of control, and is typically associated with authoritarian tradition where panopticism is used to maintain order and security. The "ordered" vision of public space is rivaled by the "unmediated" view, which conceptualizes public space as the site where "the voiceless" can materialize their claims and make their demands heard, as a medium for the contestation of power wherein it provides visibility to subaltern groups, and as the space in which identity is constructed, reified, and contested. In short, the unmediated view envisions public space as the crucible of democracy. I support this unmediated vision in arguing that public space is an ideal model for democracy. *Democracy as public space* puts power back in the hands of the people and allows us to move beyond technocratic, "top-down" models of development.

Furthermore, a geographic analysis of the neoliberal doctrine of "order" reveals the "good governance" agenda as mere pretence. Democracy is widely recognized as the only system of government to offer true legitimacy, and as such, neoliberals the world over pay lip service to democracy in an effort to facilitate the complicity of national populations in allowing the market to reign supreme. Moreover, the neoliberal promotion of an "ordered" vision of public space, most overtly via its corollary found in private space, explains why authoritarian governments, as long as they espouse the free market, are so complacently accepted by the global neoliberal intelligentsia agenda. While "order," "stability," and "security" appear as worthwhile goals, we must ask why "order" always seems to benefit the preservation of the status quo, and also in whose interest our nations and cities are being "secured." As Don Mitchell (2003b: 230, original emphasis) points out, ". . . the crusade to 'secure the city' is not new, and every attempt to reorder the city has served *particular* interests." The preoccupation with "order" in Cambodia is viewed in this study as serving the interests of capital at the global level, and political elites at the level of the nation-state. However, these "particular interests" are fiercely contested by Cambodians themselves. This contestation is strongly evidenced in the burgeoning geographies of protest that have emerged in Cambodian public spaces in the post-UNTAC years. The Cambodian experience is of course not unique, and my findings resonate within a larger, global pattern of increased calls for order and stability *vis-à-vis* democracy as global marketization intensifies. The violent responses to protest movements challenging neoliberal policies in cities as dispersed as Stockholm, Lilongwe, Genoa, Seoul, Quebec, Prague, Asuncion, Seattle, Port Moresby, and Istanbul serve as instructive examples of how the unmediated usage of public space and the very practice of democracy have come into conflict with the neoliberal order.

Thus the major claim I advance is that unfettered and intense marketization is the foremost causal factor in Cambodia's inability to consolidate democracy, and further explains why authoritarianism remains the principal mode of governance among Cambodia's ruling elite, an inclination that is often elicited through the execution of state-sponsored violence, or *violence from above*. By examining Cambodia's public space, such violence is revealed to be utilized and legitimated in the name of promoting "order" and "stability," so that the flow of capital and the freedom of the market are not interrupted. It is argued that "order" preserves an economic system that serves to maintain the power and privilege of indigenous elites at the expense of the poor, which in turn entrenches patron–client relations as the elite are positioned to informally control markets and material rewards. Finally, I contend that hypocrisy is inherent to the "good governance" agenda, a condition that is made luminous through Cambodia's geography by way of the (re)production and contestation of public space, where the neoliberal doctrine is spatially manifested in a way that is irreconcilable with democratic politics in Cambodia.

In seeking answers to why democracy remains unconsolidated in Cambodia following the UN's massive peacekeeping operation of the early 1990s, the predominant explanation to emerge among Cambodian observers is that Khmer culture is ill-equipped to manage political conflict in a peaceable manner. Scholars such as Steve Heder (1995), Pierre Lizée (1993), Abdulgaffar Peang-Meth (1997), and David Roberts (2001) have all published works that, to varying degrees of lucidity and sophistication, identify a supposed "cultural trait" of absolutism as being the primary and intractable obstacle to greater democracy in Cambodia. However, when placed under close scrutiny, such *culturalist* interpretations lack reasoned explanatory power, and bear all the same hallmarks as the racial explanations that suffused "development theory" in the bygone era of colonialism. The axiom that opens this introduction suggests that Cambodia's political culture is not nearly as absolutist as some of the country's commentators would have us believe. In addition, this maxim further hints that Cambodians have internalized the notion that power never goes uncontested. While the view that Cambodia retains a "culture of violence" – as though violence is some sort of inheritance from time immemorial – is utterly pervasive in Cambodian studies (see Becker 1998; Bit 1991; Curtis 1998; Faulder 2000; Meyer 1971; Moreau 1998; Jenks Clarke 2001; Kurlantzick 2000; Peang-Meth 1991; Prasso 1994; Roberts 2001; Sodhy 2004; Verkoren 2005), some scholars have challenged the conventional view of implicating Khmer culture as the source of Cambodia's democratic woes, and have provided their own non-culturalist accounts of why Cambodia's path to democracy has been such a tempestuous ride. For example, Caroline Hughes (2003b) identifies a context in Cambodia whereby political empowerment among average Cambodians has not been forthcoming because democracy came into being as a donor mandate, rather than as an indigenous movement.

Hughes's (2003b) concern with the wisdom of installing democracy in Cambodia in a "top-down" approach is not misplaced, as democracy is said to be a system of government that represents the will of the collective, and as such should be an endeavor that is driven from the "bottom up." The major argument concerning Cambodia's transitional political economy advanced by Hughes (2003b: 220) is that:

> Broadly speaking, co-optation and monopolization of local political economies by the partisan state in the 1990s has led to a substitution of internationalization for democratization in Cambodian society. This is problematic in that [it] . . . has exacerbated elitism in Cambodian society, and has prompted the emergence of new hierarchies in which those most able to operate in an internationalized sphere are increasingly distanced from the grassroots.

I very much agree with Hughes on this point, and the conclusion I draw from this observation over the course of this study is that neoliberalization in Cambodia has narrowed the potential for Cambodians to become involved in democratic processes. In contrast, Hughes (2003b: 220) argues that:

> This conclusion has major implications for the ability to promote short cuts to democracy in an environment of severe material dearth. The experience of Cambodia suggests that the contribution of international resources specifically dedicated to the enabling of political participation does widen opportunities for this beyond the narrow sphere of the partisan state.

Hughes (2003b: 220) provides the caveat that "these opportunities are mostly limited to an internationalized elite, and are much less observable in rural areas," yet she contends that this is primarily "because international intervention has rarely penetrated far into rural Cambodia, where the political terrain remains monopolized by partisan state authorities." The implication of Hughes's argument is that economic liberalization has not penetrated deeply enough into rural areas for political participation to flower, and furthermore that there is a linear "staging" to democratization, whereby only economic liberalization and growth will overcome the "material dearth" that is said to hinder democracy. Thus, rather than challenging neoliberalism's uneven development, Hughes seemed to have internalized the logic of its doctrine.

Many scholars of Cambodia share this *de facto* pro-neoliberal view (see Ear 1997; Kao Kim Hourn 1998; Kevin 2000b; Markussen 2008; St. John 1997; Tith 1998; Un 2006), while very few have offered any kind of challenge (see Hendrickson 2001; Le Billon and Springer 2007; Peou 2000; Richmond and Franks 2007). More recently Hughes's (2009: 8) interpretations have done a complete turnaround, and she now argues that "the intrusions of donors take place within a neoliberal framework that works against the prospects for popular participation in a public sphere of political engagement and debate." This seems more tenable, although her understanding of neoliberalism is remarkably undertheorized. Rather than offering any explanation as to what she might mean by a "neoliberal framework," Hughes instead treats neoliberalism as an academic buzzword. Such inclusion without explanation ultimately undermines the forcefulness of Hughes's otherwise impassioned argument, as neoliberalism is simplistically reduced to an agenda that is tantamount to IFI and bilateral donor intervention. Accordingly, Hughes fails to grasp how Cambodian elites have internalized neoliberal discourse, and further, how this discourse circulates through Cambodian society, both informing and being reconstituted by civil society networks and the population at large via governmentality. Instead, she considerers neoliberalism as a "political straitjacket that limits the potential for the emergence of a genuinely empowered national public sphere that can provide a setting for deliberation and accommodation" (Hughes 2009b: 3). Such reductionism serves to replicate the idea of neoliberalism as monolithic inevitability, so although the concept of neoliberalism is now acknowledged in her work, the potential for emancipatory politics is crippled by her implicit perpetuation of the notion that "there is no alternative."

The arguments presented in this book are removed from, and offer a counter to the reductionist, neoliberalist, and culturalist strains of thought that pervade recent studies of Cambodia's political situation. I argue against *culturalist* interpretations based on their proclivity for essentialism, and their tendency to lend credence to the claims of "Asian values" politicians who seek only to legitimize their own hold on power. Such arguments are further viewed as doing a disservice to all Cambodians because of their implication that there is something "wrong" with Cambodian culture and thus a priori Cambodian people themselves. I also dispute the notion that the political turmoil in present-day Cambodia is an outcome of the market not having penetrated deeply enough into the fabric of the Cambodian landscape. To the contrary, in contributing to the growing number of studies that identify linkages between neoliberalization, authoritarianism, and violence (see Auyero 2000; Benson et al. 2008; Borras and Ross 2007; Bourgois 2001; Canterbury 2005; Coleman 2007; Cooper 2004; Escobar 2004; Farmer 2004; Gillespie 2006; Giroux 2004; Goldstein 2005; Manalansan 2005; Marchand 2004; Sánchez-Prado 2006; Wacquant 2001; Uvin 2003), I argue that neoliberalization and the construction of a new political economic order is the source of the Cambodian government's ongoing tendency toward authoritarianism and its penchant for using violence as its overarching *modus operandi* of governance. I further want to argue against the reductionist views that treat neoliberalism as a ubiquitous and monolithic force by challenging their consideration that individuals, cities, and states have no choice but to kneel before this new global sovereign. Such thinking is deeply problematic and disabling to any liberationist struggle.

Chapter 2 reviews the literature on democracy, development, and public space and establishes a framework for understanding public space as a potentially emancipatory process and democratic crucible. The chapter begins by assessing the meaning and value of democracy in moving toward a participatory interpretation of the concept. An analysis of cultural arguments related to democracy follows, where I address and dismiss the charge that democracy is culturally inappropriate for non-western societies, an argument that most often takes shape under the rhetoric of "Asian values." Similarly I challenge the notion that political and civil liberties are a luxury that the Global South poor have no concern or need for, commonly identified as the "Lee Thesis." I then proceed with a discussion of the development discourse, where I assess the colonial origins and ethnocentric character of development and dissect the "good governance" agenda. A framework for moving beyond Eurocentric and "top-down" approaches to development is then presented in the form of *democracy as public space*. Here I suggest that civil society is inadequate as a means of providing indigenous ownership of the simultaneous project of development and democracy, as it is an entity that offers little opportunity for the development agenda to be set by the people most directly impacted by it. Only an open and unmediated public space can provide the opportunity for democracy to emerge, and it is thus a highly contested domain, where Global South political actors of all stripes, both rich and poor, and the machinations of globalized capital continually stake out their claims. Such contestation is then argued to illustrate that a democratic space is never free from the risk of disorder, an observation that places democracy in conflict with the need for "order" and "stability" so that capital should flow smoothly. Public space, while having the potential of being truly democratic, is thus often also a space of violence, which is impelled and manifested both as *violence from above* and *violence from below*. Thus, what I have termed a *disquieting nexus* exists between violence and democracy, as violence that originates "from below" and is driven by a demand for equality and with the goal of egalitarianism is often seen as the only endeavor that can democratize a political system. Yet an *irreconcilable schism* emerges when violence is recognized as anathema to the very principles of democracy.

Chapters 3 and 4 contextualize the theories and geographical framework laid out in Chapter 2, and weave together Cambodia-specific literature with empirical findings obtained from research conducted in Cambodia over seven months, from June to December 2004, and a further nine months, from November 2006 to August 2007. Through an examination of public space, Chapter 3 surveys the events and circumstances of Cambodia's transitional political economy beginning with the international response to the genocide, through the UNTAC years, and up until and including the 1997 coup d'état when the road to democratic consolidation was tested and ultimately undermined by donor responses to this incident. I begin the chapter by examining Cambodia's historical background to provide the necessary context for understanding the country's UN-sponsored transition in 1991. I then address the Paris Peace Accords as a moment when marketization took off in Cambodia, and argue that such neoliberal reform was incorporated into and reinvigorated the politics of patronage. The prospects for a "neutral political environment" are then assessed in light of the ruling party's tight control of public space. It is argued that the conditions of surveillance and media domination more closely resembled a panaopticon than a context that might allow for free and fair democratic elections, yet the international community scarcely cared as democracy played a rhetorical role to the primary objective of stability so that markets could successfully emerge. The close relationship between neoliberalism and neoauthoritarianism in the Cambodian context is then identified, and in doing so I contend that a political economy perspective is more productive to understanding the Royal Government of Cambodia's (RGC) actions than *culturalist* notions of absolutism. The pandemonium that swelled in 1997 then becomes the focus, where I am particularly concerned with the Cambodian People's Party's (CPP) quest for hegemony that precipitated a brutal grenade attack on members of the opposition party and their leader, Sam Rainsy, and a few months later a murderous coup d'état. I survey the responses of Cambodia's donor community and contend that their showing of profound indifference speaks to a situation where economic interests take precedence over even the faintest conception of democracy.

Chapter 4 provides an analysis of Cambodia's political economy in the post-coup era up to the present day by tracing the contemporary developments in the country's ongoing battle for public space and democratic accountability. Here I examine the conditions under which the 1998 elections took place, calling into question the donor community's haste in deeming them "free and fair." Following the announcement of the election results, Cambodians took to the streets *en masse*. This collective awakening underlies what later became known as the Democracy Square Movement and the authoritarian response that followed, the implications of which I assess in terms of Cambodia's burgeoning democracy. I then focus my analysis on the city-level project of beautification, and examine how and why this became the RGC's new mode of control of Cambodia's public spaces as overt control became less tenable. I also reflect on the Cambodian government's appeal to American concerns for the "war on terror," and how this has been used as a pretext to silence members of the opposition party and other groups who call into question the CPP's legitimacy as the country's ruling party. Set within the context of Cambodia's post-transitional stage where democratic consolidation should be forthcoming, I then revisit the notion that patron–clientelism has been reinforced as neoliberalization intensifies. The Cambodian government's movement back toward overt control of the country's public spaces following the anti-Thai riots of January 2003 marked a new tenor in the run up to national elections later that same year. Cambodian protesters were once again entangled in direct violence and confrontation with police and army personnel as the country saw a return to widespread crackdowns on public gatherings. The election of 2003 resulted in political stalemate, and I analyze how the CPP nonetheless continued to govern the nation with little concern for the wishes of the people in spite of the growing popularity of rival parties. Such authoritarianism and disregard for public concern is argued to be symptomatic of the larger patterns of neoliberalization in the country, where labor, land, and indeed life itself are continually threatened by the machinations of Cambodia's neoliberal order. These developments are then related to Cambodia's contemporary political economy of violence and authoritarianism by reflecting upon the Cambodian government and donor community's shared concern for "order" and "stability" as a method for promoting market consolidation and further neoliberal reform. In particular, I question its implications for a viable public space and hence a deeper sense of democratic empowerment in Cambodia. Finally, Chapter 5 questions both the potential for future conflict if Cambodia's neoliberal order continues to operate without the consent and popular approval of the citizens it is supposed to represent, and importantly the possibility of revolution should a democratic conception of public space be continually suppressed.

Empirical findings were derived from three qualitative methodological tools: (1) participant observation; (2) a content analysis of newspaper articles pertaining to neoliberalism, violence, democracy and public space, collected from a local English-language newspaper, *The Cambodia Daily*, over a one-year time period (from 1 November 2008 to 31 October 2009), which are presented as headlines collected in tables throughout the two empirical sections[1]; and (3) in-depth interviews with over one hundred individuals covering a wide range of Cambodian political actors, cutting across political, generational, gender, urban–rural, and economic divides, including, among others, nongovernmental organization (NGO) leaders, human rights workers, International Financial Institution employees, university students, teachers, market stall owners, homemakers, motorbike-taxi drivers, politicians, garment factory workers, civil service personnel, and government employees. *The Cambodia Daily* was chosen in favor of other newspapers because it is the longest-standing English-language daily newspaper in Cambodia. *The Cambodia Daily*'s coverage of local issues is also arguably more comprehensive than that of *The Phnom Penh Post*, which has only recently gone daily after nearly two decades of bi-weekly service.

The aim of fieldwork conducted for this book was to produce a critical ethnography in which Cambodian participants felt empowered rather than exposed by the study. Thus, the purpose of this research was two-fold. First, it provided a forum for collaborative, qualitative research between myself and Cambodian individuals, "giving voice to the voiceless" to reveal the participants' understanding and meaning of their perceptions and experiences of both political violence and democratic processes. This is an attempt to overcome some of the silencing that has been characteristic of Cambodia's current political situation. A second motivation for this research is a concern with devising ways to minimize the scope and potential of violence, while simultaneously empowering those subjected to it. The origins, meaning, and implications of political violence (originating both "from above" and "from below") and its relation to observed behavior in Cambodia cannot be known without research (Jenks Clarke 2001). Smyth (2001: 4) suggests, "Sound research carried out in violently divided societies may, if effectively communicated to the appropriate actors, eventually lead to an improved response to the management of conflicts." As Stanko and Lee (2003: 11) advise, "After all, violence is preventable. The more we gather knowledge about it, the better off we are to contribute to its minimization in society."

A critical ethnography that explores the "particularities" of the research participants' lives (Abu-Lughod 1991) affords practical advantages in allowing an understanding of the perceptions and experiences of Cambodians more sensitively than could other approaches. It also allows for the "democratization" of my research project by giving "voice" to participants through the sharing of their life histories, which is a necessary approach since I share Staeheli and Lawson's (1994) view that speaking *for* other people is ethically contentious. Helen Jenks Clarke (2001: 92) argues, "it is important for Cambodians to be involved in research in order to regain knowledge that has been lost and to empower them for the future." Accordingly, I was bound by an ethical responsibility to listen to the voices of my participants and I planned for a certain degree of flexibility in my research project so as to be inclusive of the goals and wishes of the Cambodians I have attempted to represent. And while it is perhaps impossible to overcome the "un-get-roundable fact that all ethnographic descriptions are homemade, that they are the describer's descriptions, not those of the described" (Geertz 1988: 144), I follow Nolin and Shankar's (2000) lead by employing a persistent, scrutinizing, and self-conscious critical reflexivity throughout the research process. By using sensitive, collaborative, and critical ethnographic methods, I believe I have ensured a high degree of honesty about the nature of the subjectivity that shapes my analysis and findings.

The voices of the Cambodians that speak in this study communicate a strong desire for democracy. The precarious conditions that exist because of a democratic deficiency are reflected in the voices of Cambodians themselves, as participants have shared their perceptions and experiences of violence, and how *violence from above* influences their visualizations and materializations of public space. The newspaper headlines collected in this study similarly show a marked contestation of public space in Cambodia, and corroborate the anger and distress vocalized by participants. Together, these sources indicate that many Cambodians have simply had enough exploitation at the hands of the market, and are no longer willing to accept an undemocratic polity. Ultimately, I seek to challenge the wisdom of market fundamentalism. While neoliberals tout the power of the market as an agent of social change and worthy of praise, the contestation of public space in Cambodia reveals the market's status in the country cannot be assumed. If the market continues to operate unimpeded, it will invariably lead not only to intensified misery and suffering among the Cambodian people, but also it will march inexorably toward its own self-destruction. Indeed, Cambodia has been through the cycle of ruin and rebirth all too recently under the rise and fall of the infamous Khmer Rouge regime. We would do well to heed the warning of the Cambodian proverb that opens this introduction, as those who do not learn from history are invariably doomed to repeat it.

2 Caught in the headlights of "culture" and neoliberalism

Public space as a vision for democracy and "development from below" in the Global South

> There are those who like to speak and take no action, but what kind of result can arise from such an endeavor? They put much reliance on luck and fate, only to discover that they have achieved little.
>
> – Cambodian proverb.

Democratization in non-western contexts has become the focal point of "development" in recent years, where increasing globalization has unquestionably played a significant role in the diffusion of democratic ideas. The relationship between democracy and globalization is so apparent that the international pressures for democratization must be considered in any discussion of democratic development. This is not to say that the domestic factors of democratization can be ignored, and indeed scholars such as Rita Abrahamsen (2000: 8) maintain that "the neglect of the interplay of the internal and the external severely impoverishes contemporary explanations of democratization." Accordingly, I follow Abrahamsen's advice and analyze both the internal and external factors that shape the process of democratization in non-western societies. In doing so, I organize the discussion in this chapter around the two pillars that both those who accept and those who reject the universality of democracy repeatedly refer to, namely culture and economics. Far from being opposed to democracy as many scholars have argued, an analysis of culture reveals it to be inconsequential to democracy, allowing us to move beyond the notion of "Asian values" and its ideological, although euphemized, counterpart "illiberal democracy." I address the economic focus of democratization specifically in terms of its liberalization as being the primary focus of "development" as currently conceived through the neoliberal paradigm of "good governance."

In recent years, "development from below" has become a slogan used by development planners of all stripes, thus debasing the original connotation of the concept. However, the paradigm originally set out by Stöhr and Taylor in their 1981 edited book *Development from Above or Below?*, identified "development from below" as "A change in the level of decision making . . . and in the basic concept of development (going from the present monolithic concept defined by economic criteria, competitive behaviour, external motivation, and large-scale redistributive mechanisms to diversified concepts defined by broader societal goals, by collaborative behaviour and by endogenous motivation)" (Stöhr 1981: 39). Taylor and Mackenzie resurrected the theory in 1992 with the book *Development from Within*. Here, Taylor (1992) identifies the rhetorical use of "development from below," along with the skepticism of indigenous planners who viewed the concept as simply another example of the theories and prescriptions of the Global North being applied to the Global South, as the key reasons for abandoning the term. Chosen to replace "development from below" is "development from within," which again stands in contrast to the "top-down," "development from above" paradigm that views people as objects of development who must be "modernized," "mobilized," or "captured." The basic objective of "development from within" is "to allow local people to become the subject, not the object, of development strategies. Given the opportunity to do so, they have shown themselves to be perfectly capable of making rational choices regarding their own destinies" (Taylor 1992: 257).

My arguments mirror "development from within," where participation is recognized as both the goal and the means of development. However, I have retained the designation of "from below" in favor of "from within," as I believe this more accurately identifies the starting point from where participation, development, and democracy is to be impelled. "From within," without retracing Taylor and Mackenzie's entire theory, is vague enough to imply that any actors from within the nation-state, including the state itself, can or should drive the development agenda. Conversely, the designation "from below" puts this decision solely in the hands of the people, where they can collectively determine the scale at which development will be conceived and take place. In this regard, I am silent on institutional proposals concerning "development from below" as this is something to be designed by the people themselves.

Based on these understandings, this chapter sets out a framework for conceiving public space as a vision for democracy and development "from below" in the Global South. I present public space as an opportunity to move beyond the ethnocentric and paternalistic "top–down" perspective that characterizes both the neoliberal approach to development and, as we shall see, civil society. A move toward "development from below" in the form of *democracy as public space* is recognized as an affront to the interests of both indigenous elites and global capital, and accordingly I examine the contested nature of public space. Public space is recognized as the battlefield on which the conflicting interests of the Global South's modern-day aristocracy and proletariat classes are set, as well as the object of contestation itself.[1] Moreover, within the spaces of the public the materialization of violence is acknowledged as both an outcome of attempts to impose an "ordered" view of democracy originating "from above," and as an act of resistance and liberation "from below" by those who seek truly democratic spaces of unmediated interaction. This violence reveals the paradox of democracy, or what I have called the *disquieting nexus*, in that democracy, although premised on the notion of non-violent mitigation of conflict, is never free from the threat or manifestation of either *violence from above* or *violence from below*.

Ultimately, this section's discussion of culture, the "development discourse," and the contestation of public space allows us to move beyond essentialist accusations of an "undemocratic culture" as responsible for the continued predilection for authoritarian modes of rule in the Global South. It allows us to see the structural constraints placed on elites by the neoliberal doctrine, and in so doing we are better positioned to understand that the current struggle for democracy in the Global South, as well as its associated violence, is fundamentally a clash between the machinations of global capitalism on the one hand, and the attempts of the poor, marginalized, and "propertyless" to insert their voices into the "development" policies and practices that are adversely affecting their lives on the other.

Toward a definition of democracy: Participation, process, and value

Democracy is a notoriously nebulous and hence difficult term to define. To some it means ensuring citizens have equal political rights while defending large areas of society and the economy from "political intrusion." To others, we achieve democracy only when powerful elites no longer foil the aspirations of the masses (Pinkney 1994). Engrossed in layer upon layer of philosophy and propaganda, it is tricky to choose the criteria by which one may categorize a political regime as "democratic" (Gupta 1990). Indeed, the boundary between "democratic" and "non-democratic" is often hazy and imprecise, an ambiguity that "is further complicated by the constraints on free political activity, organization, and expression that may often in practice make the system much less democratic than it appears on paper" (Diamond, Linz, and Lipset 1989: xvii). Adding to this dilemma is the degree of reverence the term "democracy" has attained (Arat 1991; Lummis 1996). In his well-known essay "Politics and the English Language," George Orwell (1993: 163) stated, "It is almost universally felt that when we call a country democratic we are praising it: consequently the defenders of every kind of regime claim that it is a democracy, and fear that they might have to stop using the word if it were tied down to any one meaning." Thus, as a political term, the word "democracy" is mercilessly overworked, "a debased currency in the political marketplace" (Schmitter and Karl 1993: 39), used to justify terror and compromise, revolution and mediocrity.

However, it is worth noting that words often have more than one meaning, and their meanings change through both time and space, dependent on the individual, ideology, paradigm, culture, or context. Zehra F. Arat (1991) suggests that the meanings ascribed to the word "democracy" vary from "a way of life" to "a form of government." Schmitter and Karl (1993) corroborate this notion and emphasize that there is no single form of democracy, and with great significance in light of recent world events, they argue that Americans should be careful not to confuse the concept of democracy with their own institutions. Diamond and Plattner (1993: xi) assert that democracies can vary considerably in the degree to which consensus versus competition, shared power versus majority rule, and public authority versus private action are encouraged. Furthermore, "These variations ... may have far-reaching implications for the quality and stability of democracy" (Diamond and Plattner 1993: xi). And while "the specific form democracy takes is contingent upon a country's socioeconomic conditions as well as its entrenched state structures and policy practices" (Schmitter and Karl 1993: 40), it is important not to degrade our conception of democracy based on cultural relativism, for "to accept this cultural relativist position is to deny any universal meaning to the word and, in the process, to indemnify the most scurrilous of dictatorships and to undermine the legitimacy of democratic and reformist oppositions" (Hewison, Rodan, and Robison 1993: 5).

Given the untidy meaning of democracy in contemporary discourse, to say that you are for democracy may be taken as a sign of bad taste in some circles (Lummis 1996). Consequently, in stark contrast to the wide range of politicians who (mis)appropriate the label, scholars may hesitate to use it without adding qualifying adjectives, due to the ambiguity that surrounds "democracy" (Schmitter and Karl 1993). Indeed, for these reasons, Robert Pinkney (1994) demands that academics clarify the type of democracy they are discussing. Nonetheless, that the word "democracy" is used to both self-designate and presumably legitimate so many existing structures, and to indicate the desirable end-state of so many political, social, and economic pursuits, is a reflection of the political climate of our time (Diamond, Linz, and Lipset 1989). For better or worse, as Schmitter and Karl (1993: 39) are quick to point out, "we are 'stuck' with democracy as the catchword of contemporary political discourse. It is the word that resonates in people's minds and springs from their lips as they struggle for freedom and a better way of life." As such, if the term is to be of any use in analysis and practice, it is imperative that we are as precise as possible about what it is that we mean by "democracy" (Diamond, Linz, and Lipset 1989).

It is perhaps easiest to start by suggesting what democracy is not. While influential writings by Schumpeter (1975), and later Huntington (1991) and Przeworski (1999) may have hit upon the most common conception of democracy in equating it solely with regular elections, Schmitter and Karl (1993) suggest this is a misleading notion called "electoralism." This is not a sufficient condition for the existence of democracy, but instead "the faith that merely holding elections will channel political action into peaceful contests among elites and accord public legitimacy to the winners' – no matter how they are conducted or what else constrains those who win them" (Schmitter and Karl 1993: 42). C. Douglas Lummis (1996: 18) makes a similar critique when he calls free elections an "important democratic method," but qualifies this in

suggesting that under certain circumstances elections may be a way for dem-
agogues or rich landowners to obtain and retain power. An electoral definition
of democracy specifies only the form and not the "spirit" of democracy. Thus,
Dipak K. Gupta (1990) contends a nation may have a superficial democratic
arrangement without having a democracy in the truest sense of the term.

Even if elections are free from coercion and fair in terms of universal
voting rights, to focus exclusively on the formal prerequisite of active voting
rights and not on normative concepts such as "the public good" or "social
justice" is to fall short of an adequate definition (Schmiegelow 1997b). Yet,
Diamond, Linz, and Lipset (1989) insist that democracy should be separated
from the economic and social system to which it is joined, and instead focus
exclusively on governmental structure. I am convinced that such a severance
ultimately fails to address the most basic tenet of democracy, that is, to
address and satisfy the needs of the people. As Giovanni Sartori (1995: 102)
suggests, democracy "is only shorthand for . . . an entity composed of two
distinct elements: (1) freeing the people (liberalism) and (2) empowering the
people (democracy)." Within Sartori's definition rest the rudiments of
democracy. When we reduce democracy to its most fundamental conception,
it joins *demos* (the people) with *kratia* (power). If democracy is fundamentally about empowerment, how can we ignore issues of "social justice,"
and if democracy also means the people, how can we ignore "the public
good?" The project of empowerment is ill fated without attention to social
and economic justice as well as the public good; and putting power in the
hands of the people necessarily entails their participation.

Schmitter and Karl (1993:42) recognize the importance of participation
in suggesting that for a political system to be considered democratic it must
offer "a variety of competitive processes and channels for the expression of
interests and values – associational as well as partisan, functional as well
as territorial, collective as well as individual." Moreover, for Schmitter and
Karl (1993), democracy is a system of governance in which citizens, acting
indirectly through the competition and cooperation of their elected representatives, hold rulers accountable for their actions in the public realm.[2] This
implies very similar criteria to Robert A. Dahl's (1971) concept of polyarchy,
which denotes a system of government emphasizing: (1) meaningful competition among individuals and organized groups (i.e. political parties) for government positions and hence power, through regular, frequent, free, and fair
elections; (2) a highly inclusive conception of citizenship so that no major
adult social group is excluded from political participation in the selection
of both leaders and policies; and (3) extensive civil and political liberties to
allow for pluralism of information and organization (i.e. freedom of expression, freedom of the press, freedom of assembly), especially the freedom to
criticize government leaders and the existing social and economic systems,
and to ensure the integrity of political competition and participation (Dahl
1971; see also Diamond, Linz, and Lipset 1989; Diamond and Plattner 1993;
Sato 1997, for overviews of Dahl's concept). Although they do not label it as

such, Arat (1991), Hewison, Rodan, and Robison (1993), and Neher and Marlay (1995) all echo Dahl's concept of polyarchy in their conceptualizations of democracy by emphasizing the same three basic tenets. Schmitter and Karl (1993), on the other hand, do recognize Dahl's concept of polyarchy, but extend it by placing even greater emphasis on participation in maintaining that citizens must be able to influence public policy through various non-electoral means in between election times, via interest-group associations and social movements.

Democracy has gone through a historical process of elimination and arrived at a point where "liberal democracy" has become the dominant form (Pinkney 1994). However, in stark contrast to Francis Fukuyama (1992), who trumpeted "liberal democracy" as the "end of history," Dahl and his followers seem to recognize the potential of democracy to move beyond its current incarnation toward a more participant and ultimately egalitarian form of democracy. This is the style of democracy I advocate in this study. Yet, I am still cognizant that every democratic system enjoys varying degrees of equality and popular participation, and thus may be constrained by the presence or threats of veto by indigenous elites, the military or foreign powers as Pinkney (1994) suggests. This recognition does not deviate from Dahl (1971), as he chose the term polyarchy in favor of democracy to acknowledge the notion that democracy is never a complete project, but rather always in a process of becoming. As Larry Diamond (1993: 4) suggests, "democracy may approach the 'equilibrium version'" of the process but is open to improvement or deterioration. Iris Marion Young (2000: 5) calls democracy "a matter of degree," to Tatsuo (1999: 29) it is an "unfinished project," and Neher and Marlay (1995: 6) remind us that "No government, even that of so-called models such as Great Britain, the United States, or Sweden, is perfectly democratic" (see also Diamond 1999). Indeed, as Hibbs (1973: 117, original emphasis) points out, "in virtually all the recent comparative politics literature, democratic political development is viewed as a *process* or framework that structures political activity rather than as a *condition* of socioeconomic equality, high mass social welfare, and the like." Nevertheless, it would do us well to remember that the *process of democracy*, while by no means the end of political struggle, often offers people better opportunities to pursue such goals as economic equality and social justice through the mechanism of participation (Stepan 1993). Lummis (1996: 15) asserts that "Democracy is not everything, but something. When the word is used in the right place, at the right moment, it is fresh, clear, and true." In line with Carole Pateman (1970), who claims that democracy cannot exist without a participatory society, I believe the "moment" of illumination that Lummis (1996) speaks of is the very moment of political participation.

Finally, we might rightly ask why democracy is important at all. Certainly, its importance is not derived from democracy being "the only model of government with any broad ideological legitimacy and appeal in the world today" (Diamond, Linz, and Lipset 1989: x). C. Douglas Lummis (1996: 28, original emphasis) reminds us that "all other theories and ideologies point to . . . democracy negatively, as the specific thing they do *not* achieve, the area they carefully avoid, the black hole at dead center in their scheme of rule or management." Thus, the onus should not be on the democrat to explain why she or he values the collective empowerment of the people. If we are able to define the people holding power as "a system under which the legitimate members of a given society participate with a reasonable degree of equality in the decision-making process," as this study advocates, "then a . . . society of hunters and collectors is a democracy. Thus, it may be said that democracy is a political system as old as [hu]mankind" (Sato 1997: 81). Indeed, it was only with the advent of agricultural food production that social changes allowing for state formation and social stratification occurred, and democracy came to be replaced by other forms of government such as aristocracy (oligarchy) and monarchy (despotism). The ancient Greeks merely rediscovered what had been lost for millennia, and in so doing, they inspired the modern resurgence of democracy. Ultimately, given the temporal prevalence of democracy, the burden of explaining the value and importance of a political system should rest firmly on the shoulders of alternative theories to democracy where the people do not rule. It is these theories that must justify the absence of democracy, and explain why it is necessary or better to give power to the few rather than to all.

Negotiating the boundaries of culture: Debunking the "Lee Thesis" and the myth of "Asian values"

The idea that democracy can be an internally driven process in the non-western world is fiercely contested, as democracy has long been associated with so-called "western civilization."[3] A prominent feature of democratic theories, both classical and modern, is the notion that democracy requires a distinct set of cultural values, that is, a so-called "democratic culture," in order to emerge, exist, and endure (Diamond 1993; Harrison and Huntington 2000; Llosa 1993; Tatsuo 1999). Przeworski, Cheibub, and Limongi (2003) break these cultural arguments down into three categories: (1) *strongly cultur-alist*, which is the view that some cultures are simply incompatible with dem-ocracy; (2) *weakly culturalist*, which maintains that a democratic culture is required for democracy to materialize and survive, but is moot on the question of the compatibility of democracy with the traditions of particular societies, since these traditions are malleable, subject to invention and reinvention; and (3) the *non-culturalist* view, which contends that culture has no causal power with regard to democracy whatsoever. Culturalist critiques of non-western democracy, which often suggest that human rights are not universal and use either blatant or euphemized "Asian values" arguments as a lynchpin, are profoundly flawed in several key ways.

We can begin by pointing to what is perhaps the most *strongly culturalist* argument of all, which states quite simply that emphasis on democracy and political freedom is an explicitly "western" priority, one that acts in opposition to "Asian values," which are supposedly more concerned with discipline than with freedom (Sen 1999a; 1999b). However, to speak of values as being "Asian" is to attribute them to 60 percent of the world's population, and in so doing, the argument fails to capture the diversity of cultures and regimes found on the continent. As Schmiegelow (1997b: 28) points out, "The very diversity of the political and cultural landscapes of the countries of the Asian region casts doubt on any effort to demonstrate that there is such a thing as an 'Asian political culture' or an 'Asian' meaning of democracy" (see also Donnelly 1999; Tatsuo 1999). Stretching this critique back further into the annals of the past and regionalizing it to "Southeast Asia," we can subject Stanley J. Tambiah's (1977) work on "the galactic polity" to the same critical scrutiny. Tambiah glosses over the geohistorical specificities of what he calls the "traditional kingdoms" in an attempt to universalize particular cultural formations and political characteristics as both innate and timeless to the region as a whole. The purpose is to provide a framework for understanding contemporary political inclinations and developments in the region. Yet Donald K. Emerson (1984) and Jim Glassman (2005) have sufficiently debunked such homogenizing arguments in recognizing "Southeast Asia" as an imagined geography, one that was actively produced as a bounded unit of study despite its cultural heterogeneity, political economic disunity, and considerable geographic variation.

Similarly, John Gray (1998: 193) criticizes the very idea of "Asia," calling it "as much a chimera as 'western civilization'," an idea that is corroborated by Amartya Sen (1999a: 232), who says that "attempts at generalization about 'Asian values' . . . cannot but be extremely crude." Many *culturalist* scholars are aware of such crudity, as well as the stigma attached to "Asian values," in that it is a priori an acceptance of authoritarian rule. Nevertheless, some scholars choose to tread a very similar path to "Asian values," often couching their arguments in euphemized language. Bell and Jayasuriya (1995: 5–7), who forward an "illiberal democracy" argument rooted in culture, provide us with one such example:

> In the non-Western world . . . freedom was, and for many still remains, anything but an obvious or desirable goal. Other values and ideals were, or are, of far greater importance to them – values such as the pursuit of glory, honor, and power for oneself or one's family and clan, nationalism and imperial grandeur, militarism and valor in warfare, filial piety, the harmony of heaven and earth, the spreading of the "true faith", nirvana, hedonism, altruism, justice, equality, material progress – the list is endless. . . . it goes without saying that most Asians do not feel a burning need to free individuals from the "despots", "guardians", and impersonal forces governing the internal workings of economic enterprises, schools, families, religions and the other "unfree" social institutions that Western liberal democrats worry about.

This statement is interesting in that it fails to explain how concepts such as "justice" and "equality" can be achieved without freedom, and furthermore it remains to be seen how exactly one can determine the "desirable goals" of a population without some form of democratic action to determine these collective goals. In other words, democracy is needed to determine what the "desirable goals" of a society are, not the dictates of a leader, and least of all a confused scholar. What is most interesting about Bell and Jayasuriya's statement is the weight of authority they place on their own voices in assuming they know what "most Asians" think. This raises the most fundamental question of culture and identity: who speaks for whom?

In this postcolonial era of relativism, the answer to this question may seem at first glance to be axiomatic, since many of us may be much more comfortable with articulations of individual cultures coming from within cultures as internal processes of dialogue and reflection rather than from external accounts, which may feel like inaccuracies at best, and impositions at worst. This, of course, is not a "cut-and-dried" issue so to speak, as it invokes ethnography's ongoing "crisis of representation," or the "insider" versus "outsider" debate. In addressing this debate, I start with a simple point that is not often considered: plurality of voice comes not only from among cultures, but also from *within* cultures. Bruce Berman (1993: 9) sums this truth up nicely when he states, "No culture speaks with a single voice; no culture actually exists in a single definitive account. To claim to speak for a particular culture is a claim for power and an act of stereotyping often no less pernicious than those imposed from the outside." Thus, even if Bell and Jayasuriya were to know what "most Asians" think, the universality of democracy would remain unaffected. If there is even one voice in any given culture that favors democracy, on what authority can we reject democracy on a cultural basis?

James Clifford (1988: 8) views questions of "who speaks for whom" as "symptoms of a pervasive postcolonial crisis of ethnographic authority," a corollary to which is the question, "What are the essential elements and boundaries of culture?" This query deserves some exploring as all strongly culturalist arguments necessarily have a very limited and rigid understanding of what culture is. Answering Clifford's question about what constitutes the essential element of culture is no easy task, and it is a subject of debate that continues to seethe in academia. Indeed, there is very little that we can say about culture that is concrete, and the concept itself is best described as amorphous. Rather than defining culture itself, the primary question of culture should be about what *processes* rather than essences are involved (Clifford 1988; Gupta and Ferguson 1997). Gupta and Ferguson (1997: 4) argue, "all associations of place, people, and culture are social and historical creations to be explained, not given as natural facts," a contention that is also shared by Clifford (1988: 9), who views cultural identity, "not as an archaic survival but as an ongoing process, politically contested and historically unfinished." Thus, culture and identity are engaged in a continuous and perpetual process of becoming (much like our definition of democracy), and "are never given but must be negotiated" (Clifford 1988: 275). Culture is of course not only inventive, but as a concept is itself also invented. As Clifford (1988: 273) explains, European theorists used "culture,"

> to account for the collective articulation of human diversity. Rejecting both evolutionism and the overly broad entities of race and civilization, the idea of culture posited the existence of local, functionally integrated units. For all its supposed relativism, though, the concept's model of totality, basically organic in structure, was not different from the nineteenth-century concepts it replaced. Only its plurality was new.

Although culture "operates in anthropological discourse to enforce separations that inevitably carry a sense of hierarchy" (Abu-Lughod 1991: 137–38), and has simply replaced ideas of "race" and "civilization," the new *plurality* of culture also provided us with new orders of difference that are important to identity formation. As Berman (1993: 9) explains,

> without the existence of other cultures, or recognizable orders of difference, it would be virtually impossible for us to develop the concept of culture or the knowledge that we or anyone else has a culture. If there were a single homogeneous culture throughout the world we would be no more able to conceive of culture or know we had one than fish are conscious of the water in which they swim. . . . Our cultural consciousness and identity thus is constituted by the existence of other peoples and their cultures, and through a continuous dialogue of insider and outsider perspectives.

The continuous dialogue Berman speaks of has continued to foster new identities, and ultimately has been an incredibly powerful counteractive force to the process of cultural homogenization. Clifford (1988: 261) points out, "It is worth noting . . . that we-they distinctions of the kind Said condemns are . . . useful to anti-imperialism and national liberation movements." Historically then, in an ironic twist, Said's (2003) concepts of "Orientalism" and "othering" could be turned against colonial oppressors to join the arsenal of Scott's (1985) "weapons of the weak," serving to invigorate identity and spur Anderson's (1991) "imagined communities," thereby planting potential seeds for democracy insofar as establishing the idea of "we the people."

So far, the discussion may lead us to conclude that there may still be some value to *weakly culturalist* arguments, given that I have thus far shown cultures to be mutable. However, this very amorphousness has made culture easy prey for the resurgence of arguments that echo "scientific" racism. Thus, as Clifford (1988: 273) asserts, "the fundamental question is posed: on what basis may human groups accurately (and we must also add morally) be distinguished?" Przeworski, Cheibub, and Limongi (2003), who reject all variations of culturalist arguments, pose the question slightly differently when they tell us that if such views are to produce a compelling explanation of the origins, life, and death of democracy, they must specify what exactly it is about culture that actually matters. Harrison and Huntington (2000) and the other contributors of their edited book *Culture Matters: How Values Shape Human Progress* have heeded this call and provide one such example of recapitulated racism, as they forward a pernicious thesis that suggests that "culture" explains why some countries are undemocratic and underdeveloped.[4] In essence, Harrison and Huntington, along with the other *Culture Matters* authors, replace the "racial" inferiority argument with "cultural" inferiority, without recognizing that both are equally repugnant. Furthermore, Harrison and Huntington (2000) seem to recognize that culture is not so easily homogenized, and advocate various education programs that teach the "right" cultural values (i.e. western ones), while suppressing the "wrong" cultural values (i.e. non-western ones). One of the *Culture Matters* contributors, Daniel Etounga-Manguelle (2000: 66), obviously firmly lodged in the neoliberal camp that favors SAPs as solutions to Global South economic woes, goes so far as to suggest that Africa requires a "cultural adjustment program." It is this type of strident insistence concerning the "right" cultural values for development and democracy that has forced non-western countries to go on the defensive (Vatikiotis 1996), a posture that may ultimately hinder the move away from authoritarian rule.

Continued authoritarianism often comes in the form of the "East Asian challenge to human rights" as identified and articulated by Daniel A. Bell (1996). Bell (1996) argues that it is not appropriate to respond to this "Asian" challenge to human rights with the claim that human rights are universal, and hence cannot be restricted under any circumstances. According to Bell (1996: 648) "certain rights may conflict and . . . consequently governments may either have to sacrifice some rights in order to safeguard more important ones or to sacrifice a certain right in the short term in order to secure more of that same right in the long term." Bell uses a euphemistic gloss to disguise the essence of his argument, which is that at certain times rights *need* to be violated. Of course, it is the power holders that ultimately choose both when and what rights are dishonored. Which means that the state can justify abuse whenever it pleases, and for whatever reason it sees fit. Accordingly, the curtailment of human rights such as freedom of expression, speech, and assembly may be used to justify, legitimize, and perpetuate despotism in the name of the so-called "more important" issues such as "order" and "stability." Indeed, Bell demonstrates that authoritarian modes of thought in Asia often receive indirect support from lines of reasoning in the west itself. As Sen (1999a: 233–34) explains:

> There is clearly a tendency in America and Europe to assume, if only implicitly, the primacy of political freedom and democracy as a fundamental and ancient feature of Western culture – one not to be easily found in Asia. . . . But support for such components can be found in

many writing in Asian traditions. . . . championing of order and discipline can be found in Western classics as well. Indeed, it is by no means
clear to me that Confucius is more authoritarian in this respect than, say,
Plato or St. Augustine. The real issue is not whether these nonfreedom
perspectives are *present* in Asian traditions, but whether the freedom-
oriented perspectives are *absent* there.

Indeed, freedom-oriented perspectives are not absent in Asia, and Sen
(1999a; 1999b) identifies a number of examples, the most obvious of which
is that of Buddhism.

In Buddhist tradition freedom is given great importance, with plenty of
room for individual volition and free choice (Sen 1999a; 1999b). Even in the
teachings of Confucius, often selectively used among champions of "Asian
values" to make their case, there are notions of freedom to be found: "When
Zilu asks him 'how to serve a prince,' Confucius replies, 'Tell him the truth
even if it offends him' " (Sen 1999a: 234–35). Sen (1999a: 239–40) suggests
that the main point to be grasped is that

> the modern advocates of the authoritarian view of "Asian Values" base
> their reading on very arbitrary interpretations and extremely narrow
> selection of authors and traditions. The value of freedom is not confined
> to one culture only, and the Western traditions are not the only ones that
> prepare us for a freedom-based approach to social understanding.

This is corroborated by Przeworski, Cheibub, and Limongi (2003), who
argue that many western religious traditions have undemocratic elements
such as the legitimation of economic inequality and the ethic of self-interest
in Protestantism, even though many Protestant-dominated countries are
democratic, meaning that one can selectively pick and choose their cultural
traits to support an argument. Indeed, it is hard to forget the anti-democratic
machinations of the now democratic, but previously tradition-bound societies of Germany and Italy (Schmiegelow 1997a).

Seizaburo Sato (1997) identifies the less common, but no less culturalist
theory that democracy cannot take root in a country with a high degree of
ethnic and cultural heterogeneity and internal division. Empirical evidence
from Asia reveals that democracy is firmly in place in the ethnically diverse
India, while Singapore, consisting of primarily ethnic Chinese, has yet to
establish a viable democracy. Furthermore, Japan, Sri Lanka, the Philippines,
and Papua-New Guinea all provide examples of long-standing Asian democracy, making it clear that democracy can indeed take root in the non-
western world. It is thus far too simplistic to state that Asians and more
generally non-Europeans have anti-democratic cultures.

The second pillar of negation concerning democracy as a non-western
enterprise, namely economics, is very much entangled with the first pillar
of culture. Economic arguments come in two variations. The first variant

suggests that if given the choice between having political freedoms and satis-fying economic needs, poor people would invariably choose the latter because these needs are of more immediate concern. That is, political and civil liber-ties are luxuries that only the people of western nations can afford (Tatsuo 1999). The second variation is the claim that these freedoms hinder economic growth or the "Lee Thesis," named for Lee Kuan Yew, former prime minister of Singapore.

To counter the first argument, that people of the Global South are indiffer-ent to political and democratic rights, we can point out that this claim is based on too little empirical evidence, and to the extent that there has been any testing, the evidence is at odds with this claim (Ake 1993; Przeworski, Cheibub, and Limongi 2003; Sen 1999a; 1999b). Clearly, the authority of this argument is questionable, as the only way of verifying this would be to put the matter to a democratic testing. Furthermore, "The exercise of basic polit-ical rights makes it more likely not only that there would be a policy res-ponse to economic needs, but also that the conceptualization – including comprehension – of 'economic needs' itself may require the exercise of such rights" (Sen 1999a: 153). In other words, how can we know what the "eco-nomic needs" of Global South peoples are, without allowing them to define such needs themselves? Clearly, as Partha Dasgupta (1993: 47) argues, the notion that the poor do not care about democratic freedoms "is a piece of insolence that only those who don't suffer from their lack seem to entertain."

In addressing the "Lee thesis," Sen (1999a) indicates that this argument itself does not negate the notion that democracy is desired in the Global South. Instead, it attempts to undermine it purely on the basis of an economic argument. However, since political liberty and freedom have importance of their own, the case for democracy and civil and political rights remains unaffected. This point is corroborated by Arthur MacEwan (1999), who regards democracy as not simply a goal of development but as an aspect of the process itself. From another angle, Sen (1999a: 150) argues there is little general evidence that authoritarian governance and the suppression of polit-ical and civil rights are advantageous in encouraging economic development: "Systematic empirical studies give no real support to the claim that there is a general conflict between political freedoms and economic performance." The historical record clearly indicates that authoritarian governments have per-formed poorly in terms of addressing economic needs and improving people's material well-being (Olsen 1993; Pinkney 1994), so much so that the dicta-torial NICs (Newly Industrialized Countries) and "Tigers" of Asia can easily be seen as anomalies. Indeed, it is apparent that those countries that have reached the highest level of economic performance, both today (Neher and Marlay 1995) and across generations, are overwhelmingly stable democracies (Diamond and Plattner 1993; Olsen 1993). This is the argument used by the International Financial Institutions (IFIs), and a notion I return to below.

While a persistence of anti-democratic behavior undoubtedly exists in many countries, including those in the west, making blanket assumptions about culture lacks any reasoned explanatory power, and furthermore gives an impression that one should simply allow despots to reign. Nevertheless, in rejecting recourse to culture as an explanation for the life and times of democracy, it is important to understand the historical origins of many Global South democracies. That non-western nations experience an inordinate amount of external pressure to democratize is also significant to this discussion

The discourses of development and democracy: Colonial origins, good governance, and the neoliberal order

In contrast to the significant amount of opposition to the idea that democracy can be an internally shaped process in the non-western world, the notion that democratic development in the Global South is largely driven by external factors is well documented and widely supported. Abrahamsen (2000: 22) suggests this external process is primarily fashioned by what she calls the "development discourse," which "can be seen to have produced a form of knowledge about the Third World that has facilitated and legitimised certain forms of administration and intervention. Development discourse produced and constructed certain subjects, and put them in a hierarchical and unequal relationship to each other." In this way, the development discourse has effectively normalized the right of the Global North to intervene, control, and reshape the practices and ways of life of the Global South (Abrahamsen 2000). The origins of this discourse are to be found in colonialism (Cowen and Shenton 1995; Crush 1995; Escobar 1995; Pinkney 1994; Preston 1996; Rist 1997). Exploring the links between development, democracy, and colonialism is clearly beyond the scope of this book; however, it is important to note that much of the modern development discourse retains the ethnocentrism and paternalism of colonialism. Within two of the most common contemporary approaches to development, namely modernization theory and neoclassical growth theory, the echo of colonial Eurocentrism is not only audible, but rather comes through like a deafening roar.

Modernization theory is premised on paternalism, where so-called "backward" peoples, who are conceived as having no agency, must be taken care of by the west (Crush 1995; Escobar 1995; Preston 1996; Rist 1997). Under the trusteeship of the west, which comes largely in the form of foreign aid, the "backward" peoples will modernize to become like "us," and thus development and democracy will follow, as "they" are re-created in "our" image (Crush 1995; Leys 1996; Rist 1997). Arturo Escobar (1995: 39) argues that, behind the humanitarian concern of modernization theory are "new forms of power and control, more subtle and refined," which result in "Poor people's ability to define and take care of their own lives [being] eroded in a deeper manner than perhaps ever before . . . [as] the poor became the target of more sophisticated practices, of a variety of programs that seem inescapable."

Neoclassical growth theory, on the other hand, views endless growth as the solution to poverty, which in the current development discourse is the essential trait of the Global South (Escobar 1995; Rist 1997). Poverty is conceptualized in terms of economics, whereby the poor are defined as lacking the material possessions of the rich, and similarly poor countries are defined in relation to the standards of wealth of Global North nations (Crush 1995; Escobar 1995). Inherent to this dichotomy of course is a certain ethnocentrism, as "they" (the poor of the Global South) are defined in relation to "us" (the rich of the Global North). However, the dichotomy of "us" and "them" can perhaps be considered as part of an operational theory for the power and purpose of development, which Jonathan Crush (1995: 7) suggests is clear if we read "Global North" for "Europe" and the "Global South" for "the Orient" in Edward Said's (2003) definition of Orientalism: "a systematic discourse by which Europe [the Global North] was able to manage – and even produce – the Orient [the Global South] politically, sociologically, militarily, ideologically, scientifically, and imaginatively." Thus, Crush (1995: 7) argues that, "Development is . . . fundamentally about . . . the spatial reach of power and the control and management of other peoples, territories, environments, and places."

If we accept Crush's argument, then development as a concept is about as far away from democracy as anything we can possibly conceive of, and surely nothing could be more undemocratic than development. This presents a problem that demands a solution since I am attempting to argue that development *is* democracy and vice versa. The answer is *not* to be found in the idea that democracy is the most apt political orientation to foster economic growth. However, this is the most common brand of thinking with regard to democracy in the world today. It is promoted by the WB and IMF under the rhetoric of "good governance," which represents yet another variation of the modern "development discourse."

The concept of "governance" inextricably links democracy with economic liberalism, and thus it follows that democracy will lead to "good governance," rather than "bad governance," only if the electorate chooses a government that adheres to a free-market ideology (Abrahamsen 2000). This, of course, is an intrinsically undemocratic provision, in that it attempts to limit the range of political choice by predetermining the economic model, while preferences of the people are demoted to second-order importance. Elaborating further on the role of the "good governance" agenda, Abrahamsen (2000: 56) suggests it serves to construct economic liberalism as a force for democracy, using this simple equation: "coercive power is perceived to reside exclusively in the state and public institutions, and any reduction in the size or reach of the state is therefore regarded as conducive to democratization." Of course, the development of a market economy does not automatically produce a democracy (Sato 1997), so "good governance" relies on an implicitly culturalist argument to support its primary contention. That is, a market economy free from government interference allows investors and entrepreneurs to pursue their own self-interest and thereby energize and grow the entire economy, and with this growth comes a sense of well-being that fosters greater inter-personal trust and competence in people, which in turn foster the necessary "cultural traits" for democratic citizens (Neher and Marlay 1995).

"Good governance" optimizes the neoliberal view that has dominated the discussion of economic development in recent decades to become the ortho-dox position in modern development theory. Gray (1998: 21) challenges the neoliberal order by contending that "At the global level, as at that of the nation-state, the free market does not promote stability or democracy." The supposed nexus between capitalism and democracy is indeed ambiguous (Pinkney 1994; Rapley 2002), yet it is clear that the social and economic inequalities linked to capitalist competition prevent equality in two different ways: (1) those with superior economic resources have more influence and bargaining power *vis-à-vis* the holders of state power; and (2) they are more capable of "setting the agenda" because of their economic strength and higher education (Abrahamsen 2000; Arat 1991).

It is in this context, Abrahamsen (2000) suggests, that "capitalist dem-ocracy" can be termed an oxymoron. Lummis (1996) echoes this point by contending that the free market serves to divide society into rich and poor, a division that is incompatible with democracy, as the freedom espoused is primarily freedom for the corporation, and corporate capitalism has itself become an anti-democratic system of rule. Abrahamsen (2000: 45) is equally skeptical, indicating that the "good governance" discourse is "not simply a humanitarian effort concerned to promote development and democracy, but rather a development discourse intrinsically linked to larger discursive prac-tices through which global power and domination are exercised." Tony Evans (2001) supports this sentiment by arguing that democracy promotion has more to do with the promotion of global economic interests than with delivering human rights to the poor and excluded of the Global South. IFI insistence on sustained economic liberalization has ruled out reforms to create a more just and equitable social order. Ultimately, political equality cannot be achieved without some degree of economic equality, and without it democracy is liable to become "a vehicle for the maintenance of elite dom-inance" (Abrahamsen 2000: 76). In addition, as democracy becomes increas-ingly entangled in the processes of globalization, dreams of economic equality become evermore illusory. Thus, while all Global South countries are not equally at the mercy of international capitalism, Pinkney (1994) recognizes a greater difficulty in establishing and maintaining democracy with increased global integration. Western powers may be quick to subvert democratic progress and sustain authoritarianism, as this form of rule is more compat-ible with the machinations of global capitalism premised upon "order." This is Paul Cammack's (1997) position in arguing that the orthodox view of development has maintained a high level of anxiety *vis-à-vis* democracy, precisely because, once democratization is initiated, sovereign nations prove to be much more difficult to control. The nature of Global South economic dependence on the Global North can thus be viewed as maintaining societies where ruling elites collaborate with international capitalism while the majority of the population remains in poverty (Berger 2000; Chossudovsky 1997; MacEwan 1999; Riddell 2003a), a situation that is far from conducive to democratic consensus.

The concept of "globalization" is enormously vague, and while it may be difficult to define positively, Gray (1998: 56) is acutely aware that "A universal state of equal integration in worldwide economic activity is precisely what globalization is *not*. On the contrary, the increased interconnection of activity throughout the world accentuates uneven development between different countries." How exactly does increased global interaction "accentuate" uneven development, and what exactly are the implications for democracy? Abrahamsen (2000: 43) does a great deal to illuminate these very linkages by explaining that the institution of governance and democracy as the primary goals of development was made possible by a shift in the global balance of power following the end of the Cold War:

> The end of the bipolar world system signalled the arrival of the west's indisputable hegemony over the Third World. Aid recipients had no alternative but to rely on the west for assistance, and the collapse of Communism as an alternative, non-capitalist development model made donor states more confident of the superiority of their own economic and political solutions.

The post-Cold War reality effectively means that there is only one political-economic model available to the Global South: economic liberalism in the form of SAPs designed by the WB and IMF (Dasgupta 1998; MacEwan 1999; Rapley 2002).

A typical SAP espoused by the IMF and WB entails four basic components: (1) a removal of the state from the workings of the economy, such as reducing government spending and encouraging privatization so as to free the market from state interference; (2) currency devaluation and a freeze on wages regardless of the prevailing rate of inflation; (3) the elimination of subsidies on basic consumer items such as public utilities and transportation in an attempt to reduce expenditures; and (4) the liberalization of trade (Hippler 1995; Milward 2000; Riddell 1992). These measures are supposed to ensure economic stabilization and pave the way to "development" (read growth). However, there is growing recognition that SAPs place an extraordinary burden on the poorest segments of society and foster conditions of increased impoverishment, which subsequently provides opportunities for social unrest and violence to flourish (Adewumi 1996; Iadicola and Shupe 2003; Riddell 2003b; Vanderschueren 1996; Welsh 2002). Nonetheless, because SAPs require profound sacrifices from those subjected to them, particularly the poor, they are extremely unpopular among the general population, and as such require a proclivity for authoritarianism by the incumbent regime to see them through (Arat 1991; MacEwan 1999; Mohan 2000; Vashee 1995).

Indeed, an increasing number of scholars have joined in the chorus of criticism against WB and IMF policies due to their dogmatic focus on economic liberalization to the neglect and peril of social justice (see Berger 2000; Dasgupta 1998; George 1987, 1992; Killick 1995; Korner et al. 1986; MacEwan 1999; Mohan, Brown, Milward, and Zack-Williams 2000; Rapley 2002; Riddell 1992, 2003a, 2003b). So while the neoliberal agenda will argue *ad nauseam* that there is nothing undemocratic about a substantial economic gap between rich and poor so long as it is guided by rules such as equal opportunity, elections, and political rights, economic inequality is clearly not compatible with democracy, as the poor will use their political power to plunder the rich, or the rich will use their wealth to disempower the poor. Moreover, the policy advice provided by the IFIs does not entail recommendations that guide Global South nations toward strengthening their economy and increased self-sufficiency. Rather, the IFIs guide the Global South toward increasing dependency and debt, as they are encouraged to qualify and apply for more credit (Berger 2000; Chossudovsky 1997; Dasgupta 1998; George 1987, 1992; Korner, Maass, Siebold, and Tetzlaf 1986). In turn, this cycle of dependency weakens the roots of democracy in developing countries by "distorting the views of the national bourgeoisie, by restricting the autonomy of the national government, by skewing the income distribution, by setting priorities on economic stability as opposed to equality, and by equipping the authoritarian institutions with coercive tools of the most advanced technology" (Arat 1991: 74–75).

Furthermore, "development" under SAPs is characterized by external control and local political emasculation, which implies that multi-party democracy has no meaning at all in polities where aid dependency defines the boundaries within which domestic economic policy is formulated. Multi-party democracy is rendered meaningless in Abrahamsen's (2000: 145) view insofar as "Opposition parties may criticise the effects of adjustment [SAPs], but should they attain political office they would have to fall in line with the 'Washington consensus' in order to attract vital foreign funds." John Rapley (2002) corroborates this view, and notes the further contradiction of pushing democracy while "rolling back" the state out of the economy. He asserts, "In poor societies, states need to mobilize popular support for both democracy and state legitimacy, and are handicapped by the lack of resources that retrenchment [which comes part and parcel with the good governance agenda] leaves in their hands" (Rapley 2002: 134).

If retrenchment means locals are no longer in control of resources, it also means that in order to fall in line with neoliberal prescriptions, the ruling class in the Global South, who could previously siphon their income straight from government coffers, must come up with unique coping mechanisms to maintain their wealth and privileged position *vis-à-vis* society. William Reno (1995) calls this process "shadow state politics," which refers to the system through which leaders are drawing authority from their abilities to informally control markets and material rewards. Rather than oppose the dominant paradigm of neoliberal reform, Global South governments assimilate IFI interests and then reshape them into instruments of power.[5] The "shadow state" response allows elites to amass extraordinary amounts of wealth that are pocketed rather than put back into developing the country, as this money is obtained through unofficial channels (Reno 1995). Such practices also allow systems of clientelism and patronage to continue. Thus the neoliberal axiom which asserts, "if individuals are left to pursue their narrow self interests, society as a whole benefits" (Rapley 2002: 52), is clearly erroneous. Rather only an elite few along with their circle of patrons benefit, while the supposed "trickle down" effect fails to materialize as the forthcoming developmental rewards promised to those on the bottom are swallowed in the vagaries of the "shadow state" and thereby increase the gap between rich and poor.

By promoting democracy and economic liberalism as inseparable largely through the imposition of SAPs, the process of democratization has been prevented from progressing beyond the electoral stage, and as such, it effectively rules out social reforms toward a more equitable social order (Chossudovsky 1997; MacEwan 1999). Abrahamsen (2000: 134) suggests that it is in this way that the "good governance" discourse has fostered the creation of what can be called "exclusionary democracies," which "allow for political parties and elections but cannot respond to the demands of the majority or incorporate the masses in any meaningful way." This mirrors Schmitter and Karl's (1993) concept of "electoralism" discussed above, a conception of democracy that this study has rejected.

Furthermore, the "good governance" discourse not only sanctions the right of the Global North to intervene in the Global South to promote their particular vision of development and democracy, but has also marginalized alternative interpretations (Abrahamsen 2000; Dasgupta 1998). Consequently, "good governance" also "serves to shield the West from democratic scrutiny. The rich countries are automatically regarded as democratic and able to democratise the Third World as part of the larger development effort" (Abrahamsen 2000: 23) In this way, the current development discourse not only reconfirms the unequal power relationship between the Global North and the Global South, but it is also an intrinsically undemocratic order. Commenting on the prospects of this very arrangement MacEwan (1999: 152) states: "Undemocratic processes tend to yield undemocratic outcomes. The more thoroughly economic change is structured undemocratically, the more difficult it is likely to be for democratic transition [and consolidation] to occur." It is in this manner that globalization is not working to advance human freedom, but rather "leaving things to the market" has resulted in the emancipation of market forces and economic affairs from social and political control (Berger 2000; Gray 1998; MacEwan 1999; Riddell 2003a). By allowing such freedom to world markets, Gray (1998: 208) warns that the "age of globalization will be remembered as another turn in the history of servitude."

So how is it possible to reconcile democracy and development, rescue the pair from the intellectual trash bin, and remove the paternalistic and ethnocentric character that continues to dominate these concepts? Perhaps the place to begin is with the recognition that we are all prisoners of our own subjectivity, as it is impossible for the individual to remove the self entirely from her or his own societal and cultural context. This is not to resort to cultural relativism, but rather the recognition of both cultural and individual pluralism. Jonathan Crush (1995: 19) applies this line of thinking to the milieu of "development from above" which characterizes modern development discourse by suggesting that, "To imagine that the Western scholar can gaze on development from above as a distanced and impartial observer, and formulate alternative ways of thinking and writing, is simply conceit." If we accept this position, then all notions of "autonomous development" or "development from below" as alternatives to development are absurd, a point that Cowen and Shenton (1995) emphasize. Amid such skepticism, the prospect of eliminating ethnocentrism from "development" looks bleak. However, Escobar (1995: 53) argues the exact opposite of Cowen and Shenton, suggesting that, "Understanding the history of the investment of the Third World by western forms of knowledge and power is a way to shift the ground somewhat so that we can start to look at that materiality with different eyes and in different categories." That is, recognition of the western origins of "development" affords us the necessary critical reflexivity.

In such reflexivity, Kathryn Manzo (1991) finds embedded in the writings of dependency theory, liberation theology, feminist ecology, and participatory action research, a strong counter-modernist impulse. Counter-modernism, through its scrupulous questioning and unrelenting critique, begins to provide the basis for thinking and writing beyond development. However, Crush (1995: 18) warns that, "Self-reflexivity now unfortunately tends to be viewed more as a means of establishing authority than visualizing how alternative worlds might be imagined and made." Yet he is not entirely pessimistic, and indicates that in moving beyond the Eurocentrism which pervades "development" theory and practice, "The place to start, perhaps, is by asking what development has meant for those spaces and peoples who it defines as its objects" (Crush 1995: 21). Generally there are three common answers to this question: (1) the impact of development has been very negative; (2) people would have been worse off without it; and (3) a minority of people benefit from "development" while the majority do not.

While recipients of "development" can be seen as either victims or beneficiaries, Crush (1995: 22) criticizes that they are nonetheless represented as "homogenized, voiceless subjects of outside forces," and thus he contends that, the "power of development" is the power to "generalize, homogenize, [and] objectify." Ultimately, in resolving this issue of *development as ethnocentrism* we may need to return to the notion of subjectivity. Crush (1995) advocates using such cultural, societal, and indeed personal subjectivity as a means to move beyond the ethnocentrism and homogenizing power of development, where individual biographies and autobiographies of the development experience represent a possible resolution. This is indeed a very good start, but it still supposes the presence of an ethnographer gathering, analyzing, and synthesizing these accounts, and as such, this approach is not entirely free from the "development from above" perspective. In what at first may appear to be a perpetual vicious circle, I believe the ultimate solution to the ethnocentrism of democracy and the "top–down" approach to development is to be found in democracy itself.

We must recognize that democracy was once a critical and revolutionary word, and perhaps now more than ever the word itself has been stolen by those who seek to rule over the people to add legitimacy to their rule (Lummis 1996). This applies equally to those countries still experiencing authoritarian rule, as it does to those who have already made the transition to democracy, because the contemporary reality of exporting and promoting democracy is so thoroughly entangled in the neoliberal "new world order" that democracy has lost its very essence. It is clear that the current relationship between globalization and democracy is precarious in that the former partner dominates and controls the latter. However, this need not necessarily be the case, as it is the IFIs' insistence on inserting economic liberalism into the equation that is ultimately distorting and undermining the relationship between globalization and democracy. To rectify the distortion of this pairing would entail setting a new priority for Global South democratization where inclusive participatory politics are seen both as instrumental *and* constitutive to development (Sen 1999a; 1999b), rather than simply focusing on the former as the WB and IMF currently do. Sen (1999a: 53) articulates this very argument suggesting that "The ends and means of development call for placing the perspective of freedom at the center of the stage. The people have to be seen, in this perspective, as being actively involved – given the opportunity – in shaping their own destiny, and not just as passive recipients of the fruits of cunning development programs." That is to say, if democracy and development are to be meaningful, they must be a simultaneous project where one does not precede or take precedence over the other. In this view, "democratic development" is not merely a catchphrase devoid of any real meaning. Rather, it is the insistence upon giving equal voice and agency to all members of humanity and putting "the power of development" into the hands of the people.

Giving agency and voice to all members of society, including those made voiceless from poverty, means that the conceptualization of economic development will surely mean more than simply growth. As MacEwan (1999) argues, a democratic economic development strategy is one that situates people in a position to exercise political power and participate in the decisions that affect their economic lives. It places people in a position where their lives are their own making, and not dominated by either the state *or* the market. It is axiomatic that a substantively democratic strategy will deliver the benefits of development to the population generally. As MacEwan (1999: 2) notes, "what else could be the result of people having effective power?" Such "effective power" would equalize the distribution of income and lead to improvement in the basic standard of living of all, not just a privileged few. In contrast to the environmental plunder and community breakdown caused by self-serving Global North corporatism and its counterpart found in the Global South "shadow state," MacEwan (1999) contends that democratic economic development, with political participation as its defining feature, could lead to the preservation and repair of the physical environment, as well as the preservation and strengthening of social communities. The prospect of such a participatory model depends crucially on open public debates and discussions, and accordingly many scholars have looked to the concept of "civil society" as providing a model. In the following section, I explore the idea of "civil society" as a democratic force, but ultimately choose to move beyond this concept in favor of *democracy as public space*.

Democracy as public space: Beyond civil society to the "space of appearance" and "trials by space"

Jean Grugel (2002) argues that any explanation of democratization must pay adequate attention to the concept of civil society as it offers a resource for subordinated groups *vis-à-vis* the dominant class's instrumentalization of the state. Nara Ganesan (1997) suggests that civil society promotes democratization because it functions as "pressure from below." Diamond (1989; 1992) contends that civil society contributes to democracy by providing continuous checks on the persistent tendency of the state to centralize and increase its power, and to avoid civic accountability and control. Stepan (1988: 3–4) has defined civil society as "that arena where manifold social movements (such as neighbourhood associations, women's groups, religious groupings, and intellectual currents) and civic organizations from all classes (such as lawyers, journalists, trade unions and entrepreneurs) attempt to constitute themselves in an ensemble of arrangements so that they can express themselves and advance their interests." The preceding depictions indicate that civil society is often conceptualized as "outside" the state, or encompasses the entire non-state (market-regulated, privately controlled, or voluntarily organized) realm (see Diamond 1992, 1994; Haynes 1997; Keane 1988). Lummis (1996: 30) criticizes civil society as having "about as many definitions as definers," but concedes that in general it refers to the "sphere of society which organizes itself autonomously, as opposed to the sphere that is established and/or directly controlled by the state."

   The political engagement of civil society is frequently thought of as a way to promote democratization through pressure from below, simultaneously representing a goal to strive for, a means to achieve it, and a framework for engagement over ends and means (Edwards 2004; Grugel 2002). From both a conceptual and empirical perspective, civil society possesses a tremendous amount of internal heterogeneity and is accordingly a contentious concept with a myriad of meanings imbricated in scalar contexts ranging from the local to the global (McIlwaine 2007). The concept is more appropriate considered in the plural rather than the singular, yet despite a proclivity to homogenize important lines of differentiation (Mercer 2002), the development literature nonetheless contains extensive writing, both in terms of concrete examples and on the different theoretical approaches to understanding civil societies, especially in relation to democracy building.[6] Some studies are beginning to identify a dialectic between civil societies and states (Glassman and Samatar 1997; Mercer 2002), making depictions that conceptualize civil societies as "outside" the state, encompassing the entire non-state (market-regulated, privately controlled, or voluntarily organized) realm (Haynes 1997), increasingly problematic. Civil societies are more appropriately conceived as a public sphere of interaction between state and market, being at once both mediated by and a mediator of the political and the economic. Nonetheless, only a concept of civil societies properly differentiated from the economy (and thus the bourgeois) can form the basis of a critical sociopolitical theory where the market has already or is in the process of developing its own autonomous logic. Otherwise, the undifferentiated version of civil society embedded in the slogan "society versus the state" would lose its critical potential (Cohen and Arato 1992). In other words, for civil societies to retain their dramatic oppositional role under authoritarianism and democratic transitions, a three-part model distinguishing civil society from both state and economy is required. Yet while such differentiation is a theoretical possibility, the pragmatism of its practice is not as forthcoming.

Diamond (1992) argues that in the transition from authoritarian rule, the emergence of civil society marks the turning point from fear to public action in the struggle for democracy. The reason for the emergence or persistence of authoritarian rule in the first place is because powerful elements of society, typically landowners, bankers, and industrialists, accept or actually collaborate with it, and, according to Diamond (1992), civil society turns these powerful actors against the state. What Diamond is alluding to is that civil society can and should replace "the most oppressed class" or "the vanguard party" as the agent of historical change (Lummis 1996). However, the difference is that, unlike a class or party, civil society does not rise up and seize the power of the state for the people. Instead, by rising up it empowers itself, so that landowners, bankers, and industrialists (the bourgeois) may stand against and marginalize the state. However, in doing so, they come to control the state themselves. This brings us back to where we started: capital in control of the state and orientating it in an authoritarian arrangement to effect its exacting logic. This vicious circle is perhaps expected in light of the unremitting theoretical misconception that the state and capital are distinct spheres, rather than integral parts of the totality of capitalism (Yeung 1998). Anderson's (1991) account of imagined communities lends credence to the conceptual fusion of capital and the state. In this view, the nation – and its subsequent expression as statehood – is founded upon the decidedly capitalist enterprise of colonialism. Although local expressions of capitalism were present prior to the colonial encounter, the historical experience of colonialism intensified and internalized capitalist relations in the colonies through the very processes of imagining communities. In other words, because civil societies are often simultaneously enmeshed in processes of capitalist usurpation and notions of statehood, an interlocking of three thematic nuclei (Slater 1989), they may also be viewed as colonial transplants. This matter is important because Habermasian ideas concerning civil society (and indeed public space) are the product of "western" thought, which I am attempting to bring to bear as a vehicle for understanding "non-western" contexts. Through colonial occupations we can discern a coalescence of this foreign character of civil societies around indigenous elites, who are at once both those groups to whom Habermas (1989) attributes the capacity to commandeer the state, and the class that assimilated and came to embody the logic of capital. Thus, indigenous elites represent the pivots for making the translation of civil societies across cultures. Yet, as Glassman's (1999) conception of the internationalization of the state recognizes, distinctions between so-called local and global elites have become increasingly blurred as their interests and character converge under globalized neoliberalism. What we are left with is a transnational capitalist class (Carroll and Carson 2006).

Given the apparent interface between capitalism, the state, and a civil society, the latter is not only easy prey for corporatism (Wiarda 2003); rather corporatism is to at least some degree constitutive of civil societies. This certainly falls in line with the qualitative hollowing-out process of state restructuring espoused by the neoliberal agenda where the state becomes differently powerful as emphasis on markets takes on primary importance (Peck 2001), but it does little to address inequality and certainly does not empower existing marginalized groups. On the other hand, neoliberal prescriptions and their resultant renewed commitment to authoritarianism in the Global South (Canterbury 2005) may lead to a different fate for civil societies. Jones, Jayasuriya, Bell, and Jones (1995: 167) observe that

> The technocracies of Pacific Asia have spawned civil societies that are notable for the extent of their state dependence. Civil society is state regulated and affords little opportunity for the development of a critical public realm. The state in fact functions as the gatekeeper licensing civil discourse and managing its terms of debate.

Caroline Hughes (2003b) describes this very situation as having occurred in the context of Cambodia, where the conception of civil society is simply nongovernmental organizations (NGOs) (see also Kao Kim Hourn 1999), who work very closely with the government, and are subject to at least some degree of surveillance since they must be registered (Curtis 1998; Peou 2000).

Although NGOs are a commonplace proxy for civil societies, acknowledging that "NGOization" conditions civil societies does not mean that they are equivalent concepts (Yacobi 2007). Nonetheless, Cambodian civil society suffers from being highly professionalized, legalistic, technocratic, and extremely hierarchical with authoritarian-style internal governance, where the top often represents an international patron (Curtis 1998; Hughes 2003b), tendentially linking it to neoliberalism. Mohan (2002) describes similar disappointments with Ghanaian civil society. Such civil societies offer another variation of the top-down perspective, where the agenda is set either by government (making the designation "nongovernmental" oxymoronic), an international patron (bilateral donors), or the IFIs, such as the WB and IMF. Thus, although many civil societies embrace (at least outwardly) a democratic ethos, which makes them part of the struggle to found a democratic public space, often they not only fail to challenge the status quo of the government, but in line with Harvey's (2005) contention that NGOs are the "Trojan Horses" of neoliberalism, some civil societies may *a fortiori* work to reinforce the hegemony of the neoliberal order.

Hadenius and Uggla (1996: 1621) advocate a definition of civil society that "denotes (a) a certain area of society which is (b) dominated by interactions of a certain kind. The area in question is the public space between the state and the individual citizen." Spatialized notions of civil societies such as this are becoming increasingly common (see Grugel 2002; Lewis 2002; McIlwaine 2007), an understanding I follow up on not to circumvent the concept altogether, but to infuse it with some precision in bringing civil societies closer to the emancipatory potential they are frequently used to envisage. An ideal version of civil society would "not seek to force the state to found liberty but rather struggle to found a space of liberty itself" (Lummis 1996: 36). It is the *making* and *taking* of space and place that allows us to move toward a truly participatory model of democracy. J. Nicholas Entrikin (2002: 107–8, emphasis added) articulates this very point with eloquence and precision:

> If Robert Sack is correct in arguing that place and self are mutually constitutive, then the means of creating the ideal self for sustaining the project of democracy have parallels in place-making. In constructing places we seek to have them match our projects and ideals, both individual and collective. In democracies such ideals include the desire to build places that promote social justice, tolerance, and inclusion and that offer public gathering spaces or places reflecting collective values about community and the natural environment. At the same time, we also recognize that dysfunctional, in this case undemocratic, places exist, such as those that promote injustice or that unfairly exclude. Viewed as a form of life and as a *process*, democracy involves in part the making, unmaking, and remaking of places.

Since democracy is meant to be, and by definition should be inclusive, it is specifically those spaces and places that are *public* that are of primary importance. Thus, public space can be regarded as "the very practice of democracy" (Henaff and Strong 2001b: 39). In addition, public space can be "interpreted to include democratic ideals, good citizenship, civic responsibilities, and essential social compact that constitutes the core of civil society"

(Banerjee 2001: 10), but *potentially* without the hierarchy, international patrons, government appropriation, and co-option of the modern aristocracy that problematize civil society.

Only a conception of civil society rooted in public space is sufficient for a participatory vision of democracy, recognizing that "voice to the voiceless" is not something to be handed to people by civil society, governments, the market, or IFIs. Rather, it is something to be *taken* for themselves. Thus, the relationship between democracy and space is crucial, since democracy requires places not only where people can gather to discuss the issues of the day and work on solving problems (see Arefi and Meyers 2003; Cybriwsky 1999; Fyfe 1998; Habermas 1989; Halbert 2002; Mattson 1999; McInroy 2000; Seidman 1989; Staeheli and Thompson 1997), but also places where rights and ideas can be contested (see Burk 2003; Dean 2003; Goheen 1994, 1998, 2003; Herbert 1998; Lees 1994, 1998; Low 1996; Mitchell 1997a, 2003a, 2003b; Sennett 1970; Tan 2002; Yeoh and Huang 1998).[7] In other words, public space is both the expression of democracy and the proof of its existence (Giorgi, Crowley, and Ney 2001).

Public space can accordingly be defined as "an unconstrained space within which political movements can organize and expand into wider arenas ... politicized at its very core," and tolerant of "the risks of disorder (including recidivist political movements) as central to its functioning" (Mitchell 1995: 115). According to Lynn A. Staeheli and Albert Thompson (1997: 30), "liberal political theory rests on the assumption that the public sphere can be equally open and accessible to all members of a polity," while suggesting republican theory differs only insofar as to incorporate "responsible behaviour" into this notion. Thus, a democratic society values public space as a forum for *all* social groups, maintaining that there should be no structural deterrents prohibiting the ability of individuals to participate in public affairs. This conception of public space is corroborated by geographers Peter G. Goheen (1994: 431), who regards public space as "a place where ... collective rights to performance and speech are entrenched," and Susan Ruddick (1996: 133, 135, original emphasis), who views public space "as a crucible of participatory democracy" and the "*active medium* through which new identities are *created or contested.*"

The notion that public space is important for identity formation is well recognized in Human Geography (see Bondi and Domosh 1998; Cope 1996; Lees 1994; McDowell 1999; Osborne 2001; Rendell 1998; Valentine 2001). Indeed, this creative process works both ways, as identity itself is important in forming the contours of public space.[8] While public space allows unique individuals to join in collaborative efforts and still maintain their distinct voices (Schutz 1999), representation itself, whether of oneself or of a group, demands a physical space (Mitchell 1997a, 2003b). Mitchell (2003b: 33) calls this the "logic of representation," which concentrates on the right of individuals and groups to make their desires and needs known and represent themselves as legitimate claimants to public considerations.

The right to representation is not always recognized, and as such, public space as a concept can also refer to the nature and extent of social and political interaction and communication available to a person (M. Taylor 1991; Mah 2000). Hannah Arendt (1958) calls this the *space of appearance*, or the space within the world that men and women need to appear. Action and speech require such visibility because, for democratic politics to occur, it is not enough for a group of private individuals to vote separately and anonymously. Instead, because belonging to any public requires at least minimal participation (Warner 2002), individuals must come together and occupy a common space where their commonalities and differences can emerge (Howell 1993). While visibility is recognized as central to the functioning of public space (Goheen 1998; Villa 2001; Weintraub 1995), Arendt (1958: 199) argues this view should be extended to include a degree of theatricality because "Wherever people gather together, it [the *space of appearance*, or public space] is potentially there, but only potentially, not necessarily and not forever." Gill Valentine (1996: 216) corroborates this notion by suggesting that public space is not just "there," but "is something that is actively produced through repeated performances."

Notions of theatricality recognize that space is produced, an idea made popular by Henri Lefebvre (1991) in his influential book *The Production of Space*, where he draws a distinction between the visualization and administration of space on the one hand, and its materialization on the other. In Lefebvre's (1991) terms, public space that is controlled by government or other institutions, or whose use is regulated, is referred to as *representation of space*, whereas public space as it is actually accessed and used by various social groups is called *representational space*. This is an important distinction because it draws attention to the difference between the "official" status of a space and the actual ability of various individuals and groups to use it (Arefi and Meyers 2003), and it also hints at the underlying contestation of all public space insofar as it recognizes that all space is socially constructed. The idea that space is "not merely an empty container waiting for something to happen, but *is both constructed by and the medium of social relations and processes*" (Cope 1996: 185, original emphasis) captures the concept of "spatiality," which recognizes that society and space are inseparable (Massey 1994; Soja 1989). Thus, we should acknowledge that representation not only demands space, but also creates it.

Eugene McCann (1999: 179–80) contends that the benefit of Lefebvre's theorization of space is "his insistence on the importance of representations of bodily, lived experiences of space." This addresses the fundamental difference between public space and the public sphere, which are often conflated in the literature and "do not map neatly onto one another" (Duncan 1996: 130). The public sphere, which in its original Habermasian sense is effectively silent on space (Howell 1993), can be defined as the abstract domain of our social life that is separate from the coercion of state power, where public opinion is formed (Seidman 1989; Habermas 1989; Ku 2000). On the other hand, public space must be taken literally as an actual *physical* space precisely because this physical dimension gives a powerful *visibility* to political struggles and action (Goheen 1994, 1998; Hershkovitz 1993; Tan 2002; Zukin 1995). The necessary physicality of public space is not an idea shared by Henaff and Strong (2001b), who have argued that when democracy is no longer direct, it only functions as a "virtual public space." However, this notion is misguided as even representative democracies bear witness to public protests launched "on the ground" in material spaces, and such activities provide non-electoral feedback into "virtual public space" (which is really the public sphere) of the representative democracy. Furthermore, as Don Mitchell (1996a: 127–28) argues, "Activists do not dance on the head of a pin, any more than angels do," and thus public space cannot be established in the abstract (Mitchell 1995; 2003b). Accordingly, newspapers, radio, television, and the Internet are part of the public sphere and not public space.

Mitchell (1995; 2003b) argues against the notion of these electronic spaces as a public space because they are highly structured and dominated by corporate and/or government interests, and thus they can "do a lot to enhance existing power structures" (Calhoun 1998: 381). The Internet in particular has been championed as a revolutionary tool with the potential of invigorating democracy (see Baber 2002; Banerjee 2001; Crang 2000; Henaff and Strong 2001b; Weber 2001). However, Dean (2003) contends such views are overly optimistic, and corporate control of the Internet has made it a "zero institution," leading not to democracy but rather to "communicative capitalism." Although opposed to the Internet as public space, Mitchell (2003b) is not quite as dismissive and suggests the Internet can provide a network that allows social groups to organize. However, he warns, "All the web communications in the world would not have nearly shut down the Seattle meeting of the World Trade Organization or destroyed the Genoa talks. But people in the streets did" (Mitchell 2003b: 147).

Lefebvre (1991: 416) refers to the *taking* of space that Mitchell alludes to as "trials by space," and he further argues that groups "cannot constitute themselves . . . unless they generate (or produce) a space. Ideas, representations or values which do not succeed in making their mark in space . . . lose all pith and become mere signs . . . abstract descriptions . . . or fantasies." This suggests the critical importance of physical space in understanding democracy as public space, but Lefebvre's statement is also indicative of how some groups have been excluded from the democratic process. That is, they have failed to "make their mark" in public space. Thus, paradoxically, public space has also long been a place of exclusion (Miles 2002; Mitchell 1996b, 2003b).

Although a great number of scholars have long recognized the democratic character of public space (see, for example, Agacinski 2001; Carr, Francis, Rivlin, and Stone 1992; Fraser 1990; Habermas 1989; Halbert 2002; Henaff and Strong 2001a, 2001b; Howell 1993; Ku 2000; Levine 2002; McInroy 2000; Mattson 1999; Sennett 1978), this idea itself is very much contested. Miles (2002: 256) argues that, "Public space has . . . a problematic relation to democracy" and asks, "How many women or people of colour . . . gaz[e] on a spectacle of difference in which they do not participate?" There is a vast literature on the exclusion of women (see Bondi 1996; Bondi and Domosh 1998; Day 2001; Duncan 1996; Massey 1994; McDowell 1999; Moghadam 2002; Rendell 1998; Ruddick 1996; Yeoh and Huang 1998), ethnic minorities (see Burk 2003; McCann 1999; Ruddick 1996; Tyner 2002), gays and lesbians (see Casey 2004; Duncan 1996; Hubbard 2001; Ingram, Bouthillette, and Retter 1997; Leap 1999; Valentine 1993), the elderly and the young (see Elsley 2004; O'Neil 2002; Valentine 1996, 1997), and homeless people from public space (see Daly 1998; Davis 1992; Mitchell 1997b, 2001, 2003a). Feminist scholars in particular have contested the idea of public space based on its support for the dichotomy of public/private. Bondi (1996) contends that the public/private dichotomy has attracted a great deal of attention within feminist studies because it relates closely but problematically to social constructions of gender and sex. Steinberger (1999: 296) has argued that notions of public and private are "deeply and ineluctably enmeshed, the one with the other, so much so that the distinction between them, even if pressed only gently, often seems to quickly evaporate." However, Nancy Fraser (1990: 57) contends that many feminists refer to public space as everything that is outside the domestic or familial sphere and thus in its usage, "feminists conflate three analytically distinct things: the state, the official-economy of paid employment, and arenas of public discourse."

Aside from their apparent malleability (Goheen 1998), notions of "private" and "public" are further complicated in that their meaning and usage are imbued with "local specificities of time and place" as they differ according to societal and cultural context (Drummond 2000: 2379). However, this is not to suddenly adopt a position of cultural relativism, and it should be clear that all the *culturalist* arguments, both weak and strong, that pertain to democracy as outlined above apply equally to public space. We should cast aside any suggestion that participation and hence public space is a "cultural value." A desire to participate in the affairs of one's community or country is not a cultural value, nor an outcome of material wealth, but an intrinsic component of the human animal as a social being. The applicability of public space to non-western settings is conveyed in a number of recent articles (see Abu-Ghazzeh 1996; Arefi and Meyers 2003; Cybriwsky 1999; Drummond 2000; Edensor 1998; Embree 2002; Hee and Ooi 2003; Hershkovitz 1993; Law 2002; Low 1996; Moghadam 2002; Slyomovics 1995; Thomas 2001; Tan 2002; Yeoh and Huang 1998). Recognizing local contexts of public space simply means that "any social order will be a product of social practice – the politics of the street" (Mitchell 2003b: 9–10).

Accordingly, in overcoming the theoretical hurdle of the private/public dichotomy, and to better understand what makes space *public*, I follow Mitchell's notion of the "politics of the street" and also the suggestion of Henaff and Strong (2001a), who look to the criteria that must be met for one to enter a particular space. A space is said to be *private* when a given individual or group are recognized by others as having the right to establish entrance criteria, a corollary to which is that private space is imbued with meaning by way of acknowledged ownership.[9] A space is *public* by contrast precisely because, whereas there are criteria that control admission, the right to enforce those criteria is always in question. That is, public space is open to those who meet the criteria, but it is not controlled in the sense of being owned and thus "is always a contestation over the legitimacy of what can be brought and what can be excluded from the life one chooses and is required to have in common with others" (Henaff and Strong 2001a: 4).

Therefore, we should be careful not to dismiss public space altogether, as the importance of public space rests in its *potential* to be a site of political participation. Although he argues against the idea of *democracy as public space*, Miles (2002: 256) inadvertently lends his support when he asks: "was public space ever a site of mass democracy, except when crowds . . . took matters into their own hands?" While public space is never perfect and may very well be exclusionary to certain social groups, public space remains the only site where claims can be made visible and contested (Duncan 1996). Where else but in public space can excluded groups make themselves seen and demand their inclusion? If at different times spaces may "change in their role for accommodating different social groups" (Atkinson 2003: 1830), surely contesting one's exclusion and *taking* public space forces the very issue and can potentially secure such change and accommodation. As Mitchell (2003b: 132) states, "Women, some of the propertyless, and people of color have only won entrance to 'the public' through concerted social struggle, demanding the right to be seen, to be heard, and to directly influence the state and society." To demand inclusion in a space often means forcibly occupying the space of exclusion, which requires an awareness that the idea of public space has *never* been guaranteed, and by its very definition *must* be contested.

The contestation of public space: Capitalist machinations, neoliberalism revisited, and the disquieting nexus

Democracy is not a tidy process and has a degree of inherent uncertainty and instability that reflects the openness of public discussion concerning community principles and standards, and the possibility of sudden changes in collective goals. As Entrikin (2002: 109) argues, "Unlike the paradises of popular imagination and the world's great religions . . . in which permanence is part of their perfection, the places of democratic societies . . . must always be in process, constructions to be maintained and repaired." Through the *process* of public space the collective interest is defined, and it is for this reason that public space lies at the heart of democracy. However, this *process* is also why public space is the subject of continuous contestation. Mitchell (2003b: 129, original emphasis) argues that if public spaces arise out of "a dialectic between representations of space and representational spaces, between the ordered and the appropriated, then they are also, and very importantly, *spaces for representation*." That is, public spaces gain political importance when they are *taken* by marginalized groups and restructured as *spaces for representation*. Accordingly, it is paramount to view public space as a medium that allows for the contestation of power.

The notion that public space is the site of power relations persists both spatially and temporally, where such contestations focus on issues of "access" ranging from basic use to more complicated matters, including territoriality, representation, control, and symbolic ownership (Atkinson 2003; Hee and Ooi 2003). Mitchell (1995: 115) elucidates this sentiment by asserting:

> Whatever the origins of any public space, its status as "public" is created and maintained through the ongoing oppositions of visions that have been held, on the one hand by those who seek order and control and, on the other, by those who seek places for oppositional political activity and unmediated interaction.

Public space as a *process*, like its counterpart in democracy, is never a complete project, but is instead always in a constant state of flux between those who seek to deprive it and those who seek to expand it. In other words, public space is both a product of, and the site of conflict between the competing political ideologies of "order" and "stability" on the one hand and unmediated interaction on the other.[10]

Although Carr, Francis, Rivlin, and Stone (1992: xi) claim to advocate a "supportive, democratic, and meaningful" conception of public space, they instead exemplify the ordered approach as they suggest that public space can be "the setting for activities that threaten communities, such as crime and protest." However, the right to protest is what makes public space "supportive, democratic and meaningful," as it provides those without institutionalized power the opportunity to change the status quo. Crime, on the other hand, is most often conceived of in terms of property rights (McIlwaine 1999),[11] and accordingly it is the victims of capitalism (i.e. the poor), or the "propertyless" (i.e. homeless people), who are recast as the transgressors of public space (see Davis 1992; Mitchell 1997b, 2003).

Hee and Ooi (2003) take a different approach to the ordered view of public space in contending that the public spaces of both the colonial and postcolonial city are constructions of the ruling elite. Certainly, elites and incumbent regimes attempt to enforce their *representations of space*. However, this ignores the element of contestation, and the prospect of *spaces for representation* to emerge. Lefebvre (1991: 381–85) reminds us that there is no fixity to space, as the (re)production of space is a "continual struggle between the state . . . trying to produce and maintain a seemingly homogeneous but fundamentally contradictory abstract space, on the one hand, and subaltern groups . . . asserting their 'counter-spaces' and constructing their 'counter-publics', on the other." Lees (1994) offers Beijing's Tiananmen Square as a case in point, inasmuch as the people *took* this previously state-controlled space, and although it was physically recaptured by the state, it remains ideologically contested as it continues to fire the imagination of people's movements both in China and around the world.[12] Thus, "The values attaching to public space are those with which the generality of the citizenry endows it" (Goheen 1998: 479), and not simply the visualizations and administrations of the reigning elite.

Representatives of mainstream institutions such as governments and the IFIs challenge the collectively endowed values and espouse the "ordered" view of public space because they seek to shape public space in such a way as to limit the threat of democratic social power to dominant social and economic interests (Fraser 1990; Harvey 1992, 2001). Although they never achieve total political control over this space, they do attempt to regulate public space by keeping it relatively free of passion (Duncan 1996). To remove the passion from public space, corporate state planners attempt to create spaces based on a desire for security more than interaction and for entertainment more than democratic politics (Boyer 1992; Goss 1996; Jackson 1998). Michael Sorkin (1992) refers to this process as "the end of public space," and in the context of Los Angeles, Mike Davis (1992) argues that architecture, urban planning, and an aggressive police force have effectively militarized large sections of the city and criminalized much of the public activity of the poor. Richard Sennett (1978) forwards a similar argument in *The Fall of Public Man* by proclaiming public space dead and public life meaningless, killed by capitalism. The "ordered" view of public space is premised on a perceived need for order, surveillance, and control over the behavior of the public (Fyfe 1998; Mitchell 1996b, 2003b). Meaning, in this view public space is no longer truly *public*, but rather it becomes *illusory public*. That is to say, *representations of space* come to dominate *representational spaces*.

The processes of increased surveillance, commodification, and "private" usage have become known in the literature as the "disneyfication" of space (see Boyer 1992; Cybriwsky 1999; Goss 1996; Jackson 1998; Sorkin 1992; Stormann 2000). In this view, the urban future looms as a universal Disneyland, "where a sanitized, ersatz architecture devoid of geographic specificity draws citizens away from a democratic, public realm into plastic temples of consumption" (Lees 1994: 446). The "disneyfication" of space accordingly entails a growing disaffection of people from the potential of unmediated social interaction and escalating control by powerful economic and social actors over the visualization and materialization of space (Mitchell 1995; 2003b). In this light, the struggle for democracy is inseparable from public space, as it is not *what* is said that is at stake, but rather *where* it is said. Public protest is easily silenced when the important gathering places in a city have all become highly policed public space, or its corollary, private property (Mitchell 2003a). That is why Mitchell (2003b: 152) argues that it is "necessary to oppose the usurpation of public space and its privatization at every turn," because "Whether challenged from the left or the right, the established power of the state and capital are threatened by the exercise of public rights within public space" (Mitchell 2003b: 150).

While public protests may initially appear to be limited in scope, that is, focused only on a single issue, more often overt acts of protest are "manifest expressions of deeper, broader, latent dissatisfactions" (Willner 1972: 353). The "latent dissatisfactions" in today's existing and emerging democracies are primarily related to the strains of capitalism and the neoliberal order. Indeed, Mitchell (2003b: 137) argues that in the contemporary city "the neoliberal assault on all things public is in full swing." However, the struggle that surrounds capitalism has not resulted in "the end of public space" (Lees 1994; Mitchell 1995, 2003b). Instead, it represents the very heart of public space: contestation. In the post-Cold War world of widespread liberal democracy and pervasive neoliberalism, the contestation of public space has come to be fundamentally about contesting the machinations of capitalism (Harvey 2001; Purcell 2005). So while opportunities for *taking* space are steadily diminishing as new forms of surveillance and control are implemented (Mitchell 1995; 2003b), in contrast to the death knell of public space rung by Sorkin (1992), Davis (1992), Sennett (1978), and others, the "disneyfication" of public space is being fiercely contested on a global scale, from Quebec City to Cancun and Seattle to Genoa (see Wood 2004; Purcell 2005).

Space itself can never become completely dominated; as Massey (1994: 156) reminds us, space by its very nature is "full of power and symbolism, a complex web of relations of domination and subordination, of solidarity and cooperation." Accordingly, while the "ordered" view attempts to dominate space, resistance from the unmediated vision of public space will always be there to meet it, since as James C. Scott (1990) reminds us, hegemony is never fully achieved. And while resistance is seldom overtly confrontational, as the struggle for democracy truly emerges, the "weapons of the weak" (Scott 1985) will inevitably become more manifest once the visible battle for space begins to take shape in the form of protests, rallies, marches, and other spatially defined "arts of resistance" (Scott 1990; Pile 1997). Furthermore, whatever rights to public space have been won, they have often only been achieved through forceful struggle by people willing to break existing laws, and thereby exposing those laws to be oppressive in their geography if not their actual wording (Mitchell 2003a; 2003b). In this sense, "There never 'really' is public space, [but] it is always there for the making" (Mitchell 1996a: 130). The production of public space, then, is always a dialectic between its means and its "end."

The preceding interpretations of public space highlight one central theme: public space is ideally a medium that allows for *embodied* self-representation. Thus, when public space is deprived, individuals cannot "situate" their self-representation in the existential realm. Consequently, contestation is impermissible and self-representation becomes (almost) *disembodied* in form. We have seen that public space is in a constant state of flux between those who seek to deprive it, and those who seek to expand it. That is, "Public space is the product of competing ideologies about what constitutes space – order and control or free, and perhaps dangerous, interaction" (Mitchell 2003b: 129). When the pendulum sways too far in the direction of the "deprivers," the resulting deprivation of public space has two apparent consequences: (1) the erosion of individual volition resulting in a submissive population, presumably the desired effect by those who seek to undermine public space; or (2) the materialization of violent outbursts against those who oppress public space, which represents a rebellion against an oppressive dominant–subordinate relationship (Davies 1973), and is the undesired effect of the "ordered" view. Maxwell Taylor (1991: 159) places emphasis on the latter consequence by suggesting a "lack of public space is related to the development of political violence." Bhikhu Parekh (1981: 95) elaborates on both points by suggesting that through the deprivation of public space:

> an individual's life acquires an eerie sense of unreality, as happens in a mass society and under tyranny when isolated individuals, thrown back on themselves, live a "shadowy" existence and search for reality in intense private sensations or acts of violence.

In this "search for reality," the expression of violence becomes the only practicable form of public self-representation, and in this sense can be an invigorating and liberating process for those who participate (Arendt 1958). As Taylor (M. Taylor, 1991: 167) argues, "through the absence of public space, the independence of action (which we call freedom) becomes limited . . . this absence results . . . in the conditions that enable and facilitate the expression of extremes of violence."

Such outbursts of violence can be thought of as *violence from below*, sometimes referred to as political violence (see Hewitt 1993; Hibbs 1973; Honderich 1980; Zimmerman 1983), which serves to counteract *violence from above*, often called state-sponsored violence (see Iadicola and Shupe 2003; Tilly 2003; Ungar et al. 2002). Rapoport and Weinberg (2001: 5) define political violence as "illegal physical attacks, or threats, on persons, property, institutions, and symbols in order to destroy, alter and sustain systems or policies . . . and the persons responsible may be outside or inside governments." Therefore, since both the dominant and subordinate pole can engage in violence (see Bill 1973; Davies 1973), and both sides may be politically motivated, each source of origin is appropriately thought of as political violence. Furthermore, the internationalized and internationalizing character of the contemporary state (Glassman 1999) should alert us to the complexity and ambiguity that underpins contemporary expressions of so-called state-sponsored violence. In short, the chosen terms more accurately reflect where violence is impelled from within the local-cum-global socioeconomic hierarchy. In any case, for "outbursts" of *violence from below* to have meaning to both the "deprived" and the "deprivers," they must necessarily occur in public spaces, and they are thus a reassertion of the perpetual contestation of public space.

Often it is only by being violent that excluded groups have gained access to the public spaces of democracy and acquired what Lefebvre (1996) refers to as "the right to the city" (Hewitt 1993; Honderich 1980; McCann 1999; Mitchell 1996b, 2003b). This is the paradox of democracy, because without competition and conflict, there cannot be a democratic polity. However, any society that sanctions political conflict runs the risk of it becoming too intense, producing a conflict-ridden society where civil peace and political stability are jeopardised (Diamond 1993; Mitchell 1996b, 2003b). Democracy on the one hand is predicated upon the idea of non-violent management and resolution of conflicts, or in other words, the idea of trading bullets for ballot boxes. However, on the other hand, many democracies are born in the violence of revolution and "few see or wish to see how intimately related ballots and bullets are" (Rapoport and Weinberg 2001: 5; also see Le Vine 2001). The classic passage by Thomas Jefferson (quoted in Le Vine 2001: 261) which states "the tree of liberty must be refreshed from time to time with the blood of patriots and tyrants," suggests that violence might be considered imperative to democratic renewal. Jefferson's quote also hints at the emancipatory potential of violence, where despite arguments from those who seek to protect the status quo in the name of "order" and "stability," *violence from below* may generate reallocations of wealth and open paths to political empowerment (Apter 1997; Hewitt 1993; Honderich 1980; Iadicola and Shupe 2003; Mitchell 2003b).[13]

Ekkart Zimmermann (1983) argues a fundamental conflict between violence and democracy, and contends that the most successful groups reach their goals without resorting to violence. However, we must remember that what constitutes "violence" (much like "crime") is often defined "from above" (McIlwaine 1999). That is to say, violence is defined as legitimate or illegitimate as it relates to whether it furthers or threatens the social order of a society. Iadicola and Shupe (2003) suggest an example of this is that *violence from above* is often defined as legitimate and is often not considered violent but rather as a defensive or peacekeeping action. A corollary to this is that "those who are more powerful in the society have a greater ability to commit violence and the violence they commit is more likely to be defined as legitimate, and thus not problematic" (Iadicola and Shupe 2003: 39). Consequently, the exclusion of *violence from below* in public space is frequently simply the exclusion of the "unruly" – those who are a priori defined as "illegitimate," "violent," and a "threat" to the existing order (Mitchell 2003b). This is a point also taken by Charles Tilly (2003), who purposefully omits the terms "riot" and "terrorism" from his typology of violence because they "embody a political judgment rather than an analytical distinction." Moreover, the "existing order," increasingly means the economic order, as there is a "growing corporate stamp on the monopoly on violence" (Atkinson 2003: 1834), which was formerly the hallmark of the nation-state (Hirsch and Perry 1973). The corollary of the corporatization of violence is neoliberalism.[14]

Taylor (M. Taylor, 1991: 178) articulates that a "lack of public space appears to be . . . an attribute of ideological control." In the world today, the dominant ideology of control is increasingly market fundamentalism. The vision of public space as a place of unmediated interaction, and one that understands a space's very "publicness" as something inherently good where a *collective* "right to the city" is accepted and understood, is increasingly threatened everywhere where neoliberal ideology has spread its wings.[15] The biggest threat to public space comes not from those actions labelled as "disorderly" or "violent" by the existing order, but rather "from the steady erosion of the ideal of the public, of the collective, and the steady promotion of private, rather than democratic, control of space as the solution to perceived social problems" (Mitchell 2003b: 137). Amid such widespread privatization (of space and otherwise), spending cuts, and globalization, all of which are concomitant to IFI promotion of SAPs, Mark Ungar (2002: 49) maintains that "violence has become both an outlet of societal prejudices and an attempt by embattled nation-states to regain their footing."

Violence from above comes attendant to both "roll-back" neoliberalism, where regulatory transformation sees the state narrowly concerned with mobilizing and expanding markets to the peril of social provisions, and "roll-out" neoliberalism which concentrates on bellicose regulation, disciplining, and containment of those dispossessed or marginalized by earlier stages of neoliberalization (Peck and Tickell 2002). Accordingly, the prevalence of violence in much of the Global South results from changes in state power. Joel S. Migdal (1988) has identified two facets to a "weak state": (1) "state autonomy," which concerns the relative distribution of power between state and society, particularly between the state and dominant interests in the private sector of the economy; and (2) "state capacity," which draws heavily on the Weberian dichotomy of patrimonial and rational-bureaucratic polities, where little distinction is made between the personal interests and official duties of decision-makers in the executive, legislature, and/or bureaucracy. The changes in state power that mark a state's neoliberalization thus appear to coincide with the conditions that underline a "weak state," as the desires of the capitalist class coincide with, and indeed come to dominate, the policy orientation of the state.[16] Weak states, or those where state power is lacking both the capacity to meet the rights and demands of citizens and the autonomy to improve the living conditions for the majority of the populace, have contributed to high death tolls in Asia by exacerbating conflict, perpetuating inequality, and resorting to repression to protect their power (Welsh 2002). "Strong states" by comparison have appropriate capacity, accountability, adherence to democratic ideals, and are "developmental" insofar as they are geared toward the promotion of public welfare, which ultimately works to deter violence.

If development produces negative consequences, it is virtually certain that violence will continue (Apter 1997). Thus, insofar as neoliberalization has increased the gap between rich and poor, as long as modern development continues on the reckless premise of unlimited growth and the universalization of the market, not only will new landscapes of coping be required to assuage the damage done (Riddell 2003b), but the prospect and probability is that violence will escalate. Under neoliberalism, proponents like Dollar and Kraay (2002) argue that absolute poverty levels have been on the decline since the early 1980s. However, the reliability of such global statistics has come under fire (Wade 2004). Poverty reduction statistics do not recognize spatial and temporal variations in inflation. What a dollar buys in year and/or place "A" is not the same as what a dollar buys in year and/or place "B." The World Bank uses U.S. data when computing inflation, which is a "lowball" estimate for most Global South countries, and if China is excluded, the 1990s actually show an increase in global poverty (UNDP 2002). Nevertheless, violence explodes most frequently out of a sociopolitical atmosphere where identifiable programs of modifying change have been implemented, particularly when the social, economic, or political position of the subordinate group has been improved (Bill 1973). Thus, even if we accept the validity of IFI statistics, the potential for violence is not abated, as neoliberalism ignores the "paradox of prosperity" in assuming that absolute rather than relative affluence is the key to contentment, making the global neoliberal regime inherently unstable (Rapley 2004). Socioeconomic inequality is on the rise (UNDP 2002), and has been so marked under neoliberalism that Harvey (2005) contends it is structural to the entire project. Accordingly, as the egalitarian dreams that fuel democracy are continually broken under the spell of neoliberalism, violence is an inevitable outcome. It is not poverty that provides an impetus for violence, a problematic assertion not least because poverty *is* violence effected at the structural level (Iadicola and Shupe 2003). Rather, it is relative inequality – and the awareness of such disparity resulting in humiliation – that often sparks resentment and impels violence from below, which may also proliferate where participation in organized violence opens avenues to political and economic power.

A major dilemma of violence is that *violence from below* is likely to be met with renewed *violence from above*. Victor T. Le Vine (2001) has argued that when democracies break down they usually do so when citizens become accustomed to resorting to violence to get what they want.[17] Tilly (2003: 41), who argues that, "Where participation in organized violence opens paths to political and economic power, collective violence multiplies," corroborates this point. Preventive measures used to realize the "orderly" view of public space, such as prohibition of assembly and anticipatory arrests, may reduce the frequency and scale of demonstrations in the short term, but they ultimately alienate the population and spawn more violence as they increase the likelihood of clashes between police and activists on an extended timeline (Hewitt 1993). This is precisely why Warner (2002: 70) maintains, "any distortion or blockage in access to a public [space] can be so grave, leading people to feel powerless and frustrated." Violence begets more violence, which counteracts the ultimate goal of a non-violent society.

The relationship between democracy and violence is a *disquieting nexus* because even under the best circumstances it is morally ambiguous. In Apter's (1997: 2) words, "Like the evil to the good it can represent the dark side of politics or its most shining project." Violence can serve to include the excluded and grant "the right to the city" (Hewitt 1993; Honderich 1980); but at the same time it is also vile, abhorrent, and dehumanizing. The brutality of violence not only desecrates those who are directly affected by it, but it also tears at the social fabric, subverting the level of trust, interconnectedness, and indeed the "publicness," necessary for societies to function. As noted above, public space allows for *embodiment* of the self, but the publicity of violence "brings one to experience one's own embodiment in a totalizing way that language fails. Violence turns a speaking body dumb" (Bar-On 2002: 14). The conception of democracy as a *process* is even more fitting in this context, as there is always the threat (either latent or manifest) that the public violence inherent to the democratic process will ultimately tear it apart. To break this cycle of violence a democracy *must* recognize the right to protest. Yet confoundingly, the right to protest is a struggle that is often only won through violence (Mitchell 1996b; 2003b).

In acknowledging the paradox of what I have termed the *disquieting nexus* between violence and democracy, we can rightly ask if democracy is even a worthwhile project. I believe democracy is still a defensible mode of power on at least three levels. In the first instance, when democracy is radicalized and conceived as public space, it has the potential to counteract the technocratic elitism that currently informs the "development discourse," because agency and voice is generated from the "bottom up," rather than from the "top down." The second argument for democracy rests on the assumption that the violence democracy engenders is far less damaging than the violence generated "from above" under authoritarian regimes. Any reading of recent human history clearly illustrates that the most extreme cases of mass human mortality, including not only war and genocide, but also famine (Sen 1999a), have occurred under authoritarian regimes, not democratic ones (Tilly 2003). Finally, and most importantly, we would do well to recognize that what initially appears as a *disquieting nexus* may actually be an *irreconcilable schism* given democracy's espousal of non-violence. Thus, when democracy takes on violent means, it changes into something else with a close resemblance, but nonetheless with a content that is fundamentally irreconcilable with democratic praxis.

Conclusion

Powerful elites, both indigenous and extraneous to the Global South, will fervently try to impede any move toward a participatory "from below" vision of development and democracy, but such is the nature of democracy, ever a process, ever a contestation. Indeed, democracy is not achieved by the "hidden process of socioeconomic development" bringing a country to a point where it has the necessary "prerequisites" or economic conditions (Diamond 1992: 5). Nor is democracy the outcome of an "appropriate," inherent, or habituated culture. Democracy is born of struggle, and it is in this exertion that a path to social justice may be opened. If violence is more likely to occur in the context of hierarchical structures (Iadicola and Shupe 2003), then a democracy founded on egalitarian principles and social justice, one that accepts social and economic rights as having equal importance to political rights, offers a lasting preventive measure against violence. In order to reduce violence, there needs to be a move toward conditions that promote strong developmental states, not in the "Asian-way," but in terms of increasing social equality through attention to a broad distribution of resources (Welsh 2002). We must resist naturalizing market relations, as doing so constrains the policy environment for states and consequently denigrates their capacities (Peck 2001). Clearly, there is a need for a vision of public space that extends beyond the market to communicate and establish alternatives to neoliberal hegemony.

Public space offers a spatial medium to the frustrations subalterns feel with regard to systems of hierarchy, neoliberal or otherwise. It allows them to locate their anger in a material sense, thereby opening public space to new visualizations, which may bring about new administrations. It is clear that social discontent gives rise to anger, which in turn results in expressions of *violence from below* (Feierabend, Feierabend and Gurr 1972: 3). If those on the bottom perceive those on the top as unwilling to listen, evidenced through a denial of public space, then tensions will mount and may boil into violence. The contestation of public space is paramount because while elite challenges may be fierce, they are never insurmountable. While struggle is the only way to achieve democracy and social justice, it is never without danger of such violence. Mitchell (2003b) argues that cracks do occasionally appear in the façade of incessant repression, and *violence from below* can be a tempting approach to ensuring that a perceived oppressor is brought to its knees. Yet Dahl's (1971: 15) axiom which states, "The likelihood that a government will tolerate an opposition increases as the expected costs of suppression increase," illustrates that *violence from below* is not always necessary, and simply the threat of civil disobedience may be enough to democratize a repressive regime. Nonetheless, pressure for democratization still demands the continual assertion of physical presence in public space if dissidents are ever to be seen and heard (Mitchell 1996).

Public space is the stage on which the conflicting ideologies of "order" and "stability" on the one hand, and unmediated interaction on the other, are set. The current predominance of the neoliberal doctrine means the "ordered" vision of public space has become the only model available to the Global South insofar as this view represents the interests of capital. The implication of this, an assertion corroborated by Canterbury (2005), is that the answer to why there is a proclivity for authoritarian rule in the Global South is not to be found in "culture," but rather in the contextual embeddedness of neoliberal reforms and the resultant unequal political-economic arrangements of neoliberalization. In deconstructing the neoliberal order, this chapter has attempted to reveal its charlatan character, where "development" and "democracy" are rhetorical washes that obscure continued disempowerment and ongoing impoverishment for the poor. Yet in spite of such adverse conditions, the struggle for democracy, for social justice, and for "the right to the city" persist in seeking to establish a different kind of order, one built on the needs of the poorest and most marginalized segments of society. Even a people that has lost its collective political memory and has been oppressed or mystified into believing that the power of the government is a personal attribute of the King, a divinely ordained punishment, an inheritance from colonial masters, a market commodity, an IFI provision, or something that grows from the barrel of a gun, may still make the discovery that the real source of power is themselves (Lummis 1996). It is in spaces of the public that the discovery of both *power* and *self* is made, and it is in the contestation of public space that democracy lives.

3 From genocide to elections to coup d'état

Public space in Cambodia's transitional political economy

In the water, crocodiles; on land, tigers.

– Cambodian proverb

It is hard to pinpoint a time in Cambodian history when the people's troubles began, as it would seem that the country has always been caught between Scylla and Charybdis. The precarious circumstances in which Cambodia has often found itself have to a great extent been influenced and determined by its geography. Located in the very heart of Indochina, Cambodia sits on the fringes of two of the world's most influential cultural traditions, the Indo and the Sino. The place name "Indochina" can only begin to hint at some of the difficulties Cambodia surely faced as two very different cultural influences staked out their claims in the Mekong Delta region. Even closer to home, the land of Cambodia sits directly between two powerful neighbors, the Thai and the Vietnamese, both of whom have long had an interest in determining the affairs of the Cambodian people. More recently, the French saw Cambodia, along with Laos and Vietnam, as an opportunity to buttress their position in the Far East against the influence of other European colonizing nations. In the 1960s and 1970s Cambodia bore witness to a high stakes and deadly proxy war fought between the Soviet Union and the United States (US) in neighboring Vietnam. Despite the best efforts of Cambodia's leader at the time, Prince Norodom Sihanouk, this Cold War showdown spilled over into Cambodia's borders, setting off a series of events that ultimately resulted in genocide. Cambodia was once again a victim of its own geography.

With the global triumph of capitalism in the late 1980s, Cambodia entered its latest position between the proverbial "rock and a hard place." This precarious arrangement is reflected in the country's recent United Nations' (UN) sponsored transition to democracy. The quest for democracy, although fiercely desired by Cambodians themselves, and seemingly promoted by foreign interests, has in fact been severely threatened, and in some cases even attacked by members of the international community. From one side, bilateral and multilateral donors have placed extraordinary constraints on the Cambodian government through their fundamentalist espousal of liberalizing the Cambodian economy. The preoccupation with "order" and "stability" has not only implicitly supported authoritarian modes of governance, but has also undermined the burgeoning of democracy's most essential component: public space. From another perspective, some scholars of Cambodia have done a disservice to all Cambodians by essentializing Khmer culture as "absolutist" and thus unsuitable for democracy. In some instances, this charge is so forceful that it echoes the rhetoric of staunch "Asian values" politicians. However, in spite of these "crocodiles" and "tigers," Cambodians have begun to find ways to realize their dream of democracy, most notably by carving out *spaces for representation*. This chapter begins with a brief historical overview of Cambodia's *geography of vulnerability* before moving into an analysis of the transitional period where the spatial contestations of Cambodia's transformed political economy are brought to light.

Wither Angkor: Cambodia's historical geography of vulnerability

Between the ninth and fifteenth centuries AD, the Khmer-speaking kingdom of Angkor, centered at Angkor Wat, was the most powerful presence in Southeast Asia, extending its influence over much of present-day Laos, Thailand, and Vietnam (Chandler 1996; Corfield and Summers 2003; SarDesai 1994). Yasovarman I (889–900) founded the first Angkor city, and Suryavarman II (1112–50) commissioned Angkor Wat, marking the apex of the Angkorean civilization. Jayavarman VII (1181–1219), was the most prolific Angkorean temple builder of all Angkorean kings, and under his authority, the huge temple complex of Angkor Thom was constructed (Chandler 1996; Mabbett and Chandler 1995; SarDesai 1994). However, it was Jayavarman VII's preoccupation with temple building that helped cause his kingdom to decline, as resources were depleted and labor was forced, causing discontent (Peang-Meth 1991; SarDesai 1994). Religion also played a major role in the decline of Angkor, as Theravada Buddhism replaced the Brahmanic cult of the divine god-king, or *Devaraja*, under Jayavarman VII. The spread of Buddhism into the kingdom, preaching individual salvation through one's own efforts, interrupted the old way of thought and encouraged the Khmer people, who had faced much hardship under Jayavarman VII's reign, to accept the peace and tranquility offered by the new religion (Chandler 1996; Peang-Meth 1991; SarDesai 1994). Following a series of attacks from the Champa kingdom (later absorbed into modern Vietnam) to the east, and the Thais from the west during the thirteenth and fouteenth centuries, the Khmer abandoned Angkor Wat in 1431, and moved their capital to Phnom Penh (Chandler 1996; Hood and Ablin 1990; Reddi 1970; SarDesai 1994).

According to David Chandler (1998a), Cambodia's physical geography is essential to understanding Cambodian history, and particularly the country's relations with neighboring Vietnam and Thailand. Chandler (1998b: 35) declares that, "Cambodia has been harassed, dominated, protected, exploited, and undermined by Thai or Vietnamese regimes," contributing to what can ultimately be seen as an *identity of vulnerability* among Cambodians. Cambodia has few natural barriers, and accordingly it was "often invaded by Thai or Vietnamese armies which, in turn, would be expelled by forces assembled by the other neighbour" (Chandler 1998a:14). The pattern of foreign intervention was very apparent by the end of the sixteenth century. At this time, most of the Khmer royal family was in exile due to incessant Thai incursions into Phnom Penh, and the Khmer prince who occupied the throne served merely as a Thai vassal (Hood and Ablin 1990). This period also saw extensive territorial loss to the Vietnamese, which was exacerbated in the 1630s when Cambodian King Chey Chettha II married a Vietnamese princess and allowed the imperial court in Hué to set up a customs post in the Khmer town of Prey Nokor (later renamed Saigon) (Chandler 1996; Corfield and Summers 2003). Over the next two hundred years, thousands of Vietnamese people immigrated into the Mekong Delta region still referred to by many Cambodians as *Kampuchea Krom* (Lower Cambodia) (Chandler 1996; Kiernan 2001; Takei 1998).

In 1794, Cambodia's western provinces of Battambang and Siem Reap, the latter containing the majority of Angkorean ruins including Angkor Wat, came under the direct control of the Thai and remained so for over 100 years (Chandler 1996; French 2002; Keyes 2002; Reddi 1970). The process of Cambodian territorial loss reached its apex in the mid-1800s when newly installed dynasties in Hué and Bangkok grew "strong, competitive, and ambitious" (Chandler 1998b: 35), and with the kingdom of Cambodia on the brink of disappearing, the Cambodian King petitioned for French protection (Corfield and Summers 2003; SarDesai 1994). Lindsay French (2002: 437) indicates that, "Under the French Protectorate (1863–1953) the authority of all political and administrative figures was subordinated to the colonial regime, but the underlying structure of local and provincial authority remained intact." Although referring to any colonial system as "peaceful" is a disreputable gloss of the violence inherent to this form of rule, Michael Vickery's (1986: 6) suggestion that, "despite neglect and exploitation, [Cambodia] was peaceful [under French protection]; at least there was no attempt to overturn the system or expel the French. There was endemic banditry . . . but it was without political context and not a major threat to the Protectorate," hints at how this power sharing arrangement made Cambodia's colonial experience somewhat less hostile than was the case elsewhere in the region.

Four years after the establishment of the French Protectorate in Cambodia, the Thai relinquished their claim of suzerainty in all of Cambodia except the western provinces by signing the Franco-Siamese treaty of 15 July 1867 (Dommen 2001; French 2002). The primary goal of French policy was to prevent any further Thai intervention in Cambodia (Dommen 2001), and Thai influence in Cambodia steadily declined, especially after 1907 when France made Thailand relinquish the provinces of Battambang and Siem Reap

(Chandler 1998b; French 2002; Keyes 2002; Kiernan 2001). On the other hand, Vietnamese influence continued to play a prominent role in Cambodia's *identity of vulnerability* in the late nineteenth and early twentieth centuries, as Vietnam was part of French "Indochina" and, as such, hundreds of Vietnamese worked as civil servants in Cambodia, and thousands more came to settle in the country (Chandler 1998a).

David Chandler (1998b: 35) argues that, "Cambodia's geographic vulnerability, along with the small size of its population, heightens its people's sense of insecurity vis-à-vis their neighbours and restricts Cambodian governments to a cautious, even-handed foreign policy." Cambodia's "even-handed foreign policy" manifested itself as political neutrality during the American war in Vietnam. Unfortunately, this stance only delayed the inevitable, as it was simply a matter of time before the war spilled over into Cambodia (Chandler 1991; Kiernan 1996). March 1969 marked the beginning of widespread and sustained B-52 bombings of Cambodia (Blum 1998; Shawcross 1979). Over the next fourteen months, in a campaign that lasted a total of almost four years, no less than 3,630 bombing raids were flown over Cambodia, driving the North Vietnamese and Viet Cong forces ever deeper into Cambodian territory (Blum 1998). Naturally, the bombardiers followed in hot pursuit of the Vietnamese Communists, with Cambodian casualties rising exponentially. By the time the United States exited the war in Indochina, half a million tons of bombs, or nearly three times as much as America had dropped on Japan during all of World War II, were unleashed on Cambodia (Chandler 1991, 1996; Owen and Kiernan 2006). The result for Cambodia was sweeping devastation of the country's natural environment, two million internal refugees, and the loss of approximately 600,000 human lives (Herman 1997; Kiljunen 1984). The "decade of the genocide" had begun (Kiljunen 1984), but sadly, even darker days lay ahead for Cambodia.

Western politicians have repeatedly and inexcusably downplayed the United States' role in the rise to power of the barbarous Khmer Rouge regime. However, William Shawcross (1979: 396) illuminates the American connection by simply stating, "the Khmer Rouge were born out of the inferno that American policy did much to create." Ben Kiernan (1993a: 217) argues, "Pol Pot's revolution would not have won power without U.S. economic and military destabilization of Cambodia . . . this was probably the most important single factor in Pol Pot's rise." The American bombardment had fostered extensive rural civilian support for the insurrection out of sheer abhorrence for all things "American," including the United States-endorsed Lon Nol government of the time (Chandler 1996; Church 1997; Haas 1991, Kiernan 1985), which had ousted the popular King Sihanouk from power following a coup in 1970. Journalist John Pilger (1998: 4) insists "Pol Pot and the Khmer Rouge would be historical nonentities . . . and a great many people would be alive today . . . had Washington not helped bring them to power . . . supported them, armed them, sustained them, and restored them."

On the morning of 17 April 1975, Phnom Penh surrendered to the intrepid and heavily armed Khmer Rouge forces (Carney 1989; Martin 1994). Converging on Cambodia's capital, the victorious insurgents were "ominously silent" and responded to the approval of the welcoming crowd with callous indifference (Chandler 1996: 208). What struck the people of Phnom Penh most, according to Henry Kamm's (1998: 121) interpretation of the firsthand accounts he had gathered from escapees shortly after the event, was the youth and remarkable "grimness" of the conquering soldiers who exhibited "fierce, unsmiling, automaton-like demeanour." Indeed, many of the soldiers were under fifteen years of age (Chandler 1996; Kiernan 1996). So began a period of Khmer history characterized by monumental social change and abhorrent political upheaval. Chandler (1996: 209) proclaims, "no Cambodian government had ever tried to change so many things so rapidly; none had been so relentlessly oriented toward the future or so biased in favour of the poor."

The insurgents responsible for the fall of Phnom Penh, and the seizure of Cambodian state control named their new regime Democratic Kampuchea (DK).[1] Known to the western world as the Khmer Rouge, leaders of DK were members of the Communist Party of Kampuchea (CPK) and collectively referred to themselves as *Angkar* (the Organization) (Frieson 1993; Kiernan 1996; Marston 1994), becoming so infamous for their barbarism that the very word "Cambodia" invariably conjures up images of genocide (Chandler 1998a). In a "3 year, 8 month, and 21 day" reign of terror,[2] and in accordance with their anti-urban dogma, the Khmer Rouge forcibly displaced millions of Cambodians, obliterating their individual identities, severing community and familial relations, and killing millions more through their brutal control and manipulation of space in the creation of Democratic Kampuchea.

Angkar, not to be confused with Angkor, ascertained their primary objective as that of replacing perceived "impediments to social justice and national autonomy with revolutionary energy and incentives" (Chandler 1996: 209), and sought to destroy "population groups defined by ethnicity, nationality, religion, or race . . . to create a levelled, homogeneous society" (Weitz 2003: 188). Hindrances to national autonomy included individualism, familial relations, religion, urbanism, currency, proprietorship, and the monarchy, which, ironically, the insurgents had previously fought to renew in aligning themselves with King Sihanouk (Ayres 2000; Kiernan 1996). Furthermore, the revolution resembled the Marxian doctrine of "class warfare," since DK leaders viewed Cambodia's poor as having "always been exploited and enslaved . . . [and once] liberated by the revolution and empowered by military victory, they would now become the masters of their lives and collective masters of their country" (Chandler 1996: 209).

Phnom Penh's capture, romanticized by the CPK as the "liberation" (Kamm 1998), corresponded with the Cambodian New Year and came a fortnight before the communist victory in South Vietnam. Chandler (1996) suggests the timing was deliberate, and cognate to Year 1 of the French Revolution, *Angkar* would usher in a new epoch in Cambodia, completely independent of the revolution in Vietnam. To the insurgents, 1975 was

"Year Zero" (Church 1997; Jenks Clarke 2001; Kiernan 1985, 1996), and, in the words of a DK spokesman, *Angkar's* victory marked the end of "over two thousand years of Cambodian history" (Chandler 1996: 209). However, time did not stand still in Cambodia; rather as the days and months progressed millions were expelled from their homes, separated from their families, stripped of their identity, and/or barbarously murdered.

On the very first day of the "liberation," citizens of Phnom Penh were stunned by the order that everyone was to evacuate the city (Kamm 1998; Kiernan 1996). In the weeks following 17 April 1975, the roads of Cambodia were clogged with masses of distressed men, women, and children heading away from their homes as *Angkar* troops coercively emptied the populations of cities and towns throughout the entire country (Chandler 1991; Kiernan 1996). Between two and three million people were displaced in the following two months, and facing uncertain futures, virtually everyone was forced into the countryside to become agricultural workers (Chandler 1991; Martin 1994). Correspondingly, while Phnom Penh and other urban centers were left mostly to decay, the country was sealed off from the outside world almost entirely (Chandler 1991; Jackson 1989; Kiernan 1996). The Khmer Rouge put forward several reasons for the decision to empty the cities, ranging from fear for their own security to a shortage of food in the capital (Kiernan 1996; Martin 1994; Quinn 1989). Many scholars give a very different account, suggesting the decision arose from the CPK's anti-urban ideology (Chandler 1991; Jackson 1989; Quinn 1989), and that "they saw cities as breeding grounds for counterrevolution" (Chandler 1996: 210).

Angkar situated their revolution in the public space of Phnom Penh to exhibit and proclaim their newfound authority, while simultaneously transforming the city's public space in accordance with their own anti-urban design by immediately evacuating the entire population. In this sense the CPK not only used their occupation of Phnom Penh's public space as an iconographic representation of the ultimate victory of their revolution, but seemingly tantamount to absolute mastery in the "art of control," they suppressed the potential for adversarial counterinsurgency by expelling the city's entire population to the countryside, thus eliminating the forum of urban public space altogether. This sentiment is corroborated by Chandler (1991: 247, emphasis added), who calls the decision to empty the towns "a calculated, political decision . . . with an economic and *ideological* rationale." The ideology at play was the Khmer Rouge's adoption of Chinese revolutionary thinking, that is, urban conglomerations themselves are visualized as detrimental to revolution, and thus *Angkar's* referral to Phnom Penh as "the great prostitute on the Mekong" becomes clear (Chandler 1991: 247). Moreover, in line with an ideology of absolute control, the CPK attempted to constrain space within DK so that no counter-political movements could organize and expand to overthrow their regime. Thus, whatever public space the Cambodian people had fought for and won during the long haul of history, and specifically during Cambodia's first attempt at democracy during the postcolonial Sihanouk (1953–69) and Lon Nol (1969–75) years (Chandler 1991; Corfield and Summers 2003; Peou 2000), was denied during the murderous revolution of the Khmer Rouge.

David Ayres (2000: 95) refers to the period of DK as "an era of almost incomprehensible social change," where centuries-old cultural traditions were completely devastated, social networks were torn asunder, economic activity was abolished, and state-sponsored violence and terror became unprecedented (Kiernan 1996; Weitz 2003). Conditions in Democratic Kampuchea varied both spatially and temporally, but misery and desolation were common everywhere (Church 1997; Martin 1994). It has been estimated that during *Angkar's* reign over 1.5 million, in a population of seven million, died as a direct result of the Khmer Rouge's administration and conduct (Banister and Johnson 1993; Heuveline 2001; Weitz 2003), which included cruelty and indifference, overworking people to the point of exhaustion, starvation and malnutrition, neglect and mistreatment of the sick, and the denial of medical services (Chandler 1991, 1996; Kiernan 1996; Martin 1994). As many as 200,000 more Cambodians, deemed "class enemies" by *Angkar*, were executed without trial (Chandler 1999).

However, Democratic Kampuchea would not last, and in early 1979, after months of provocation and border incursions by the Khmer Rouge, Vietnamese troops invaded Cambodia and entered a hollowed Phnom Penh on 7 January 1979 (Chandler 1991; Kiernan 1996; Martin 1994). There are several reasons for the eventual and arguably inevitable collapse of *Angkar*, including preoccupation with Vietnam, treachery from within their ranks, and the "literalness and speed" with which foreign socialist-models were followed (Chandler 1991: 236–37). In any event, what was of paramount importance to the millions of exploited and despondent Cambodians was the fact that the *Angkar* failed to maintain control of state power. In all their weariness, Cambodians must have received the news of DK's demise with exultation, as this meant a definite end to the regime's perverted conception of effecting social justice.

Following the invasion, the Vietnamese installed a client government known as the State of Cambodia (SOC), where Khmer Rouge defector Hun Sen eventually emerged as its leader in 1985 (Corfield and Summers 2003). The official name of the country was changed from Democratic Kampuchea to the People's Republic of Kampuchea (PRK). Almost immediately following the Vietnamese invasion of Cambodia, the United States began secretly backing Pol Pot in exile (Pilger 1998; Roberts 2001). In November 1980, Washington made direct contact with the Khmer Rouge when Ray Cline, former Deputy Director of the CIA, visited Pol Pot's operational base in Cambodia as a senior foreign policy advisor to President-elect Ronald Reagan (Blum 1998; Colhoun 1990). By 1981, some 50 CIA and other intelligence agents were conducting covert operations against Cambodia from the American Embassy in Bangkok and along the Thai–Cambodian border (Pilger 1997). America's objective was two-fold: (1) to appease China, enduring Khmer Rouge benefactor and adversary of the Soviet Union and Vietnam; and (2) to revive and then utilize the Khmer Rouge in putting pressure on the Vietnamese, America's source of recent humiliation in Indochina (Pilger 1998; Roberts 1997). In collusion with the US, China was supplying Pol Pot with arms (Colhoun 1990; Herman 1997; Roberts 2001). The Carter administration's National Security advisor, Zbigniew Brzezinski, stated in 1979 that he "encouraged the Chinese to support Pol Pot . . . Pol Pot was an abomination. We could never support him but China could" (quoted in Herman 1997: np).

Pilger (1998: 4) refers to the United States and China as "Pol Pot's accessories and Faustian partners for the purposes of their own imperial imperatives." This depiction of the relationship among the US, China, and Pol Pot is indeed fitting, given that for eleven years Washington and Beijing led the charge in defending the Khmer Rouge as the rightful occupants of Cambodia's UN seat in place of the Hanoi-backed Hun Sen government (Blum 1998; Roberts 2001). Without American financial support, coupled with the Chinese supplying arms, the Khmer Rouge would have "withered on the vine" (Pilger 1998: 4). Instead, the Khmer Rouge continued to wage a guerrilla war against the incumbent regime from their jungle strongholds located along Cambodia's northwestern border until finally collapsing in 1998 following the death of Pol Pot. Meanwhile, because of American disapproval for the Vietnam-installed regime in Phnom Penh, Cambodia was forsaken after ten years of abhorrent warfare and grievous poverty. Washington compelled the UN to withhold development aid and impose an embargo that barred Cambodia from all international agreements on trade and communications (Pilger 1998; Roberts 2001). To this date, Cambodia retains the shameful distinction of being the only country in the world to have been denied development aid by the UN (Roberts 1997). As for the sanctions, they were absolute; not even Cuba or the Soviet Union were treated in so severe a manner (Pilger 1997).

Cambodia opens for business: The Paris Peace Agreements, marketization, and the renewal of patron politics

Throughout the 1980s, SAPs were not part of the platform used to push markets into Cambodia. Instead, the first half of the decade saw *de facto* privatization creep across the country, and in response to the emerging sea change in global geopolitics, the Cambodian government introduced a number of economic reforms in 1989. These reforms, which consisted of a change in land tenure policy, tax and marketing policies, a new investment law designed to attract foreign capital, and a separation of the state from production through the reduction of subsidies and the privatization of state-owned businesses (Hughes 2003b; Irvin 1993; St. John 1997; Um 1990), came on the heals of Hun Sen's visit with the staunchly capitalist Thai Prime Minister Chatichai, who was very vocal in his desire to transform Indochina "from a battlefield to a market place" (quoted in Um 1990: 97). The timing of the People's Republic of Kampuchea's (PRK) reforms was not incidental, as the fall of the Soviet Union that same year signaled to Cambodian elites that the communist era had ended, leaving a return to autarky or the free-market economics of the west as the two most obvious remaining options. With Chatichai's coaxing, the PRK decided to get on board early, presumably in the hope of securing new international patrons before the rush of other former Soviet satellites came to the same conclusion. Furthermore, the lack of SAPs throughout the 1980s was not due to unsuitability of the economy *per se*; rather it was a case of Cambodia still being under Vietnam's communist wing and the west's reluctance to get further embroiled in the Indochina quagmire.

Indeed, this movement toward the free market coincided with renewed interest from the west after the decade of neglect throughout the 1980s. The PRK's economic reforms are arguably a major factor in the timing of a UN initiative to attempt to finally settle the long-burning civil conflict in Cambodia, since "the bulk of foreign capital remain[ed] poised at the door awaiting the conclusion of a political settlement that would guarantee against the threat of anarchy [*sic*]" (Um 1990: 104). The demise of the Soviet Union and the 27 September 1989 exit of the Vietnamese meant the US could end its policy of covert subversion in backing the Khmer Rouge (Blum 1998; Colhoun 1990; Herman 1997; Pilger 1997, 1998; Roberts 1997, 2001), and begin legitimately interacting with the SOC; after all, Cambodian markets were now open for business. As Khatharya Um (1990: 103) argues, "Indochina has long been a tantalizing economic prospect, with various countries having sought assiduously to circumvent their own official embargos to secure an economic foothold in Cambodia, Laos, or Vietnam." Logging, fishing, petroleum, and tourism ventures were among the many that stood to profit from opening this "booming economic region" (Wesley 1995: 64). For other countries, the interests of capital certainly played a part, but the UN proposal was also an opportunity to jettison some of the guilt that surely lingered due to the decade of international abandonment and indifference that followed in the wake of the Khmer Rouge atrocities (Boua 1993; Curtis 1998; Mysliwiec 1988; Nautiyal 1992).

With at least somewhat dubious motives (see Boua 1993; Roberts 2001; Shawcross 1994; Thion 1993), the UN in 1991 negotiated a settlement to the long-running civil war between the Coalition Government of Democratic Kampuchea (CGDK), consisting of Cambodian resistance groups including remnants of the Khmer Rouge, and Vietnam's former clients, the SOC (Brown 1993; Brown and Timberman 1998; Findlay 1995; Heininger 1994; Ratner 1993). The signing of the Agreements on a Comprehensive Political Settlement of the Cambodia Conflict (also known as and herein referred to as the Paris Peace Agreements) on 23 October 1991 marked the official beginning of what has become known as Cambodia's "triple transition" from authoritarianism to democracy, command economy to free market, and war to peace (Curtis 1998; Hendrickson 2001; Hughes 2003b; Peou 2000;

Tith 1998), which would be overseen by the United Nations Transitional Authority in Cambodia (UNTAC). Article 12 (Part II) of the Paris Peace Agreements (PPA) stated that, "the Cambodian people shall have the right to determine their own political future through the free and fair election of a constituent assembly" (Hendrickson 1998: 50).

The UNTAC was charged with the task of disarming the warring factions and creating a "neutral political environment" in which future "free and fair" elections could take place (Boutros-Ghali 1995; Curtis 1993; Doyle 1995, 1997; Findlay 1995; Nautiyal 1992; Ratner 1995; Suntharalingam 1997). The PPA further stipulated that once elected, the constituent assembly should draft and approve a new constitution and in accordance with Article 23, transform itself into a legislative assembly. Article 23 outlined the principles for a new Cambodian constitution that included human rights and basic freedoms (Hendrickson 1998). If, as Joakim Ojendal (1996: 194) contends, "one of the intrinsic aspects of the [UNTAC] operation was the establishment of an [economic] liberal order . . . [via Cambodia's] reconnection to the international economy," then the ruling SOC party seemed onboard with Cambodia's transformation to a liberal democracy even before the PPA signing. Indeed, "only with the arrival of UNTAC in 1992 was Cambodia able to fully reconnect with the world economy" (Tith 1998: 101), and the SOC's move away from a command economy in 1989 was the first hint of this, a position that was later solidified on 18 October 1991, when the SOC announced a formal end to communism. The SOC party renamed itself the Cambodian People's Party (CPP) and adopted a political platform that stated, "all Cambodian citizens have the right to the freedom of political beliefs, assembly, publication and defence in the courts" (quoted in Brown 1992: 93). The platform also espoused the continued economic liberalization away from communism toward a truly free-market economy (Brown 1992). Soon thereafter, in early 1992, Cambodia began "normalizing relations with the developed world and accepting large amounts of aid in the form of grants and loans from bilateral and multilateral sources . . . with the idea of becoming fully reintegrated into the global economy" (Ear 1997: 73). However, the attribute of "normal" to such relations can only refer to the status quo of aid dependency and debt in the Global South.

Despite signing the PPA, the adoption of a new platform, and agreeing to the eventual implementation of a new constitution based on political liberalism, it was not long before authorities violated the "democratic" spirit of these agreements. On 17 December 1991, demonstrators consisting of both government employees and students gathered in Phnom Penh to protest about high-level government corruption related to privatization (Jones and PoKempner 1993). In an early appearance of the "shadow state" at work, government staff accused their superiors of pocketing money made from selling or leasing factories and official residences to private foreign entrepreneurs (Hughes 2003b). The demonstrations proceeded without incident until 21 December 1991, when police beat two students and arrested another

(Jones and PoKempner 1993). Over the next two days police stepped up their aggressions, thrashing many protesters with batons and firing their weapons into the crowds (Peou 2000). By 24 December 1991, the police were success-ful in dispersing the demonstrations, but not without bloodshed, as eight civilians had been left dead, with another twenty-six injured. In the days following the protests the government reacted by imposing a curfew in Phnom Penh, banning demonstrations, and on 27 December 1991, passing legislation restricting permission for demonstrations it believed could lead to violence (Jones and PoKempner 1993; Peou 2000).

The government's response to this episode represents both a temporal and spatial strategy to deny the theatricality of the *space of appearance* "where collective rights to performance and speech are entrenched" (Goheen 1994: 431), by ensuring that there are no "repeated performances" of collective representation through which citizens may produce a viable public space (Valentine 1996: 216). In addition, this strategy represents an attempt to impose an "ordered" view of public space, which subverts Mitchell's (2003b: 33) "logic of representation" and ultimately works to preserve the status quo of the existing social order through the re-administration of space. That is to say, what is particularly problematic about the government's approach is its delegitimizing of demonstrations through law. Although this piece of legisla-tion predates and contravenes Cambodia's new constitution, it is still used in Cambodia, where would-be protesters require official government sanction via a demonstration license to "legally" hold a public protest. Consequently, most planned demonstrations that are critical of the government or its policies have henceforth not received a licence and have accordingly been criminalized as the "ordered" view of public space is used to limit the threat of democratic social power to dominant social and economic interests. Thus, the response of *violence from above* to "illegal" and "unruly" demonstrations is legitimized and has become a common response to public protests.

Furthermore, while the demonstrations indicated that the patronage system "is not monolithic, but contains its own tensions and contradictions that can cause outbreaks of discontent" (Hughes 2003b), the government response was clear. It conveyed a strong message that it was not going to budge on its agenda of economic liberalism, presumably because those in high positions quickly came to realize that by twisting their ability to informally control markets and material rewards into instruments of power via "shadow state" politics, they could amass extraordinary amounts of wealth. Their position of political power was guaranteed by their rising economic power, which together, both the economic and the political, were lodged in a foundation of patron–client networks. In other words, the former communists had transformed themselves into neoliberals, where the politics of patronage were retooled to accommodate this ideological shift. Patron–client ties, which are not at all unique to Cambodia and can be found in various forms in virtually every human society, have existed since the dawn of agricultural production when roving bandits (barbarians) transformed themselves into stationary bandits (monarchy) and societies became socially, politically, and economic-ally stratified (see Olsen 1993). Scott (1972: 92) defines the patron–client relationship, which is an exchange relationship between roles,

> as a special case of dyadic (two-person) ties involving a largely instr-umental friendship in which an individual of higher socioeconomic status (patron) uses his own influence and resources to provide protection or benefits, or both, for a person of lower status (client) who, for his part, reciprocates by offering general support and assistance, including personal services, to the patron.

In the Cambodian context, David Roberts (2001) paints a picture of patron–client relations as a pervasive social reality, which indeed they currently are (see Frieson 1996a; Heder 1995; Hughes 2003b; Ledgerwood and Vijghen 2002). However, Roberts goes further to suggest patron–client bonds are an ingrained cultural feature, where the use of "culture" throughout Roberts' thesis is extremely essentialist in nature. Echoing the "scientific racism" of a bygone era, Roberts (2001) repeatedly makes destructive and disparaging accusations about Cambodian culture, labelling it "violent" (2001: 52), "abso-lutist" (2001: 36), having an "innate resistance to power sharing" (2001: 27), and in perpetuating the "Great Dichotomy" of modernization theory, he labels it "traditional" (2001: 5).

Roberts (2001) forwards his *strongly culturalist* and harmful diatribes in an effort to illustrate what he sees as the cultural imperialism of "alien" values, and to prove that Khmer culture is unsuited to democracy. As an example, which is by no means isolated, Roberts (2001: 53–54) argues:

> [violent] behavior can be connected to Cambodian cultural heritage and tradition. . . . in Khmer relationships there is no mechanism or system for managing disputes. Furthermore, the intolerance of others' opinions characteristic of political, as well as social, culture aggravates the likelihood of confrontation. . . . The absence of institutions to resolve conflicts that derive from intolerance of "other" views leads to their settlement in more violent ways.

Although Roberts (2001) explicitly states he does not espouse the "Asian values" position, this can be interpreted as an attempt to cover his tracks so to speak, since his book *Political Transition in Cambodia, 1991–1999* reads as a thinly veiled recapitulation of this idea. As an example of such "Asian Values," Roberts (2001: 205) argues that economic development must precede democracy, "Because the majority of Khmers are relatively poor, voting for openness and accountability – that is, for democracy – [is] counterproductive to their economic and social requirements." In other words, Roberts is arguing that democracy is bad for Cambodia given its current cultural and socioeconomic milieu, while the patron–client system is implicitly accepted as more "appropriate." In a review of Robert's book, Raymond Zepp (2004: 61) challenges the apathetic treatment of the current status quo, and suggests, "To refer to the present patron-client system as a cultural given or even a cultural blessing to its people is to gloss over a cruel and inhumane anarchy [*sic*]. It is not a cultural system, but rather the law of the jungle, where the strong take from the weak." In other words, simply because a system of exploitation has deep historical roots in a particular geographic setting, does not mean this system is a "cultural" characteristic of the people it serves to oppress.

A further key mistake is the implication that these relations have moved through the course of history unchanged since time immemorial. Roberts fails to take notice of the ways in which economic liberalization transforms patron–client relations. The elite mold these relations via their economic strength into practices of rent-seeking, vote-buying, and corruption, while the peasantry responds to such abuse by using its "weapons of the weak" in the form of primarily negation and passive resistance, but occasionally open rebellion (Scott 1985). For the elite's part, the move to free-market economics seemed to offer "a matrix of resources that could shore up exclusionary loyalties within the weak state apparatus, and reducing the field of action for resistance in rural villages, as a means to strengthen the state militarily and politically" (Hughes 2003b: 19). Specifically, the dismantling of agrarian "solidarity groups" and the move toward private land ownership was seen as a way to undermine the subversive threat of the Khmer Rouge (Um 1990).

Cambodian elites are not unique in their desire to retain their position of power, so the need to resort to depictions of Khmer culture as "absolutist," "violent" and "inappropriate" for democracy is not only essentialist, but represents an analytical lacuna. The desire for preservation is a universal symptom of power, applying equally to authoritarian and democratic regimes. That many of the CPP's high-ranking officials were educated in the economically liberal west should not be overlooked,[3] and the move toward free-market economics, and particularly its timing, suggests that Cambodia's political elites were shrewd planners who intended this transformation as a strategic maneuver to ensure their position of power into the future. They also realized that this transformation would require a new *modus operandi*. This was to be found in building their own personal wealth, and following Marxian theory which considers capitalism as an exploitative system that allows for very few "winners," the newfound embracement of neoliberalism allowed Cambodian elites to harden their political power *vis-à-vis* society. Indeed, as Dylan Hendrickson (2001: 101) notes, "Despite rapid economic liberalization after 1991, the benefits were largely limited to the urban areas and to the country's elite classes. Cambodia's political leaders seized the opportunities to enrich themselves and strengthen their powerbases. . . ." This was done in large part through their ability to control International Financial Institution (IFI) prescribed privatization schemes, where many state-owned enterprises were either purchased by members of the ruling class themselves or used corrupt practices such as bribery to negotiate the purchase or lease of public land and enterprise.

The plunder of Cambodian forests provides a prime example of such corruption, where public lands are leased to foreign companies not only with the typical neoliberal ideology of allowing for tax holidays and renewable leases, but also under circumstances of bribery where government royalties fail to reflect the true value of the timber (Multinational Monitor 1997). As Journalist Gar Smith (1997: 28) suggests, "the price of admission to log the world's vanishing forests frequently takes the form of a political bribe," and he quotes the Associated Press who explain that "many Asian companies gain footholds through hostile takeovers or by buying concessions from locals. Often cemented by bribes, they form alliances with the elites that enable them to skirt laws, win virtually every legal case ... and sometimes affect national legislation." The impact on government coffers has been disastrous, as the Cambodian government has continually received little "official" revenue from logging operations. In 1997, the government lost US$90 million in logging revenues, but by that time, they had sold nearly all of Cambodia's available forestland to logging firms (Global Witness 1997). Global Witness, Cambodia's former official forest-crime monitor who was recently sacked under dubious circumstances of government intimidation and IFI complicity, has for years been expressing the serious concern about the situation in Cambodia. As early as 1996 they had cautioned there is not "another instance in the world where such a vast proportion of a country's forests, situated in areas with no effective government control, had been sold in such a short time, and in such great secrecy, to foreign companies" (quoted in the Edmonton Journal 1996: E7). The poor, who, as expected, receive little to no benefit from logging endeavors, have become increasingly militant in response to such activities. They have *taken* public space to bring visibility to their dismay in the hope of stemming the activities directly responsible for a decline in their ability to sustain their livelihoods. This is made evident in newspaper headlines compiled from *The Cambodian Daily* and presented in Table 3.1.

In terms of the patron–client bond itself, a clear example of how economic privilege has been manipulated to strengthen this relationship comes from Hun Sen himself. Hun Sen presents himself publicly as benevolent benefactor and friend of the people, building schools and hospitals in his own name rather than that of the state. He is able to do this because of his extraordinary wealth, and in return for such gifts, he is able to secure a strong client base, as it is only those villages with strong showings of support that receive Hun Sen's financial blessings (Hughes 2003b). In contrast to *culturalist* explanations which view patron–client relations as unique to Cambodia or Southeast Asia, and overlook the fact that the same patterns are found in the west, most overtly in so-called "corporate culture," economic ingenuity and individual cunning of the patron are a more apt explanation for the ongoing prevalence and relevance of patron–clientelism in Cambodia.

Table 3.1 Resistance to forest clearing

Headline	Date
4 Trucks of Illegal Wood Confiscated in K Cham	01-07/11/2008
Fugitive Sought in R'kiri Land Dispute Case	01-05/12/2008
Protected Wood Illegally Cut in R'kiri. Adhoc	15-19/12/2008
Mondolkiri Land Dispute Turns Violent	22-28/12/2008
Ratanakkiri Villagers Sue Keat Kolney Again	22-28/12/2008
K Cham Police Probe Shooting at Forestry Office	05-09/01/2009
M'kiri Villagers Clash With Developers in Dispute	24-30/01/2009
Families to Guard Forests in Kompong Thom	21-27/03/2009
Two Arrested, Six Sought in R'kiri Dispute	25-01/04-05/2009
Villager, NGO Allege Illegal Tree Planting on Contested Land	09-15/05/2009
Ethnic Minority Members Block Efforts to Clear Land in Kratie	09-15/05/2009
Alleged Logging Near Dam Site Worries Environmentalists	06-12/06/2009
Banlung Villagers To Protest Illegal Logging, Land Grabbing	20-26/06/2009
R'kiri Villagers Clash With Police Over Illegally Logged Wood	27-03/06-07/2009
Journalist Killed, Two Injured in Pursuit of Illegal Loggers	11-17/07/2009
Illegal Logging of Rare Trees On the Rise in Ratanakkiri	11-17/07/2009
Pursat Villagers Protest the Sale of Sacred Trees	05-11/09/2009
Mother, Son Beaten Unconscious Over Luxury Wood Argument	05-11/09/2009
Banong Families Fight S Korean Agribusiness Firm For Forest"	17-23/10/2009

Source: The Cambodia Daily: Weekly Review.

Indeed, economic liberalism has not broken the bonds of patron–client relations as is theorized by neoliberals. Instead, it has allowed them to become "further entrenched in the state due to the inability of the [weak] formal economy to offer alternative livelihood opportunities" (Hendrickson 2001: 101). Moreover, the prospects for Cambodian public space are damaged by such activity, as Hun Sen's schools and hospitals are not truly public, but rather "private" gifts from the country's leader that always come connected with the erection of a CPP party signboard, as well as the inscription of Hun Sen's personal monograph (Hughes 2001b; 2003b). The pervasiveness of this practice is very apparent when visiting Cambodia, where in contrast to CPP party signboards as a prevalent feature of the landscape, one rarely sees opposition party signboards outside of the capital.[4] The subtle inclusion of Hun Sen's insignia on "public" buildings transforms the publicness of these *representational spaces* and their potential as *spaces for representation* into *representations of space*. The prospective for dissent within such illusory public spaces is therefore negligible, as the supposed benevolence of the benefactor is visually reinforced by the physical presence of a personal or party logo. Accordingly, this strategy precludes any criticism of the patron, or at least places an unnecessary burden of risk on those who would dissent, as conflict may arise with individuals who accept such spaces as altruistic gifts and thus inappropriate locations to situate challenges to the intentions of the leader. This is clear given that even in more overtly public spaces free from the physical visual reminders of CPP authority, participants to this study commonly cited fear of conflict or retaliation should they discuss politics at all, let alone express dissenting views[5]:

"... in the very rural where, for example, they live close to a village chief or someone who are strong member of such political party and who perform on the path or who, who is performing like very strong member, and so then the other person who live close by, may feel not comfortable to talk in the public space. For example like, if they live in the same village, then they say something, if they talk something they would say 'don't tell such person like Mr. A because he or she is very strong or they are strong member of such party' so you be careful, make sure that, what we are talking about, not pass on to them."[6]

"For me I feel unsafe talking about political issues in the public space but for those who are interested in political or worried about political affairs, I think it is important for them to speak about these issues in the public spaces."[7]

"I never discuss about this [politics] with friends, family or strangers. I am afraid we will have the Pol Pot regime again. I am afraid about this, because the Pol Pot [regime] kill my parents all. If I talk or criticise, I'm worried this will happen again."[8]

"I am afraid to talk [in] the public space ... afraid. Afraid yeah ... maybe I will have the problem happen for me, so I cannot talk, discuss about this in the public space because someone [may] like the another party ... so [we are] not the same [as] each other, the same idea, so maybe [I'm] afraid they make trouble for me."[9]

"The politic cannot open, be open for me, open, to say in the public, speak in public. When I discuss in the public space I afraid when someone will have ... they like another party, they make trouble ... make trouble for me or sometimes they hurt me, has problem for me. For me this never, happen for me, but I saw someone, happen make problem with someone, I saw but for me never happen. ... I saw about the another party, someone that like the party and another person that like the different party, they kill ... they can kill, to kill, and sometimes hit each other, and sometimes they hate them."[10]

"It is important for the democracy too, for the, the people that [have an] idea to say something about the political [situation], but nowadays, in Cambodia we have the democracy but, ah, some people they afraid about the ... to discuss about the politics, because they still afraid ... Because they think it's the, many people like different party so when we discuss and talk with each other ... might have a problem. I am afraid of violence."[11]

In this pervasive atmosphere of ubiquitous fear, Hun Sen's use of personal and party insignias has introduced a panoptic condition with a largely predetermined social production of space as pro-CPP, thereby undermining the "public" status of the schools and hospitals he builds.

"Neutral political environment" of panopticon? Undermining democracy in the name of "stability"

All three elements of Cambodia's "triple transition" remain unconsolidated to this day. The first indication that the path to democracy would not be as smooth as envisioned by the PPA came when the CGDK's Khmer Rouge element destroyed any prospect for moving from war to peace soon after the UNTAC arrived in the country. Though signatories to the PPA, the Party of Democratic Kampuchea (PDK) ultimately rejected the plan when it became clear to them that they would be unable to attain political power through democratic means and resumed guerrilla activities from Cambodia's periphery near the Thailand border (Heder 1996; Kiernan 1992, 1993b; Shawcross 2002; Talentino 2003; Wesley 1995; Will 1993). Furthermore, the PDK's withdrawal threatened the entire UNTAC mission as it threw the disarmament proposal into disarray. With the Khmer Rouge ignoring the ceasefire, the other factions refused to hand their weapons over to the UNTAC. The disarmament failure subsequently had a profound effect on the second objective of creating a "neutral political environment," as the continued strength of the military, and its control by the CPP, meant it proved impossible to disentangle the CPP from the state apparatus itself (Frieson 1996b; Heder 1996; Hughes 1996; Kiernan 1992, 1993b). However, the UN mission was successful insofar as the election went ahead as scheduled in May of 1993. Three major parties competed: the CPP, headed by Hun Sen, and the two remaining CGDK elements, the Royalist Party known as FUNCINPEC, the French acronym for the National United Front for an Independent, Neutral, Peaceful, and Cooperative Cambodia, headed by Prince Ranariddh, and the Buddhist Liberal Democratic Party (BLDP), which ran independently of each other (Findlay 1995).

Providing a detailed assessment of the UNTAC's successes and failures is not within the scope of this book. There already exists a vast literature on this UN operation, where its effectiveness has been the subject of fierce debate (see Babb and Steuber 1998; Doyle 1995, 1997, 1998; Duffy 1994; Findlay 1995; Heininger 1994; Hughes 1996; Lizée 1994, 2000; Munck and Kumar 1995; Peou 1997; Ratner 1995; Sanderson 2001; Suntharalingam 1997; Talentino 2003; Tombes 1994; Will 1993). However, regardless of one's position on the utility of the UNTAC, for the purpose of this argument, it is important to recognize that the UN-sponsored transition did not end the violence. Indeed, the predominant characteristics of the run-up to the 1993 elections were the threats of violence, intimidation, and bloodshed. Although scholars such as Michael Vickery (1995) and David Roberts (2001) deny any pattern to CPP violence during the elections, both have a reputation as CPP apologists. Analyses that are more balanced suggest the CPP killed more than a hundred opposition members, and subjected the population at large to arbitrary violence and intimidation (Brown and Zasloff 1998; Doyle 1997; Findlay 1995; Heder and Ledgerwood 1996; Hughes 2003b; Peou 2000; Um 1994). Judy Ledgerwood (1996: 131) argues that such violence and intimidation was indeed widespread:

> [the electoral violence] cannot be understood as the isolated outbursts of local-level agents of an authoritarian regime struggling to retain power and privilege. It suggests that at a more systematic level the explanation lies in the ways in which those with power to propagandize and violently repress others handled the gap between political rhetoric and social reality in the new situation created by the Paris Agreements. SOC offered a continuing search for "enemies within" and an ongoing process of finding and punishing those who betray the state.

The "continuing search" refers to the Khmer Rouge's historical precedent of terror.

DK used several metaphors to define their regime, but one of the most telling is the saying "*Angkar* has the eyes of a pineapple," which, echoing Jeremy Bentham's Panopticon, suggests that *Angkar* is omnipotent as the eyes of a pineapple point in all directions (Marston 1994). The metaphor's message was clear in suggesting that so-called "enemies of the revolution" could not hide from the regime. While the CPP stopped short of resurrecting the same allegory, the intended message was effectively the same. Cambodian voters were informed via propaganda, intimidation, and violence that democracy was not available, that there was no space to define and manifest one's individual identity, nor was there space to foster meaningful social relations without fear of being questioned on their loyalty to the SOC. William Shawcross (2002: 50) suggests "the Hun Sen regime . . . did everything it could to undermine the attempt to enforce democratic political and judicial norms," which worked in collusion with the CPP's attempt to reinforce its grasp on the population by reorienting its administrative structures to party-building tasks. Indeed, the CPP appeared monolithic insofar as it maintained tight control over the bureaucracy, army, police, media, and judiciary (Doyle 1995). Kate Frieson (1996a) conveys this very point when she argues that the SOC's administrative apparatus, including the civil service, police, and military, were indivisible from the CPP. While the PPA stipulated there must be a separation of party and state, in reality the two moved closer together during the UNTAC period. In other words, the UN failed to implement its primary mandate of creating a "neutral political environment" by disentangling the CPP from the SOC, which subsequently greatly undermined the potential for the emergence of a public space since in Staeheli and Thompson's (1997: 30, emphasis added) view, public space must be "*equally* open to all members of a polity."

The Khmer Rouge also played their part by terrorizing the countryside.

David Ashley (1996) paints a picture of extensive guerrilla warfare in Battambang Province, which involved a pattern of arbitrary detention and summary execution of SOC officials, random violence against the population at large, as well as violence aimed at preventing the elections from taking place. The situation in Battambang was not isolated, and reflected a larger pattern of violence throughout the western areas of Cambodia that were still controlled by the Khmer Rouge since their fall from power in 1979. For example, on 27 December 1992, 20 heavily armed Khmer Rouge soldiers entered a village on the Tonle Sap River and massacred 13 ethnic Vietnamese and two ethnic Khmer residents. Clearly, the Khmer Rouge's racist ideology had not been consigned to the past, as the most brutal of their activities focused on Cambodia's ethnic Vietnamese. Another attack on 27 January 1993 claimed 8 lives, and 10 March 1993 marked an apex in malevolence against Vietnamese residents of Cambodia during the UNTAC period, when 29 were injured and another 33 individuals were massacred (Brown and Zasloff 1998; Chopra 1994). The PDK insurgents also utilized extensive propaganda campaigns aimed at convincing the population not to participate in the elections, with the most serious deterrent being the threat to blow up several polling booths on election day (Brown and Zasloff 1998; Heder 1996; Shawcross 2002). The prospect of a "neutral political environment" was clearly in tatters, and thus so too was the possibility of the emergence of a truly public space.

Nonetheless, the brutal pre-election conditions did not prevent the election in May of 1993. Given the potential for "political calamity and personal danger," the turnout was remarkable (Um 1994: 74). The UNTAC had managed to persuade 95 percent of the population to register to vote, and 90 percent of those registered showed up at the polls (Brown and Zasloff 1995; Findlay 1995; Frieson 1996a). The sheer number of Cambodians who came out to vote sent a clear message to Cambodia's political parties and the world: peace and democracy were overwhelmingly desired, and violence and intimidation would not be a deterrent to the Cambodian people's realization of these goals. However, despite the strong showing of the population at the polls, controversy swirled over the outcome. FUNCINPEC won the election with 45.5 percent of the votes, the CPP was placed second with 38.2 percent, while the BLDP was placed third with 3.8 percent (Brown and Timberman 1998; Gallup 2002), and although the UNTAC quickly declared the elections "free and fair," Hun Sen and the CPP refused to accept the results (Ashley 1998a; Findlay 1995; Gallup 2002). Convinced of electoral fraud, the CPP threatened succession of all the land to the east of the Mekong River (Ashley 1998a; Peou 2000; Shawcross 2002; Um 1994), which would ultimately mean protracted civil war on top of the reignited Khmer Rouge border resistance.

The most common explanation for the UNTAC's acceptance of an outcome inconsistent with the election results was that it was not in a position to confront the CPP militarily (Ashley 1998a; Boutros-Ghali 1995; Doyle 1995; Will 1993). A slightly more skeptical view suggests that Cambodia was preordained as the UN's peacekeeping model and biggest success story to date, and in order to avoid having the whole operation blow up in its face, the UN agreed to preside over the creation of an inauspicious coalition between the CPP and FUNCINPEC (Roberts 2001; Shawcross 1994, 2002). Indeed, there is a level of credibility to both of these explanations. However, Peou (2000: 255) provides a more critical appraisal in arguing that the PPA "were not designed to undermine SOC's hegemonic status. In fact, one could argue that they weakened the resistance forces and could enhance the SOC's political legitimacy by electoral means." This assessment fits neatly with the neoliberal focus on the prominence of "order" and "stability," which in Pierre Lizée's (1993) view was the true goal of the PPA as the UN was in fact looking for options that would bring stability to Cambodia, regardless of the result of the vote. In this respect, the UN took power out of the hands of the Cambodian electorate and gave it to the factional leaders. Reinforcing the powerful position of the CPP/SOC would increase stability in the short term and allow for an immediate influx of foreign companies eager to exploit both Cambodian resources and its newly opened markets following an early IFI prescription adopted by the SOC, which called for the removal of barriers impeding the establishment of foreign firms (Ear 1997).

Indeed, the victory of FUNCINPEC not only came as a shock to most observers, but also posed a significant obstacle to the machinations of foreign enterprise. Moreover, the authors of the PPA lent implicit support to the "iron fist" of Hun Sen, as he was allowed to force his way into a renewed position of power while democracy took a backseat to the "ordered" position of neoliberalism. Therefore, while Prince Ranariddh and Hun Sen became co-prime ministers, the CPP never truly shared power and dominated the new regime.[12] This was easily predictable, not because of a supposedly "absolut-ist" culture, but simply because of the continued entanglement of the CPP with the state apparatus, the failure of disarmament, and as the following section will illustrate, IFI prescribed civil service downsizing. Thus, the UN's preoccupation with "stability" over the will of the people undermined the prospect of Cambodian democracy from the very beginning, and only served to hinder the development of a viable public space.

The repercussions of the UN's decision would come back to haunt Cambodia as the shocking coup of 1997 (discussed below) would illustrate that true stability is not borne of submission to the whims of the powerful, but through the collective good of democracy. What's more, Cambodian perceptions of democracy in their country have been damaged ever since:

> "I think ... in Cambodia now ... the democracy is just only have the name. The people still afraid they still scared, could not express their own ideas and speak something ... or speak something related to the government, and its not a full democracy, has a lot of ... lack, it is lacking many kinds of things, various kinds of things ... it is still lacking."[13]

"Many people, most people of Cambodia want the democracy but they, they cannot access what they want to do. For example want to make education, but can't access . . . So I would like to give you a definition of democracy, it mean, to mean that people can do what they want, people have rights enough to, right enough to make something, right enough to talk freely. This means the people have rights enough to, to you know for example, to earn money and to go anywhere or to talk to friends or to talk about political but in Cambodia its not . . . not openly. In Cambodia right now we have a little democracy system, need especially to be improved, to be improved in the future."[14]

"I think nowadays Cambodian democracy is not clear, only speak the word of democracy. People cannot speak much if they are simple citizens or top leaders. Gasoline protests doing to keep price lower but army stop them . . . its not good. . . . I think [democracy is] important in Cambodia but right now we can't have this kind of democracy in Cambodia . . . they just speak of democracy . . . still lead to Communist control. . . . participation is part of democracy, but I don't think right now we can have this type of things, we just speak but cannot get the results. Some radio, TV programs that love in democracy, which get people to talk about democracy but they only talk."[15]

"I think the democracy in Cambodia it [is] a small . . . small idea of the group, we cannot do democracy in Cambodia, not large, so democracy can live in the white man or educational man because . . . and so democracy in Cambodia, it is small group. When we say something to the people that we don't know, we . . . sometimes we can get the, ah, dangerous from them because they, the powerful of the person who give it to Cambodia and . . . they just come from the Communist. And so in Cambodia now, they have democracy, but it is small because of before the Cambodians always get the idea from the Communist. And so when we say I think it very good for we want to speak democracy to the people that we don't know, but under democracy now, it very small, it live in the heart of the people in the Cambodia but [if] we say something to the person who have powerful, we can't dare. . . ."[16]

"Its not working, and since the year that Hun Sen made himself the president, since that year on, I feel that democracy is not working here. I feel that I'm is not living in a democratic country."[17]

"I think democracy, this is underworking. Its underworking. Not, not just little bit . . . we have just start a little bit. I, I think, I want? The word, ah, transition . . . transitional . . . transition. Yeah, yeah, I like this word. The eleven years is transitional period for democracy in Cambodia, not the full step."[18]

". . . in Cambodia we have the democracy, its good for the democracy but I'm still afraid, to talk anywhere about the politic. But Cambodia have the democracy . . . democracy but the people still afraid. We have the democracy but the people in Cambodia, we can say the people or the person who [is the] top person cannot use democracy for the bottom people . . . The top people, do not give the rights to the people who talk the democracy, democracy [means] you can talk everywhere, but when the people talk everywhere [in Cambodia today], not safe, they afraid, something that happen to them . . . Because the top people not respecting people because they have powerful, they have the power. . . . Now the democracy have in the paper, write down in the paper, but all the person not respect, or not the implementation by the law, by the democracy because have in the paper, write down in the paper. I mean the book, they have the rule and the democracy we have write down in the paper, but some people not respect. . . ."[19]

Although these accounts have a palpable degree of pessimism, all participants interviewed for this study expressed a strong desire for democracy, meaning that such cynicism has not necessarily translated into a languid attitude about democracy. Lefebvre (1991: 381–85) reminds us, the (re)production of space is a "continual struggle between the state . . . trying to produce and maintain a seemingly homogeneous but fundamentally contradictory abstract space on the one hand, and subaltern groups . . . asserting the 'counter-spaces' and constructing their 'counter-publics', on the other," and this contention seems to be implicitly understood and accepted by Cambodians. Indeed, regardless of the CPP/SOC commandeering the election results and the UNTAC's acquiesce to this subversion, Jeffery Gallup (2002: 169) contends that, "in Cambodia, elections opened up a democratic space that had not existed previously." If nothing else, as shall be seen below, the 1993 elections (re)planted the seeds of democracy in the hearts and minds of Cambodians, a (re)discovery that would become manifest in the coming years when Cambodians began to transform their "arts of resistance" from "hidden transcripts" (Scott 1990), into overt contestation in the visible domain of public space.[20] In other words, Cambodians would soon begin to demand democracy by *taking* public space.

Welcoming the false dawn: The neoauthoritarianism of neoliberalism in Cambodia

Following the elections a new constitution was promulgated, which reinstated the Monarchy and officially renamed the country the Kingdom of Cambodia. Along with renewed pledges to ensure structural adjustment and continued privatization (St. John 1995), Cambodia's experiment with economic liberalization was also signed into the law under the new constitution, as indicated in Article 56 which states: "The Kingdom of Cambodia shall adopt a market economy system" (Jennar 1995: 17). The signing of a new constitution also officially ended the UNTAC's mandate and the entire operation left Cambodia before the end of 1993 (Marks 1994). However, despite the long presence of peacekeepers, armed clashes between factional groups and armed conflict between the Khmer Rouge and the government lingered (Brown and Zasloff 1998; Jeldres 1996; Lizée 1996; Shawcross 1994; Um 1994). Similarly, it was not long before cracks began to show in the new coalition government. Many observers relate this to the imposition of a supposedly "alien" "form of politics which did not appertain to Cambodian society" (Lizée 2000: 13; see also Heder 1995; Roberts 2001). However, Hendrickson (2001) contrasts such *culturalist* explanations by arguing instead that IFI preoccupation with macroeconomic stabilization and structural adjustment undermined the potential of building political consensus, as well as subverting other programs essential to the consolidation of peace, such as addressing humanitarian needs. Indeed, neoliberalization was the order of the day as immediately following the 1993 election the Ministry of Finance, under tutelage from the WB, IMF, and Asian Development Bank (ADB), was already promising that a "stringent fiscal plan" would be in place by 1995 (Um 1994: 79).

Cambodia found itself locked into a condition of dependency on foreign assistance as nearly half of the country's budgetary allocations were being drawn from foreign aid, which translated into a limited ability to challenge the donor agenda and timetable (Hendrickson 2001; Lizée 1996). Since UNTAC, Cambodia has been subjected to a number of enhanced structural adjustment facilities (ESAFs) under the auspices of the IMF, and structural adjustment credits (SACs) from the WB. ESAFs, with disbursement beginning in 1992 to coincide with UNTAC, continued right up to 1999, when the IMF changed the language of SAPs to poverty reduction and growth facilities (PRGFs) (International Monetary Fund 2007). Since the imperatives of privatization, liberalization, and deregulation remain unchanged, PRGFs are quite simply SAPs under a new name. The IMF has continued to employ PRGFs as a primary component of its funding to Cambodia, announcing in May 2006 that a new PRGF worth U.S. $70 million had been approved conditional upon the Cambodian government rescheduling its outstanding debts (McLaren 2006). The WB has implemented SACs under various names since 1993, with a recent dispersal of U.S. $36.25 million approved on 26 July 2007 in the form of a "Rural Investment and Local Governance Additional Financing" project (World Bank 2008). These technical assistance projects have undermined government ownership and capacity in that they have been donor-driven in their identification, implementation and design (Godfrey et al. 2002). This hardly represents the "bottom-up" conception of democracy I outlined in Chapter 2, and instead is indicative of a "top-down" approach.

In a statement that appears to be emblematic of the position of the entire UN operation given its fixation on economic stability, former Secretary-General of the United Nations for Human Rights in Cambodia, Michael Kirby (1995: 31), stated: "I have always made the point that an improvement in the economy, filtering down to the average citizen, is a vitally important step on the path of rebuilding human rights in Cambodia. It helps to give a sense of well-being, purpose and commitment to society." It is not surprising that Kirby's comments echo the neoliberal theory of the "trickle-down effect" as he shifts the focus from democracy to economics as the vehicle providing individuals with a sense of agency and a participatory stake in society. However, this is a problematic conception, as it is hard to see the efficacy of the "trickle-down effect" when the gap between rich and poor has only gotten wider, while poverty has similarly increased in post-transitional Cambodia.[21] Although Article 63 of the constitution states, "The State shall respect market management in order to guarantee a better standard of living" (Jennar 1995: 18), this "better standard" was not forthcoming for the majority of Cambodians. Even Ronald St. John (1997: 187), a scholar clearly inspired by neoliberal ideology, recognizes that, "while . . . some disparities existed before [economic] liberalization, social and economic inequalities are significantly greater now." Similarly, one has to wonder how a "sense of well-being" is fostered among those Cambodians whose political, civil and social liberties have been sacrificed to the neoliberal preponderance for excesses of "anarchic [*sic*] freedom as a consequence of rampant marketization and the weakening of state authority" (Hendrickson 2001: 99). This sentiment is corroborated by George Irvin (1993: 138) who asserts:

> A rapid, unreflective transition to the market economy has driven a relatively weak state to financial crisis, raised inflation to three digit level and weakened the country's social and economic infrastructure, particularly in the rural areas. Cambodia's poor, punished by years of isolation, are now being asked to pay the further costs of reintegration into the international mainstream.

In 1994, further neoliberal reforms were ordered, as donors emphasized downsizing the civil service, which has been the traditional power base for the CPP, in an effort to build administrative capacity. Prioritizing a reduction in the civil service is one example of "rolling back" the state, and it is derived from the IFI's preoccupation with controlling public expenditures as a method of achieving macroeconomic stability (Hendrickson 2001). Such a focus is highly problematic in that it contributes to "shadow state" politics insofar as encouraging rent-seeking behavior and hardening patron–client relations as civil service members become reliant on alternative means to supplement their incomes. Indeed, following the shift to free market economics, many officials began making their living in the speculative underground economy (van der Kroef 1991). The IFIs approached downsizing as an administrative exercise, while ignoring the social and political costs. Furthermore, Hendrickson (2001) argues that such a prescription was deleterious to the stability of the fragile power-sharing arrangement in Cambodia, as the new coalition government was originally premised on the integration of large numbers of FUNCINPEC and BLDP functionaries into the CPP-dominated administrative apparatus (Hendrickson 2001). Thus, a strengthening of the Royal Government of Cambodia's (RGC) administrative capacity was required, not a weakening.

In what appears to be a calculated response to downsizing efforts, the government enshrined impunity in the law in 1994 by prohibiting civil servants, including police and soldiers, from being charged or arrested without the permission of the relevant minister (Human Rights Watch 1999). In this instance, the CPP used IFI-prescribed downsizing of the civil service to their advantage, as this amendment would further entrench their hold on power via the politics of patronage. Thus, the so-called "culture of impunity" in Cambodia (see Prasso 1994; Langran 2001; Roberts 2001) is not a cultural feature at all. Rather, impunity can be seen as another example of the "shadow state" response to neoliberal reforms. Alterations to the law serve as a more illuminating example of the "shadow state," whereas the preponderance of corporate impunity in Cambodia represents its darkest corners.

The CPP's successful commandeering of the 1993 election results, and its renewed hegemony via strengthened patron–client links surely led to a feeling of euphoria among the party's leadership. This jovial mood, coupled with what appears to be a pandering to Cambodia's new patrons in the west, led Hun Sen to proclaim 1994 as the year of the resurrection of the media (Peou 2000). Thirty-five new newspapers were founded, whereas in 1993 only thirteen had existed. However, this "honeymoon" period was short-lived. In July of 1994, the media was effectively muzzled after the government issued a list of instructions indicating what the press could and could not say (Lizée 1996; Peou 2000). This was done in spite of the fact that Article 41 of Cambodia's new constitution states, "Khmer citizens shall have freedom of expression, press, publication, and assembly. No one shall exercise this right to infringe upon the rights of others, to affect the good traditions of the society, to violate public law and order, and national security" (Jennar 1995: 14). The article itself is vague enough to provide for an interpretation that actually violates the spirit of its meaning, ultimately dismissing the prospect for a vibrant public sphere insofar as "public order" and "national security" are given precedence over the notion of a public sphere that espouses unmediated interaction.

Ultimately, the interpretation of this article that led to listing what Noam Chomsky (1991) calls the "bounds of the expressible" meant that journalists were not permitted to form their own viewpoints and convey dissenting opinions, but were instead subject to the whims of the political leadership and confined to expressing the status quo. As a result, 1994 saw several attacks against the press, including the prosecution and imprisonment of several reporters, and the murder of three high-profile journalists who were particularly critical of the new coalition government (Jeldres 1996; Neumann 2002; Shawcross 2002; Woods 1997). In April of 1995, the first action taken against a foreign journalist came when the American editor of the English-language *Phnom Penh Post*, Michael Hayes, was faced with charges of "misinformation" and "incitement." King Sihanouk stepped in and assured Hayes of an official pardon if convicted. However, Cambodian journalists were not so fortunate as four editors of Khmer-language newspapers were either fined or imprisoned (Lizée 1996; Peou 2000; Woods 1997), to which co-prime minister Prince Ranariddh, showing his "Asian values" stripes, publicly asserted "the Western brand of democracy and freedom of the press is not applicable to Cambodia" (quoted in Jeldres 1996: 155). The constriction of the public sphere has been ongoing in Cambodia, where as recently as February 2005 Hun Sen has lashed out at the media suggesting that they are abusing their "privileges" and that freedom of the press is "the freedom to create problems for society" (quoted in Yun Samean 2005a). Table 3.2 highlights recent newspaper headlines collected from *The Cambodia Daily*, illustrating that the subversion of the public sphere is ongoing.

While, journalism is part of the public sphere, which should not be confused with public space, the two are related inasmuch as the public sphere is important for mobilizing people, and encouraging them to bring their dialogue, debates, and dissent into the existential realm of public space (Mitchell 2003b). Thus, the constriction of the public sphere by the powerful is always an

Table 3.2 The constriction of the public sphere

Headline	Date
Police Investigating Disappearance of TV3 Host	08-14/11/2008
Conflicting Stories on Journalist's Arrest as Lawyer Seeks Release	15-21/11/2008
Transparency at Seminar Hailed; Reporter Removed	24-30/11/2008
Another TV Host Reported Missing, Police Say	01-05/12/2008
Police Confirm Journalist Stabbed, Died in Hospital	12-16/01/2009
Two Years on, Jailed Lecturer Awaits Appeal	12-16/01/2009
TVK's Pursat Bureau Chief Robbed, Killed	31-06/01-02/2009
Owner of Controversial Website Claims Gov't Blocked Access	31-06/01-02/2009
Lecturer Who Used Anti-Gov't Book Must Pay Fine For Release	07-13/02/2009
Net Co Denies Blocking Global Witness Website	07-13/02/2009
Confusion Remains Over Magazine Confiscations	14-20/02/2009
Senior Police Officer Held in Attempted Murder of Publisher	21-27/02/2009
Group Condemns Rising Violence Against Media	21-27/02/2009
Publisher Jailed for Defamation to Restart Paper	07-13/03/2009
Publisher of a Pro-SRP Paper to be Questioned	25-01/04-05/2009
Licadho Protests Proposed Law Limiting NGOs	30-05/05-06/2009
Show Organizers Questioned After Ambassador's Speech	06-12/06/2009
Reporter and Niece Killed in Preah Vihear, Police Say	13-19/06/2009
Jailing of Newspaper Editor Earns Wide Criticism	27-03/06-07/2009
Opposition Newspapers Losing Their Bite	11-17/07/2009
Hun Sen Says He's No Dictator, Claims He's Being Mocked	01-07/08/2009
Court Upholds Editor's One-Year Jail Sentence	08-14/08/2009
Publisher of Pro-Opposition Paper Ordered To Pay Fine	22-28/08/2009
Family, Journalists Push for Publisher's Release	05-11/09/2009
Newspaper Warned Against Naming Minister	12-18/09/2009
Decriminalize Free Speech, UN Envoy Says	26-02/09-10/2009
NGOs Petition to See Draft of Law to Govern Civil Society	26-02/09-10/2009
Lawyers to Stand Firm in Defense of Press Freedom	26-02/09-10/2009
SRP Asks King To Help Imprisoned Editor	24-30/10/2009

Source: The Cambodia Daily: Weekly Review.

attempt to mitigate and manage contestation prior to its physical manifestation in public space, where the ability to enforce "order" and control may be
much more difficult. Moreover, the effort to control the public sphere is often
an explicitly geographical project inasmuch as the potential "damage" of
dissent can be diminished by authorities through an attempt to control *where*
dissent is spoken (Mitchell 2003a), which may prove easier than controlling it
altogether. Accordingly, attempts to undermine the public sphere are often,
if not always, followed and/or accompanied by attacks on public space.
Thus, the Cambodian ruling elite's distain for dissent was not isolated to
journalism, as the freedom of assembly and expression for opposition parties
were also challenged. In late September 1995, the BLDP was victimized in
two apparent incidents of *violence from above*. Two hand grenades were
thrown at the BLDP party headquarters injuring twenty-four, and seven
others were injured when a third grenade was thrown into the grounds of a
wat (temple) where BLDP supporters were camped out (Jeldres 1996; Peou
2000). While no one claimed responsibility for the attacks, many BLDP
supporters are convinced of CPP involvement as Hun Sen was very vocal in
his opposition to the proposed BLDP party congress, claiming he was "afraid
of security problems, like grenade attacks" (quoted in Peou 2000: 307).

In light of such developments, long-time Cambodia observer Steve Heder
(1995: 425) referred to Cambodia's transition as one to neoauthoritarianism,
where "In the name of political stability and economic development, as
well as in order to fight a lingering and murderous insurgency, the country's
current 'multiparty' ruling elite coalition . . . has been working to dampen
open political contestation and to deliberalize the political atmosphere by co-
opting, cowing, or marginalizing contesting centers of power. . . ." However,
Heder (1995: 426) problematically resorts to a *culturalist* explanation for such
behaviors, citing a "general refusal of elite culture to recognize the legitimacy
of difference and opposition" a position he maintains is "widely shared."
This line of reasoning is questionable, and appears as an analytical regress-
ion of sorts given that elsewhere in the same article Heder's scrutiny is
apt. While, Heder (1995: 428) recognizes that such "dampening of political
contestation" is done in the name of "political stability and economic development" in order to see the "integration of Cambodia into the world capitalist
system," he fails to make the connection that this neoauthoritarian behavior
not only falls in line with the neoliberal canon of "order," but appears to
be a direct outcome of this doctrine. Instead, Heder relies on culture as a
theoretical crutch.

Heder simply fails to recognize that much of the authoritarian behavior
in Cambodia is defined spatially insofar as the incumbent regime seeks to
control the public activities of the citizenry in a way that it deems "orderly,"
which can in fact be read as seeking the preservation of the social and
economic status quo. Although Cambodia's international donor community
is very vocal about democracy promotion, it generally accepts the perceived
need for "order" and "stability" at face value because in point of fact it shares

the same concerns necessary for promoting neoliberalization. The concern for economics clearly pre-empts democracy as an ideal vision of public space since democratic negates the notion of public space as necessarily orderly and only accommodating to a predetermined and limited range of social behaviors and activities (McInroy 2000). Instead, the *process* of public space must be open and accommodating to all social groups, including "unruly" elements, so that the public as a whole may define the public interest. Recognizing this may help us to realize that predetermining and enforcing an economic model on a country is not only undemocratic, but is, as it happens, an act of sedition with respect to the emergence of public space. The production of space cannot be separated from the practiced economic model, as space is "both constructed by and the medium of social relations and processes" to which economics plays an unquestionably significant role (Cope 1996: 185). Thus, the pre-determination of market liberalization as the economic model imposes a public "purpose" on space in the same way as authoritarianism does.

This preordained "purpose" for public space, whether it be as a site for a docile population to witness the ostentatious awe and monolithic grandeur of the state, as in the totalitarian tradition, or a site for automaton-like citizens to consume vast quantities of material goods, as in modern capitalism, stands in stark contrast to a democratic public space, which "is used for a public purpose determined by the people acting freely and equally, bound together by spontaneous ties that are both sentimental and practical" (Tan 2002: 24). That a people may freely choose the economic policies and practices that directly affect their lives, and situate their opinions, concerns, desires, and demands in the spaces of the public appears to be a frightening proposition to the neoliberals of this world. Capitalism is premised on inequality, and *democracy as public space* threatens to reveal this truth by "fir[ing] modern imagination as the battleground where ordinary people without institutional-ized power mobilize and organize to change the status quo, to seize power from those who refuse to share it or exercise it justly for the benefit of all" (Tan 2002: 24). Thus, within the larger discursive practices of the "devel-opment discourse," the authoritarianism of Global South governments is, on the one hand, an easy and ideal scapegoat to deflect attention away from the profound socioeconomic injustices of capitalism, and on the other, a symptom of the neoliberal order many Global South governments subscribe to and abide by.

Fomenting dystopia: Hegemonic aggression, democratic transgression, and donor indiscretion

The intimidation of oppositional elements and the crackdown on both the public sphere and public space that characterized the immediate post-election years continued into 1997, with numerous attacks against the press. The two most significant incidents were a rocket attack against a television station in Sihanoukville and a grenade attack on the office of a daily newspaper in

Phnom Penh (Hammarberg 2000). While the attacks themselves were directed at elements of the public sphere, they also sent a message that the physical spaces which the public sphere occupied were not safe. However, such incidences of *violence from above* did not deter Sam Rainsy, arguably the most vocal critic of the coalition government, as he perhaps felt somewhat protected, since at that time he himself was member of the RGC. Sam Rainsy was the finance minister of FUNCINPEC, and made a reputation for himself as outspoken about government corruption. Consequently, he made many bitter political enemies, which ultimately led to his expulsion from both the party and the National Assembly without debate (Peou 1998a, 2000; Woods 1997). He went on to form the Khmer Nation Party (KNP), which was later renamed the Sam Rainsy Party (SRP). The founding of a new party was not easy for Rainsy, as the CPP attempted to thwart his efforts at every turn. This was in spite of Article 42 of the constitution, which states, "Khmer citizens shall have the right to establish associations and political parties" (Jennar 1995: 14). Throughout 1996, the party remained officially unrecognized by the RGC, and when Rainsy promised to open party offices outside of the capital, the government's attempt at controlling oppositional elements through the denial of space became clear. They responded by threatening to close down the private space of KNP headquarters in Phnom Penh. Between May and June of that same year three KNP party activists were murdered, and the CPP's domination of Cambodia's public spaces continued, as a funeral procession for one of the fallen KNP members was rerouted from passing in front of Hun Sen's house and the National Assembly (Peou 2000).

The most vicious attack on the opposition since the 1993 elections came on 30 March 1997. On that day, the KNP held a peaceful demonstration across from the National Assembly in Phnom Penh to oppose the CPP's alleged subordination of the judicial system (Hughes 2003b; Peou 2000). Two assailants attacked the demonstration with grenades. The attack claimed 16 lives and seriously injured over 100 other protesters (Hughes 2002a; Lao Mong Hay 1998b; Sanderson and Maley 1998). The apparent assassination attempt was unsuccessful only because Sam Rainsy's bodyguard acted as a human shield, dying in the process (Hughes 2003b; Peou 1998a). The demonstration had received permission from the Ministry of the Interior to hold the event, but the Ministry did not take measures to protect the demonstrators on the premise that military protection might be viewed as an act of intimidation (Peou 2000). Nevertheless, heavily armed soldiers in full battle dress were positioned only 200 meters away from the demonstrators when the attack occurred. The soldiers did not attempt to aid the wounded, or to stop the assailants as they passed right through their line (Peou 2000). Impunity, clearly prevailed in this case as no one has ever been arrested in connection with the incident (Shawcross 2002). Hun Sen has repeatedly denied any involvement, even though several eyewitness accounts indicate that Rainsy's would-be assassins went directly into the CPP's compound after passing through the line of soldiers (Economist 1997a; Kevin 2000b; Peou 2000).

A Federal Bureau of Investigation (FBI) inquiry, conducted because an American was injured, reportedly implicated associates of Hun Sen in the attack, although the report itself has never been made public (Human Rights Watch 1997). Despite "the right to strike and to non-violent demonstration" enshrined in Article 37 of the constitution (Jennar 1995: 13), the attack served as a reminder that open dissent would not be tolerated in the public spaces of the capital. Such menacing scenarios constrict the "ability of individuals to participate in public affairs" (Staeheli and Thompson 1997: 30), and whether perpetuated by individuals acting on behalf of the state or simply of their own accord, the grenade attack implies a weakened state that lacks legitimacy. In the end, the very courts the KNP was accusing the CPP of subverting in 1997 cleared Hun Sen of any involvement in the grenade attack in January 2005 by dismissing the case brought against him by Sam Rainsy (Berthiaume and Phanna Ana 2005a).

Despite the impunity that followed, the location of the attack became an ideologically important space in Cambodia's struggle for democracy. Mimicking the associations of place imbued in China's Tiananmen Square, after the attack the KNP named the park "Democracy Square." On 29 March 2000, on the eve of the third anniversary of the attack, the SRP erected a memorial stupa to honor the dead (Hughes 2001c). Thus, Democracy Square has come to represent an important symbolic space for both Cambodian democracy and identity. History is often thought of as a collective memory, where the translation of experiences into memories occurs via narrative. This translation is frequently a geographical enterprise, as collective memory is nurtured through place. As Brian Osborne (2001: 39) suggests, an awareness, or "a-where-ness," of national identity is nurtured through mnemonic devices such as "landscapes and inscapes, myths and memories, monuments and commemorations, quotidian practices and public ritual," which when "placed" in context form a *geography of identity*. Hughes (2003b: 197) conveys the symbolic importance of Democracy Square to Cambodia's *geography of identity*:

> The park is bordered to the north by the Royal Palace, offering both continuity with traditional petitions to the king for assistance by the poor and oppressed and the shadow of the king's protection to demonstrators. To the east, it faces the National Assembly Building, the repository of representative democracy. To the west, it is bordered by Wat Botum-Vadei, one of the foremost pagodas in the capital. To the south, the park faces the Hun Sen gardens, containing the Cambodian-Vietnamese friendship monument – symbolic of the origins and continuation of CPP power. A broad lawn in the middle of these four buildings, which represent different branches of power in Cambodian state and society, Democracy Square represents an important symbolic space.

Several participants of this study conveyed this same sense of symbolism by locating their own individual "a-where-ness" of this space as important site for protest by recognizing its visibility and thus its importance as a potential *space for representation*:

> "Democracy Square is a good place [for protest] because . . . this place is in front of the National Assembly so that the people who work in the . . . National Assembly know and hear about when they [the people] are doing the demonstration or complain and also its . . . its next to the Royal Palace where the King maybe hear and see also."[22]
>
> "This [is a] good place because it, ah, the place can, the people can join many people and the people discuss with each other and after make the request to the authority, local authority and have the National Assembly, have the law makers in the National Assembly, its very close. Important because very close and when the King and the top people heard and see about this, yeah, maybe they can resolve good . . . resolution . . . good resolution for the people."[23]
>
> "It is a good place also because it is in front of the National Assembly so that if we do, or if we protest something the people in the National Assembly will see us, they hear us. If we do something far away from this place maybe they cannot hear. . . ."[24]

Others placed emphasis on the historical importance of Democracy Square, illustrating how the grenade attack has entered Cambodian collective memory, thus imbuing the site with meaning as a space for protest:

> "[Democracy Square is a] good [place for demonstrations] because we have a long period, because of what happen, many people die and the grenade bomb there and people suffer a lot so we will . . . do demonstration at this situation. . . . [and] they [demonstrators] want the government to see them."[25]
>
> "If the Parliament is in another place then, the demonstrators will go to the other place and not go to this place. The demonstration, demonstrators goal is to go to the Parliament . . . I think this, this place is called the Democracy Square just only because this place is used to have many people killed and died in this places, that's why they put this . . . this name the Democracy Square in order to pay tribute to the people who died. . . . for me I think it could be a good place also because it is a public place."[26]
>
> "Sam Rainsy Party has temple small [motions with hands, referring to a stupa monument the SRP has erected on the site]. I think that its good because its in front of the National Assembly and the place is big, the park there, and the National Assembly is supposed to be representing the people of the country, so it's good to do it [have demonstrations] there."[27]

The emergent *geography of identity* related to Democracy Square has been challenged by Cambodia's ruling elite, who are very much aware of the significant association of place that exists for many Cambodians. Thus, for seven weeks following the monument's erection, the memorial stupa was the subject of a bitter standoff between SRP supporters and the RGC.

The stupa had to be replaced on numerous occasions, as it was first thrown in a sewage canal, and later smashed to pieces several times by military police (O'Connell and Bou Saroeun 2000). This public battle over the types of physical monumentation permissible in Cambodian public spaces evokes the underlying competing ideologies of an authoritarian state seeking to administer public space as a testament to its authority and strength on the one hand, and the materialization of this space by a subaltern group intent on exposing the injustice and tyranny of the state on the other. Although, the stupa in no way implicates the CPP as the perpetrators of the attack, the collective memory of Cambodians fills in this blank. The persistence of SRP supporters forced the state to concede the space. As a result, today the stupa serves as a physical reminder that will not allow Cambodians to forget this incident. Since "Political rights come into existence through struggles for recognition" (Tilly 2003: 33), the battle over the stupa represents the right of Cambodians to remember and choose their own collective identity.

As violent as the grenade attack was, the most insidious and overtly violent event of 1997 came on 5 July, when Hun Sen orchestrated a coup d'état against his co-prime minister, Prince Ranariddh, spawning two days of factional fighting in the streets of Phnom Penh (Eng 1998; Frieson 1997; Peou 1998a, 1998c). The coup resulted in over 100 extrajudicial killings of opposition members, with most of the victims being senior members of FUNCINPEC (Downie 2000; International Crisis Group 2000; Sanderson and Maley 1998). The murders themselves were nothing short of barbarous, and included decapitations, asphyxiations, and at least two cases of disembowelment (Economist 1997b). Kate Frieson (1997), who was investigating for the United Nations Center for Human Rights at the time, reported an attempted cover-up, as many of the victim's bodies were taken to *wats* (temples) throughout Phnom Penh where they were hastily cremated without any authorization (see also Peou 2000).

Prince Ranariddh himself managed to escape the chaos unscathed, and went into self-imposed exile, as did Sam Rainsy (Ashley 1998b; Doyle 1998; International Crisis Group 2000). The CPP threatened Ranariddh with prosecution should he ever return to Cambodia (Human Rights Watch 1997; Peou 2000). Hun Sen denied the bloodshed constituted a coup, calling it a pre-emptive move to avoid an impending Ranariddh coup. Peou (1998c: 91) calls this claim "illogical, since the Prince as First Prime Minister could not overthrow himself as leader of the government." To substantiate Hun Sen's claim the CPP released what became known as the "White Paper." The paper accused Ranariddh and his men of having "embarked on a campaign of provocation, which . . . only served to destabilize Cambodia" (quoted in Peou 2000: 298). The paper further presented Ranariddh as a "traitor" and a "criminal" and claimed, "One of the most serious examples of the attempt to provoke the CPP, and the immediate source of the fighting in Phnom Penh was the secret negotiations and military dealings that Ranariddh . . . had with the Khmer Rouge" (quoted in Peou 2000: 298–99).

While it is true that Ranariddh sent emissaries to visit the Khmer Rouge, Hun Sen also tried to court Ieng Sary, former Deputy Prime Minister and Foreign Minister of Democratic Kampuchea, who led a successful rebellion against the other Khmer Rouge leaders in August 1996, establishing autonomous control over a significant number of Khmer Rouge forces in the resource rich area of Pailin. Both Ranariddh and Hun Sen actually went separately and in person to Pailin in October 1996, as each was trying to negotiate the surrender of the Khmer Rouge by enticing members to defect to the government in Phnom Penh (Lizée 1997; Peou 1998c; Zasloff 2002). More to the point, the separate visits lend the impression that both Ranariddh and Hun Sen wanted defecting Khmer Rouge members in their corner of the coalition government, as this would shore up more power for their side (Ashley 1998b; Doyle 1998; Human Rights Watch 1997). Thus, both sides dealt with the Khmer Rouge independently in an attempt to attain more military strength in the coalition government (Ledgerwood nd; Peou 2000; Thayer 1998). The FUNCINPEC faction was perhaps more desperate to receive Khmer Rouge defectors, as they had been marginalized in the coalition government since it was first formed following the 1993 elections, and Ranariddh's side was no match for the CPP's military might. Nevertheless, Khmer Rouge elements fought on both sides during the 5–6 July armed confrontation (Ashley 1998b), and in neglecting Hun Sen's own covert dealings with the Khmer Rouge, the "White Paper" called Ranariddh's move tantamount to a "declaration of war" (quoted in Peou 1998c: 89). While many Cambodia observers have labeled Hun Sen's actions as a coup (Ashley 1998a, 1998b; Bjornlund 2001; Brown and Timberman 1998; Doyle 1998; Frieson 1997; Lao Mong Hay 1998a; Ledgerwood nd; Peou 1998b, 1998c, 2000), others have refuted such labeling based not only on their uncritical acceptance of the "White Paper" claims, but also because Hun Sen continued the coalition by replacing Ranariddh with another member of FUNCINPEC (Kevin 2000a, 2000b; Roberts 2001). However, Hun Sen essentially handpicked Ranariddh's replacement, Ung Huot, who amounted to little more than a puppet, and can be viewed as an illegitimate replacement on the basis of the following three points: (1) Ung Huot has recently been dismissed from FUNCINPEC by Ranariddh, who had the right to do so as party president under Provision 36 of party by-laws; (2) those party members who voted for Ung Huot lacked a quorum and thus the authority to nominate him; and (3) Ung Huot's nomination was not endorsed in an absolute majority, which required 17 members (Peou 2000).

Furthermore, David Roberts (2001) fails to provide an actual definition of a coup d'état in all of his labored analyses of what he euphemistically refers to as the "political intercourse" of 1997. In contrast, Sorpong Peou (2000) does offer a definition, and accordingly presents a much more persuasive argument. Citing the *Robertson Dictionary of Politics*, Peou (2000: 302, emphasis added) considers the events of July 1997 a coup based upon the following definition: a coup is "a swift decisive seizure of power by a political or military group from *within* the existing system." Moreover, "the organizers of a *coup d'etat* usually carry it out by capturing or killing top political and military leaders, by seizing control of key government building and public utilities, by using the mass media of communication to calm the masses and gain their acceptance of the new regime" (Peou 2000: 302). Clearly, the sudden and violent ousting of Prince Ranariddh was a coup. However, there seems to be no convincing former Australian ambassador to Cambodia, Tony Kevin (2000a: 38), who states: "ambassadors who were working in Phnom Penh at the time well know that the true origins of the factional fighting are far more complicated. The full story will be written by historians one day." Instead of simply suggesting that he and his former colleagues are the holders of "privileged information," one has to wonder why Kevin has not taken it upon himself to enlighten the world as to the "true origins" of the factional fighting. Until such a revelation occurs, outside of the flawed reasoning that accepts the "White Paper" at face value, it seems emphatically clear that the "events" of July 1997 were indeed a coup d'état.

Nonetheless, most multilateral and bilateral donors refused to label the violent clash of July 1997 a coup, and their response was largely indifferent to the impact this event had on Cambodian democracy, as they were far more concerned with "order" and "stability." Prior to the coup, donors had emphasized their support was contingent upon Cambodia's continued path toward political democracy. However, as Peou (2000: 379) points out, "a close reading of what the international community basically wanted did not contribute to further democratization. They required that Cambodia be stable. . . . Political stability for economic development was their top concern." In contrast to the 1993–95 period when donors attached few conditionalities to their aid, the year 1996 marked the beginning of donor demands, primarily directed at the promotion of stability, a demand that may have "encouraged Hun Sen to justify his coup against Ranariddh" (Peou 2000: 385). Thus, while aid was reduced following the coup from the amount of US$475 million, pledged at the Consultative Group Meeting (CGM) just days before the coup on 1–2 July, to US$375.4 million (Peou 1998a, 2000), the reduction was temporally insignificant as "stability" was soon restored with Hun Sen at the helm.[28]

In response to the coup, China did not try to hide its favoritism toward Hun Sen, saying it would not interfere with the "will of the Cambodian people" (Peou 2000: 395), a position also held by France, which made it known that it viewed Hun Sen as the only guarantor of stability (Bjornlund and Course 1998; Lizée 2000). The official Canadian stance was also soft, and expressed concern about only the ongoing violence, while urging the Cambodian parties to pursue political dialogue (Lizée 2000). Australia's position on the coup was even more controversial. Human Rights activists accused Ambassador Tony Kevin of denying asylum to opposition elements loyal to Ranariddh during the coup. In addition, Australian aid actually increased in 1997 to US$27 million, up from US$20 million the year before showing implicit consent for Hun Sen's actions where one would expect punitive action (Peou 2000). The neoliberal pragmatism of the Association of Southeast Asian Nations (ASEAN) was also evident, as the group took a far from punitive position. The group considered the CPP's use of force "unfortunate" and Cambodia's admission into ASEAN was delayed "until a later date" (Hughes 2002b; Peou 1998b), but at the same time, the principle of non-interference in the internal affairs of other states was reaffirmed and investors continued to move in to Cambodia (Peou 2000). Japan, the largest bilateral donor to Cambodia, vowed to maintain its assistance plan, and justified this position by contending that Hun Sen had promised to preserve the country's democratic institutions and coalition government (Bjornlund and Course 1998; Lizée 2000).

Washington also took a negligent stance by refusing to call the July event a coup because doing so would disqualify Cambodia from receiving aid. Contrary to the notion that US aid was cut by two-thirds (see Hughes 2002a), Peou (2000) indicates that the actual aid disbursement amounted to US $30 million, up from US$28 million the year before. Moreover, as early as late July during an ASEAN Regional Forum meeting, Secretary of State Madeleine Albright said Washington was already prepared to wipe the slate clean for Hun Sen (Peou 2000). The CPP was required only to denounce the use of force, and to allow Ranariddh to return to Cambodia and participate in the elections scheduled for 1998. The IMF did not have to get involved in responding to the incident, as it had been withholding Cambodia's SAPs since May 1996 due to its displeasure with the scandalous deforestation taking place as a "shadow state" response to its prescribed forestry concession model (see Le Billon 2000, 2002; Talbott 1998). While the WB did temporarily suspend aid to Cambodia in 1997, this seemed to be an act of solidarity with the IMF rather than disapproval of the July military confrontation, as the announcement was not made until 23 September 1997. The WB's announcement was prepared in conjunction with the IMF, who at that same time publicized that they were suspending further assistance to Cambodia, not because of the mockery that was made of democracy in July, but as a result of the RGC's "inability to meet its economic conditions" (Tith 1998: 119). Thus, "The negative responses of major donors to the coup in 1997 were not credible, and even legitimized Hun Sen's violent ascendancy in the end" (Peou 2000: 390).

The insignificant reduction in aid and lukewarm response to the coup is not surprising if we consider the fact that observers like Tony Kevin (2000a; 2000b) and David Roberts (2001) view the July upheaval as marking a transition from violence to politics, one that will supposedly bring about increased "stability" as Hun Sen has been able to consolidate his hegemonic position.

The neoliberal agenda of the IFIs and other donors has come into plain view, revealing "good governance" as the oxymoronic chimera it truly is. Meanwhile, the trampling of democratic norms, while publicly described as regrettable, are given implicit support as long as such subversions run parallel to the project of "stability" and "order." Speaking of the Cambodian context, Peang-Meth (1997: 290–91) comments on this very issue:

> In today's international arena, non-Western states have continued to embrace stability and order as a first priority, but the West, notably the United States, which has preached individual rights, freedom and democracy, has declined to intervene in conflicts where order has been preserved at the expense of human rights and freedom. The United States has, by inference, sanctioned an international norm of conduct that prizes stability and preservation of the status quo when these would be threatened by aggressive advocacy and individual rights and freedom.

Instead of coming from democratic consolidation, which is a long-term project for which the juggernaut of global capitalism is not prepared to wait, such "stability" came in the form of Hun Sen consolidating his grip on power. Thus, while Cambodia's transition to democracy lay in shambles by the end of 1997, the transition to free-market economics was in fine form as the neoliberal agenda was preserved. However, any notion that the maintenance of Hun Sen's dominance, that is, the preservation of the authoritarian status quo in Cambodia, will procure long-term stability is profoundly mistaken. As David Ashley (1998b: 71–72) contends, "*Coups d'etat*, wherever they occur, have a nasty habit of repeating themselves. The events of July 5–6 will only postpone the day when Cambodia will be able to deal with its political conflicts through peaceful and democratic means." Almost twenty years after Cambodia's transition began, truer words have not been written as political contestation in the country continues to transgress the ethos of democracy, which remains shot through with violence.

Conclusion

This chapter's account of both the historical background leading up to, and the circumstances of Cambodia's transition to democracy itself, has shown that the international community's interest in Cambodia has been far from benevolent. Instead, such attention has been a cautious and often contradictory exercise in geopolitics. Cambodia's "decade of genocide" was followed by a decade of neglect as the outside world turned a blind eye to the misery and suffering it had done much to create. The sudden renewed interest in Cambodia following the fall of the Iron Curtain is thus at least somewhat peculiar insofar as concern expressed for the political, social, and economic conditions in Cambodia could hardly be taken at face value as humanitarian. Indeed, the recent history of Cambodia tells a very different story, where most often, extraneous expressions of concern for peace and democracy were mere rhetoric designed to serve ulterior motives, namely to pry open the Cambodian economy.

This chapter has begun to uncover some of the layers of lies that have been heaped upon Cambodia's transition. It has exposed the goals of "stability" and "order" for the purpose of economic investment as taking precedence over the desire for democracy expressed by the Cambodian electorate. Concern for "stability" and "order" was reaffirmed by the UNTAC's failure to create a "neutral political environment," and their subsequent haste in deeming the elections "free and fair." While the victory of FUNCINPEC was definite, it could have been even more resounding had the UNTAC been more diligent in its attempts to disentangle the CPP from the state apparatus, which may have avoided the need for a coalition government and would not have left the CPP in such a militarily strong position. The UNTAC was not prepared for the CPP's failure at the polls, and Hun Sen was accordingly allowed to force his way into a co-prime ministerial position. Perhaps, as Lizée (1993) and Peou (2000) have suggested, the consolidation of CPP hegemony was the goal all along. In this view, Hun Sen, given his economic inclinations throughout the late 1980s, is seen to have been preordained as the ideal candidate to bring the "stability" necessary for continued economic liberalization and the "roll-out" of further neoliberal reforms in Cambodia. Indeed, Hun Sen's continual subversion of democracy in his attacks against both the public sphere and public space in the immediate post-UNTAC years was of little consequence to the donor community, as such authoritarian action was often a feature and/or outcome of instituting neoliberal reforms and represented the move toward greater "stability" in the country. Of course, bilateral and multilateral donors would quickly call for Cambodia's political parties to respect the constitution and adhere to the principles of democracy whenever *violence from above* was employed, but such criticism was always little more than lip service.

What donors really wanted was "stability" and "order," that is, the restoration of the political status quo in Cambodia so that the neoliberal agenda could be preserved, an outcome that many Cambodian observers, perhaps unwittingly, assisted by deflecting attention away from the neoliberal doctrine and the contradictions of "good governance" through their admonishments of Khmer cultural tradition as "absolutist." The subversion of democracy culminated with the ousting of first prime minister Prince Ranariddh in July 1997, which, with the exception of FUNCINPEC and of course the ever neglected Cambodian electorate, Hun Sen's coup d'état provided a convenient solution for almost everyone involved. However, while the cracks in Cambodia's democracy had become gaping fissures by the end of 1997, many Cambodians were not yet willing to give up their dream of democracy. As Chapter 4 shows, in the post-coup landscape democratic contestation has heightened dramatically, where an increasing number of Cambodians have brought their "hidden transcripts" of resistance into the plain view of their nation's public spaces.

4   Cambodia's battle for public space

The neoliberal doctrine of "order" versus the democratic expression of the people's will

Having defecated, you bury the dung like a tiger.

– Cambodian proverb.

The international community's unenthusiastic reaction to the coup of 1997 was telling in that it revealed a donor agenda where the global promotion of "stability" takes precedence over any real call for democracy. The suspicions of those few observers who had been cynical about the purpose and goals of the UNTAC mission all along could no longer be easily dismissed. While democracy was floundering in post-UNTAC Cambodia, the free market was in fine form so long as the "stability" and "order" that Hun Sen's regime represented could be maintained. Although the lie of the "good governance" agenda was now standing naked before us through the (non)actions of multi-lateral and bilateral donors in response to the coup, the 1998 elections offered an opportunity to quickly cover up this exposure. However, another exercise in electoralism rather than democracy was not what the Cambodian people had in mind, and in the post-coup landscape, Cambodians themselves would soon begin to take matters into their own hands. The *geography of protest* that had begun to emerge in Cambodia following the UNTAC mission would blossom following the 1998 elections as an extraordinary and unprecedented "from below" social movement. Since the elections of 1998, an increasing number of Cambodians have been willing to participate in the making of their society by actively *taking* space. This chapter traces the key events, voices, outcomes, and contestations of the "hearts and minds war" that has become Cambodia's battle for public space.

Violence, intimidation, surveillance, and coercion: The makings of a "free and fair" election?

International donors negotiated the return of Prince Ranariddh on 30 March 1998, after nine months in exile, and Cambodia's political leaders agreed to hold parliamentary elections again in July of 1998 (Neou and Gallup 1999; Peou 1998a). While the donor community had focused their foreign-policy responses to the 1997 coup on the need for the 1998 elections to be "free and fair" (Sanderson and Maley 1998), Ranariddh's presence did little to improve the prospects of such conditions for the election. Addressing the profusion of political killings since the July 1997 coup, and the prospects for a free and fair election in 1998, Human Rights Watch (1998a: np) reported "opposition members know that to be politically active is to court danger or even death . . . the violence has caused a widespread climate of fear, stifled dissent, and intimidation among voters" (see also Bjornlund and Course 1998). In the early months of 1998, the "cycle of violence" focused on members of FUNCINPEC, particularly those involved in efforts to rebuild the broken party structure following the coup (Bjornlund and Course 1998; Downie 2000; Grainger 1998a; Human Rights Watch 1998a). The SRP also became the focus of *violence from above*, as there were "scores of confirmed or credible accounts of intimidation by government or CPP officials" (Neou and Gallup 1999: 157). The prevalence of politically motivated homicide also tainted the campaign, including the murder of prominent SRP activist Chak Phuong and his four-year-old daughter; however, authorities continually attributed such incidents to robbery or personal revenge (Human Rights Watch 1998). The CPP was also victimized when Hun Sen's motorcade became the target of a rocket attack in a rare incident of *violence from below* (U.S. Department of State 2000). The Khmer Rouge problem continued to fester in 1998, and the insurgent group killed a number of National Election Committee (NEC) and RGC employees prior to the elections (Neou and Gallup 1999).

Although the 1998 elections saw fewer people killed than in the 1993 election, the campaign was nonetheless once again marred by coercion, intimidation, and CPP domination of the media (Downie 2000; Hughes 1999, 2001d, 2002a, 2002b, 2003b; Human Rights Watch 1998a; Peou 2000; Sanderson and Maley 1998). The CPP employed a diverse arsenal of tactics to maintain its dominance of public space during the election period. In 1997 the party resurrected its "cell system," used during the 1993 elections, where village-level CPP officials selected "group leaders," who were each required to recruit members from ten different households in the village to support the party by obtaining their thumbprints (Hughes 1999; Human Rights Watch 1998a). While this practice, along with the recording of voter registration numbers, could not be used to match a voter to a particular ballot, many voters were led to believe this was possible (Downie 2000; Hughes 1999). Some voters were forced to drink a glass of water with a bullet in it after swearing to vote for the CPP, the implication being the threat of death should the individual not vote "correctly" (Pape 1998). The CPP also illegally co-opted the apparatus of the state for its electoral campaign, as one individual I interviewed suggested that state employees, himself included, were required to campaign on behalf of the CPP.[1] However, this was not an indication of CPP loyalty as this individual conveyed his affinity for the SRP by showing me several pictures of him standing at Sam Rainsy's side during past political rallies. Thus, the 1998 elections produced a paradoxical situation in which state employees mobilized and coerced the electorate into voting for the CPP, but did not themselves support that party, a finding Caroline Hughes (2003b) corroborates.

The CPP election campaign was also characterized by the large number of "gifts" used to persuade voters, which included clothing and money, but most often monosodium glutamate (MSG), a popular Cambodian food seasoning. Voters were often told that if they accepted "gifts" but did not vote CPP, then the donations would have to be returned, raising fears in the minds of impoverished voters and meaning the "gift" was effectively payment for their vote (Hughes 1999). Many of the participants I interviewed indicated they had received gifts during the elections, and some expressed discomfort about the coercion involved:

> "I receive the, the gift, but I go . . . when I went to the vote, it's secret . . . but when they, someone give the gift to me, I must receive the gift because when I not receive, then I'm afraid someone [will be] angry [with me]. . . . When the someone from the party give the present to, to me, I must receive because I'm afraid, when we . . . I don't, ah, receive, the party, they say 'oh he don't love the party'."[2]
>
> ". . . when the commune chief go back to give the, the gift, the present to the people, so the chief of the villager, the commune chief, to take away for himself. Yeah but not divide to the people and so when he, when the population to talk about something like this [accepting a gift and then not voting for the party who gave the gift], they have problem with him, with the commune chief and then the commune chief hurt him. Maybe sometimes they threat . . . threaten me. Threaten me about, they ask 'why did you talk about this?' . . . The chief of villager, commune chief, government, yeah and especially it's [those who] have the, the power. The person [who] has the power in the community to, to threaten the people whatever they want."[3]

As an indication of just how pervasive the activity of gift giving was during the 1998 election, one participant joked with me that the CPP had become known as the MSG party.[4] Moreover, in a society where radio and television represent important vehicles for election campaigning since over 50 percent of the adult population is illiterate and newspapers have marginal readership outside of the capital, the CPP's firm grip on these forms of media made it difficult for opposition parties to broadcast policies and express opinions (Downie 2000; Samreth Sopha and Moorthy 1998). Radio UNTAC, which had allowed all parties to reach rural voters during the 1993 elections, had been dismantled, as had FUNCINPEC radio and television following the 1997 coup, which amounted to the CPP having a veritable stranglehold on access to rural voters (Grainger 1998b).

In the end, the CPP's campaign of intimidation, violence, vote buying, surveillance, and media domination paid off as the party won the 1998 elections. However, the CPP's victory was not an indication that the majority of Cambodians preferred Hun Sen's leadership. Rather, the CPP won only 42.4 percent of the vote, but through a questionable modification of the seat allocation procedure by the NEC from the "largest remainder" method of the UNTAC to the "highest average" method that favors larger parties (Bjornlund 2001; Gallup 2002; Peou 2000), the CPP managed to secure an absolute majority in the National Assembly with 64 of the 122 seats (Hughes 1999; Wayden 2000). FUNCINPEC, which obtained 31.7 percent of the vote, received only 43 seats, while the SRP received 15 seats with its 12.3 percent of the vote (Hughes 1999; Wayden 2000). Had FUNCINPEC not parted with Sam Rainsy a few years earlier, the CPP would have once again lost the election in spite of its intimidation tactics, as the percentage of the votes of the two parties when taken together, slightly outweighs that of the CPP. Ultimately, the CPP failed to capture two-thirds of the vote, and under the terms of the Cambodian constitution, it was required to form a new coalition government. The FUNCINPEC and the SRP immediately turned down the CPP's call for a coalition, as both opposition parties claimed the CPP committed massive electoral fraud (Hughes 2002a, 2002b; Peou 2000; Thayer 1998). There is indeed significant weight behind these claims given the CPP's manipulation and control of the NEC, which was supposed to be an independent and neutral body commissioned to both run the polls and hear voter complaints of fraud and irregularities (Hughes 2002a). In reality, the NEC was anything but non-partisan, as the CPP had manipulated the selection process of NEC members (Gallup 2002), resulting in its domination by the CPP (Peou 2000; Sanderson and Maley 1998). This became very clear over the course of the campaign period, as the NEC refused to investigate over 800 complaints lodged by opposition parties on the premise that they were all without merit (Downie 2000; Peou 2000).

While recognizing that *violence from above* was one feature responsible for returning the CPP to power, Hughes (1999; 2002b; 2003b) identifies a lack of public space as an even more significant factor. She explains the CPP victory in terms of a "prisoner's dilemma" whereby, ". . . the absence of any mass participatory movement for change outside of the polling booth, imposes a burden of risk on the individual voter which [she or] he may be unwilling to bear in isolation. Solidarity empowers, and without the assurance of this empowerment, the voter is less likely to resist" (Hughes 1999: 93). The spatial domination of the CPP during the 1998 elections meant that voters were significantly isolated from each other, having little idea as to how colleagues, friends, and even family were voting. However, the CPP did not act alone in securing their dominance of public space during the 1998 elections, as the opposition parties, which encouraged their supporters to keep their party affiliations and voting intentions to themselves (Hughes 1999; 2001b; 2002b), implicitly supported this situation.

Almost every participant I interviewed in both rural and urban Cambodia told me that she or he did not discuss voting preferences with anyone, including family members, at any time during the election period. The most common explanation for this was fear of conflict and violence:

"... in the village, the community or the rural area, they have some problem about political violence, problem with another party. Mostly in the rural area we have a lot of the Cambodia people vote the CPP Party, yeah so if a family likes another party they argue each other ... they, the people that support the CPP Party, they discrimination, discrimination [*sic*] with the people in the other family that choose another party, Sam Rainsy, FUNCINPEC ... discrimination, and some would threaten them."[5]

"In Cambodia ... another country I don't know [if you] can talk, like talking about whatever, like if scared, I don't know, but in Cambodia sometimes they cannot talking about politics, they scared about something when they talking, they very ... be careful about elections or about politics, political also, when they talking about political or voting preference, usually they feel scared. They want to, some people ... can, they don't feel scared or afraid because they say what they want to say, but some people [also] feel afraid about something when they speak private because ... in Cambodia unsafe and uncomfortable when we talking about political [issues]. Like they [are] scare[d] of sometimes the police, or sometimes the neighbours, like if their minds are not the same. So sometimes have problem with, like, when we speak not the same way, so have problem sometimes. Sometime the story's not ... when we talking about political, have problem for them. Usually Khmer people can't talk about government. Government and police also. They all, the[se] people [are] very high so we cannot speak about them, [because] if someone heard about it maybe we have problem so they don't want to say. Usually they like, they feel like afraid someone will kill or, sometimes, first time for the people, the small people get arrested ... but the poor people sometimes they are scared of the ... afraid of police or government to kill so they don't want to say."[6]

"When I talk the political, politics, I don't ... if the person is parallel to me, [then I] can say ah, can say ... we talk about the politics, so after I know they are parallel to me. When the people say the party that they like, so I can say I like same party. The story the same, example is, ah, you like the A party, so I say 'oh I like A party too', like this. When I meet the people, the people say first about the politics ... then no problem, but I will not say first. Afraid. I'm afraid [if] the people like another party and I like [a different] party so make the opposite [of] each other. Afraid they will hate me or hurt me. Afraid that someone will maybe try to hurt me or use the violence against me."[7]

"I used to discuss politics with my friends at school or with, the public school and we can say it, what we like of the action of the government and of the person who works in the government, we can discuss with each other. But we cannot discuss the . . . about the politics with the person who we . . . we don't know about their name, about the name . . . we can't discuss like this because the powerful . . . they can . . . they don't like us and sometimes we can get, ah . . . dangerous from the powerful party when we . . . we talk about our ideas that we don't like them."[8]

"It can be dangerous because someone might kidnap us, kidnap the children, or whatever, because the government doesn't like democracy and so the government doesn't want people to say what they want . . . If anyone tried to rebel, they would kill you or something."[9]

"I will discuss politics with family only, about the politic. Never with friends. If I discuss with another person maybe I am afraid because I . . . example if I love Sam Rainsy Party or CPP Party and we opposite each other, so when we finish discuss . . . maybe someone has a problem . . . yeah, maybe someday make a problem with me. I am afraid all things [they might do to me], hate, hit, yeah bad do something for me . . . for my family because I think, because I don't know about their minds."[10]

While many voters may have believed that their ballot was secret, as was the case with most of the interviewees in this study, other participants revealed, in a finding corroborated by Hughes (1999) and Human Rights Watch (1998a), that close CPP observation of voter behavior before, during, and after the elections, coupled with the use of forced loyalty oaths and thumb printing, frightened them or other voters into thinking that CPP authorities could inflict retribution on those who did not vote for them:

"For me I feel safety. No problem. But for the people it's not safe. For the poor people, not safe because um, of the political activists kept, keep for watching them . . . keep watching them, just try to, you know to observe, observe the activities, what the people doing. The political parties watch them. When people have to go home they have fear, someone to go and vote for that party but sit very close it, close to the election office or close to where the, where the election box or election room and then people are afraid. They're afraid when they go to the election box because the party activists are there."[11]

"[I did not feel safe] because all the place they use the army or police to guard there, and to, to threaten, threaten the people to come and vote election, so when the, during the people come and walk around and pass by they will feel very uncomfortable so . . . this is a problem that I face you know. . . . Well its better [in 2003] because, ah, some, a lot of NGO, they, most of the staff they watch at least one or two person inside so otherwise they also, know that we, ah, some safe, a bit. Better a bit."[12]

"I can't talk [about the elections] because there is always someone, like listening to you. I think they might know who I'm voting for. And sometimes if people know that you don't vote for the CPP, they might do something bad to you."[13]

"I feel unclear whether they can keep secret or not because for me, myself, I understand that when we going to vote we stay in only alone in, in one, one small room to vote. So but I don't know exactly whether they have something to put to, ah, see us, like a small camera to put, I, I am not sure whether they have this kind or not and I, I can say that I can believe . . . or I also cannot believe."[14]

Furthermore, as Sanderson and Maley (1998) point out, when individuals, authorities, or political parties wish to manipulate an election result, it is not necessary that they intimidate or coerce every individual voter, as beyond being impractical, this would tip off international observers. Thus, word of mouth about CPP surveillance during the 1998 elections was sufficient to transform Cambodia's public space into a domain of panopticism.

This transformation to a geographical imagination of pervasive surveillance was made very evident in rural areas, where rumors persisted that the CPP was using spy satellites to monitor peoples' behavior (Hughes 1999; 2003b). Several of the people I interviewed expressed awareness of this rumor. This condition of surveillance is hardly an appropriate political milieu for democracy to flourish, let alone a condition in which "free and fair" elections could possibly take place. Accordingly, the potential for transforming *representational spaces* into *spaces for representation* was bleak during the 1998 election period, a reality of which the Cambodian electorate was acutely aware. Voter apathy seems to be another factor in Hun Sen's re-election. While 97 percent of the population was registered to vote (Eckardt 1998), approximately 400,000 (or 3.4 percent) of those individuals declined to participate in the electoral process (Sanderson and Maley 1998). However, the indifference of the non-voting population is not the most troubling form of apathy. Instead, the apathy that is of most concern is that of those who see Hun Sen's iron grip as so tight, that no amount of persuasion by the Cambodian people will remove him from his well-established position of power. One participant suggested that she felt that many people voted for the CPP simply because they do not see the point in voting for another party. She indicated that while these voters may not like the CPP, they simply do not understand how a transfer of power could take place, given that Hun Sen forced his way into a coalition in 1993, and given the level of CPP control at the village level through its patron–client networks. Rather than risking retributive action, many people simply voted for the status quo.[15]

When taken together, the high levels of voter fear and intimidation, coupled with the condition of pervasive surveillance, suggest that the 1998 election was clearly not a "miracle on the Mekong" as the leader of a joint International Republican Institute-National Democratic Institute delegation, and US Congressman, Steven Solarz had proclaimed it to be (Bjorlund 2001; Downie 2000). Former UNTAC Force Commander General John Sanderson and Deputy Chief Electoral Officer Michael Maley argued before an Australian Foreign Affairs sub-committee hearing in Canberra on 24 August 1998, that

Cambodia's 1998 election was anything but "free and fair," and instead was "simply an element of the theatre by which despots seek to justify their continuation of power" (quoted in Grainger 1998c). In contrast to Jeffrey Gallup's (2002) sanguine assessment of the utility of election observers, Sorpong Peou (2000) suggests that observers supported this "theatre" in several key ways. He suggests that most election observers had little knowledge of Cambodian politics prior to this assignment, lacked appropriate language skills, and were stationed primarily in urban centers, far from the panoptic oppression of the villages (Peou 2000). In addition, while some observer groups were on the ground in Cambodia for a month or more before the elections (Neou and Gallup 1999), many more were present in Cambodia for only a few days preceding and following the election, meaning the pre-election climate of fear and intimidation went largely unnoticed (Peou 2000).

Many of the individuals interviewed for this study echo Peou's assessment. While participants generally saw the observers as a good idea insofar as they fostered a sense of safety during the actual polling day, they did not contribute to creating a climate in which Cambodians felt comfortable sharing and expressing their political convictions. That is, observers failed to counteract the CPP Panopticon to create an open *space for representation*:

> "I think the international observer, they are very, very important and they are . . . they are [more] important than the local observer because they are neutral and they . . . they don't, they are not part of any political party so that they can help observe the Cambodia elections very well. . . . They make Cambodians feel more safe, [however], I still feel, I am still dare not to speak about this problem [discussing political or voting preferences] because I, I think that they [international observers] come only a short period of time and then they go back."[16]
>
> "When the international observers come, it get warm, get warm. Its more safe yeah, and we have more justice . . . Yeah because many [people from] the international come to watch, to get more justice and safe. . . . but I'm still afraid yeah, still afraid [to discuss political preferences]. Still afraid and the, but, ah, the international observer come, cannot correct something for the election and the safe and the justice more, but the people [are] still afraid talk about the political in the public space."[17]

Some participants were particularly cynical and commented on the obliviousness of the election observers to what they viewed as a fraudulent election result:

> "I think in 1993 it was very important for UN observers in Cambodia election process was very well. Since 1998 and 2003 international observers was unnecessary because they didn't perform their duties very well . . . weren't able to help make elections fair. International communities come to observe in Cambodia but many news of fraud make

election results unclear so political parties are untrustful [*sic*] to international observer."[18]

"In the 2003, or 1998, they [international observers] tried to help, but the results were not so good, because they were not, they didn't really know the Khmer government, and the Khmer government kind of like fooled those people. For the one with UNTAC it was good, but after that, the 1998, and 2003, was not good. The international observers were not good. They did not look closely into the election. On the voting list, if they know that you don't vote for the CPP, then they can just cancel your name."[19]

"Svay Rieng Province has problems because the international observer cannot arrive here, arrive over there. Yeah so we have confuse the election, they have the Vietnamese people went to vote the election because haven't the national observer . . . arrive over there. Vietnamese voted instead of Khmer, vote instead of Khmer because the . . . haven't the international observers arrive over there"[20]

"I think that the election result is already prepared by a group of people even before the election and so I want you . . . to take this idea, or take these words to tell the international community or the people . . . your country who have some . . . who give the aid to Cambodia . . . they just stop. Stop believing the one group of people that just nowadays try to spoil . . . I want you to tell the international community that the Cambodia people are not stupid, the Cambodian people know, who, which one is wrong, which one is right, which one is bad, which one is good but the problem is that the, the people, they still don't have the ability to choose, or . . . to have what they want."[21]

There is more than a grain of truth to the last participant's concerns of someone pulling the proverbial wool over the eyes of Cambodians, as the support for the "theatre by which despots seek to justify their continuation of power" that Sanderson and Maley (1998) speak of goes much deeper than the election observers.

Support for authoritarianism stems back to those who author the observation delegations' mandates, that is, the neoliberals who hold political power in Washington, Ottawa, Canberra, Paris, and other locations that sent observers to Cambodia. Concerns about "order" and "stability" for the purposes of economic activity take precedence over any concern for democracy, and accordingly there is an inclination to quickly deem elections "free and fair" regardless of the reality of the situation and the convictions of the Cambodian people. Giving elections such a designation preserves "order" and "stability" at the risk of the chaos that might ensue should the elections receive any description other than "free and fair." While adding international legitimacy to the victors, no matter how fraudulent their path to victory may have been, is conducive to a healthy business climate, it does little to uphold a democratic ethos and serves to spread disillusion.

Taking space for representation: Expressing desire for democracy and the neoliberal response

Whereas the elections themselves had seen voters segregated from one another through CPP mechanisms of surveillance and fear, a situation that was further embedded by the well-intentioned, yet ultimately misguided actions of the opposition, the post-election period saw something truly remarkable occur. In a strong showing of solidarity, and contrary to the repeated claims of *culturalist* observers, the post-election events would prove that the seeds of democracy had indeed been planted in Cambodia's supposedly "infertile" soil, and were now beginning to take firm roots. Taking quite literally Article 35 of the constitution, which states, "Khmer citizens of either sex shall have the right to participate actively in the political, economic, social, and cultural life of the nation" (Jennar 1995: 13), people from all over Cambodia converged in Phnom Penh following the announcement of the election results, taking to the capital's streets *en masse*. Cambodians began gathering by the thousands in Democracy Square on 24 August 1998, to protest against the results of the election (Eckardt and Chea Sotheacheath 1998; Hughes 2001d, 2003b; Peou 1999, 2000).

Denying the "from below" spirit of the movement, the opposition parties claimed responsibility for the demonstrations that followed and many Cambodia watchers and foreign diplomats uncritically accepted this claim (Grainger and Chaumeau 1998). However, Cambodia observer Caroline Hughes (2003b), who was on hand during the demonstrations and conducted numerous interviews with participants, paints a different picture, suggesting it is more likely that this was a spontaneous uprising. Hughes (2003b) suggests that many of the demonstrators were refugees from the provinces who fled following rumors of retaliation against those who failed to vote for the CPP. The urban protest environment provided a sense of empowerment and solidarity, as the security provided by the gaze of the international community and media was preferable to the panoptic conditions of the rural village where individuals were required to keep their views secret if they valued their physical and economic well-being. Moreover, according to Hughes (2003b) many protesters were not only expressing dissatisfaction with the election results, but also came to express their dismay with the social and economic marginalization they faced in their day-to-day existence. This finding places Willner's (1972: 353) assertion that public protests are often "manifest expressions of deeper, broader, latent dissatisfactions" in the Cambodian context, where the "latent dissatisfactions" expressed by participants were derived from the "sacrifices" made for development under the prescriptions of the neoliberal order, that is, the grinding poverty and socioeconomic insecurity of their daily lives.[22] In this context, Democracy Square became a liberatory space in which those normally subjected to the panoptic surveillance of the village could situate their embodiment by actively *taking* the spaces of the capital for public unmediated use. In Antonio L. Rappa's

(2002: 44) words, Phnom Penh became an "accessible site of self-discovery, self-exposure, and self-flagellation" for the rural Cambodian. As we shall see below, this experience has resonated into the future, as the idea of protest has slowly diffused beyond the city.

The protests that began on 24 August 1998, lasted a total of three weeks, as demonstrators erected a tent city across from the National Assembly in Democracy Square (Hughes 2002b, 2003b; Human Rights Watch 1998b). The demonstrations took a violent turn on 7 September 1998, when Hun Sen found a pretext to move against the demonstrations following a grenade explosion near his home in Phnom Penh (Human Rights Watch 1998b; Moorthy and Samreth Sopha 1998). He called for the arrest of opposition leaders, and hundreds of riot police moved in, destroyed the encampment, and drove the protesters out of the park. Although *violence from below* was minimal, *violence from above* was apparent as the crowds were broken up by police and army personnel who resorted to using rifle butts and clubs to beat protesters into submission, which resulted in one civilian death (Hughes 2003b; Peou 2000; Post Staff 1998). However, when this failed to clear out the park, the police returned two days later on 9 September 1998, this time using electric cattle prods, gunfire, and a bulldozer (Peou 2000; Post Staff 1998). Two monks were killed in the protesters' skirmishes with police, which provoked a public outcry (Chea Sotheacheath and Eckardt 1998; Pok Sokundara and Moorthy 1998). Hun Sen quickly moved to forbid monks from taking part in protests, and then banned demonstrations altogether. Yet the people defied the ban, and the following day about 8,000 people again took to the streets to participate in a march led by a large group of monks (Chea Sotheacheath and Eckardt 1998; Hughes 2003b). Responding to the specter of *violence from above*, some of the protesters reacted with the threat of *violence from below* as several marchers were armed with bamboo sticks, stones, and even guns (Peou 2000). Thus, the totalitarian armor of Cambodia's "deprivers" of public space was starting to crack as their control over the public domain had become too intense. This dominance resulted not in the continued submissiveness of the population, but from the perspective of those in power, the undesired effect of violent outbursts "from below" against the oppression of an exploitative social order. The government crackdown continued and eventually the protests subsided, although the political deadlock persisted. In all, 26 lives were lost during the crackdown, and in the following days it another 18 bodies were discovered lying in irrigation ditches, ponds, and rivers around Phnom Penh (Bou Saroeun 1998; Peou 2000). Finally, on 25 November 1998 Ranariddh struck a deal with Hun Sen to form a new coalition government (Hayes 1998), while the SRP was left out of the deal, and viewed FUNCINPEC as having sold out to the CPP (Peou 2000).

The manifestation of *violence from above* that swelled in the post-election period can be viewed as consequential to a lack of what Taylor calls (1991: 167) "independence of action," a situation that becomes acutely manifest during election periods in Cambodia given the predominance of voter intimidation.

As Taylor (M. Taylor 1991: 167) suggests, such lack of freedom results from *violence from above* creating a virtual absence of public space, which "enable[s] and facilitate[s] the expression of extremes of violence [from below]." In this sense, the mobilization of the populace and the occasional manifestation of *violence from below* were insurrectionary acts against those in power. Cambodians were actively rediscovering that true power stems from themselves by *taking* public spaces and contesting the RGC's visualizations and administrations of these spaces by remaking them as *spaces for representation*. The RGC's use of *violence from above* and the crackdown on the demonstrations, while successful in the immediate sense, can only have alienated large segments of the population. Accordingly, this suggests a crisis of legitimacy for the RGC, which, as a state weakened by neoliberalization, cannot adequately address the demands of citizens to improve their living standards. This is why Hughes (2003b) found that so many of the demonstrators she interviewed expressed other "latent dissatisfactions."

Constrained by a market fundamentalism it willingly embraced, the violent response of the RGC is akin to a caged animal, where "showing teeth" so to speak is but a last-ditch effort to save itself and maintain its authority. "Strong" states have appropriate capacity and can legitimize themselves without recourse to violence by listening to and addressing citizens' demands, that is, through the practice of democracy (Welsh 2002). In contrast, the RGC, as a "weak" state that lacks the capacity to meet the needs of the populace, predictably takes an authoritarian stance and resorts to violence to "regain [its] footing" when citizens begin to make their demands known in the spaces of the public (Ungar 2002: 49), a pattern that continues into the present as seen in the newspaper headlines presented in Table 4.1, where *violence from above* is a persistent feature of the RGC's attempt to govern the nation. Therefore, from the perspective of a "weak" government seeking to retain power, the attempt to create and enforce an "orderly" public space takes precedence over the allowance of *democracy as public space*. Penetrating and scathing criticisms will inevitably arise to an extent unseen in accountable democratic regimes, and eventually such dissent will overthrow a "weak" government, as happened in Ecuador when violent protests against the ruling neoliberal order swept through the streets of Quito and Guayaquil in 2005 (Fertl 2005). The internalization of neoliberal ideology among Global South governments often precludes their ability to actually respond to such criticism for greater responsibility to the citizens they are meant to represent. Thus, we need not resort to cultural essentialism to comprehend the behavior of the Cambodian government, as awareness of neoliberalism as the dominating force in the current "development discourse" provides for a more considered understanding, particularly when we appreciate that this doctrine is not simply imposed by donors, but skillfully adopted and willingly embraced by the country's elites.

In spite of the massive resistance that followed the 1998 election, a movement that reflected a burgeoning of democratic empowerment "from below,"

Table 4.1 Symptoms of a weak state

Headline	Date
Forced Into Army, Villagers Fear for Livelihoods	08-14/11/2008
Guards Tortured Prisoner to Death, Family Says	24-30/11/2008
Land-Clearing Suspect Injured by RCAF Fire	01-05/12/2008
Inmates Packed in Overcrowded Pursat Prison	01-05/12/2008
Prison Using Forced Labor, Ex-Inmates Say	08-12/12/2008
Officials: Soldiers Accused in Kampot Shooting Won't Cooperate	08-12/12/2008
Overcrowding Highlights Need to Renovate Country's Prisons	08-12/12/2008
Chaos at Border When Vendors Refuse to Pay	15-19/12/2008
Military Police Shoot Protesters, Rights Group Say	17-23/01/2009
RCAF Soldiers Accused of Shooting at Villagers	07-13/02/2009
Villagers Protest After RCAF Tanks' Arrival	28-06/02-03/2009
Search on for Man Who Shot Dead SRP Activist	28-06/02-03/2009
Air Force Captain, Two Others Arrested in Park Ranger Killing	07-13/03/2009
Two Arrested in Killing of Stung Treng SRP Activist	21-27/03/2009
Villagers Shot At by Authorities Come to Phnom Penh to Protest	21-27/03/2009
Police Pay Family of Man Who Died in Custody	04-10/04/2009
Police Tortured Man To Death, Rights Group	04-10/04/2010
R'kiri Villagers Accuse Authorities of Intimidation	25-01/04-05/2009
Villagers Feel Duped Into Joining the Army	25-01/04-05/2009
Gunfire, Then Pact Ends Garment Worker Protest	16-21/05/2009
Since March, 3 K Cham Prisoners Denied Hospital Care Have Died	30-05/05-06/2009
22-Year-Old Man Dies in Prison of Suspected Fever	13-19/06/2009
Soldiers Shoot, Injure Ethnic Minority Villagers in R'kiri	20-26/06/2009
Human Rights Groups Say Prisons Are Overcrowded, Unhygienic	20-26/06/2009
4 RCAF Soldiers Arrested in Connection With Killings	20-26/06/2009
Suspect Dies in Custody; Family Faults Police	27-03/06-07/2009
Warrant Issued for RCAF Captain After Murder	04-10/07/2009
Military Police Officer Accused of Shooting Handcuffed Man in Back	18-24/07/2009
Men Injured by Police in Protest Shooting Accused of Defamation	29-04/09/2009
SRP Urges Minister to Investigate Activist's Murder	05-11/09/2009
Officials Summoned Over Shooting of Villagers in Siem Reap	12-18/09/2009
Ratanakkiri Judge Denies Harassment Accusations	12-18/09/2009
Father and Son Shot Dead in Firefight with K Cham Police	09-16/10/2009
Villager Claims Forced To File False Complaint	17-23/10/2009
S Reap Villagers Claim Harassment at Land Dispute Meet	17-13/10/2009

Source: The Cambodia Daily: Weekly Review.

the international community was quick to declare the elections "free and fair" so that it could return to *business* as usual with the Phnom Penh government. This position represents an affront to the will of the Cambodian people, clearly illustrating the willingness of donors to lend support to an unpopular[23] and authoritarian-style leader in the name of "order" and "stability" (read business interests and capital) in favor of the potential for democratic awakening. Indeed, to some, the donor community's espousal of democracy now appeared as little more than a bold-faced lie:

"Some people in the international community just come to do business, and play with the prostitutes, so I don't have any confidence in them. And also in 1998, a lot of Cambodian people [were] doing the demonstration about the election results in Phnom Penh, but the international community still recognize and support the election results. . . . I also want the international country [to] stop betray[ing] the Cambodia people because I think that when they donate the aid to Cambodia, I think some countries also have their own interests [in mind]."[24]

This participant's cynicism is mirrored by Abdulgaffar Peang-Meth (1997: 286), who recognizes that "Order and stability seem more highly prized values than the democratic principles that once drove much of international interaction." However, Peang-Meth fails to make the connection to neoliberalization, and instead depends on the same cultural crutch that many Cambodian scholars seem content to rely on. Although slightly skeptical about the "price" of development, the following passage indicates that Peang-Meth (1997: 290) implicitly accepts the neoliberal rhetoric insofar as "stability" and "order" are viewed as worthy goals:

The primacy of order and stability provides greater opportunity for economic growth and development. This economic prosperity would eventually lead to the desire for freedom, human rights, and democracy, completing the socio-economic-political circle. The question is: what price should a society incur to achieve stability and order, however important these goals may be?

Despite being Cambodian himself, Peang-Meth's statement is damaging to Cambodian democracy in the first instance because he implies democracy is currently not desired by Cambodians because of the country's economic dearth.

Peang-Meth's implication contradicts the strong voter turnout in all the elections held since the signing of the PPA, the findings of a recent survey by the Asia Foundation (2003), the convictions of his fellow Cambodian scholars, Lao Mong Hay (1998a), and Kao Kim Hourn (1998, 1999), as well as my own findings, where regardless of socioeconomic status and political convictions, participants universally expressed a desire for democracy:

"I think it is something that we want, we want it ourselves but because from that three years of genocide that kept people, um, like having those bad memories and not feeling comfortable or confident to do anything. Now its more open and everything and of course the democracy . . . I'm sure its, the democracy have its [has a] positive way and negative way, this advantage and disadvantage, but I think if you add, if you divide it in two columns I think you more, have more advantages than disadvantages."[25]

"The Cambodian, they need the, the democracy because democracy the people . . . can say, the people can say, the people can live, the people can go and come everywhere by the law, by the law of the assembly, and if we live in Communist we cannot go and say by our minds. So they need the democracy because democracy . . . make our hearts very light and very free from everything. . . . Democracy, it means . . . they use the idea of the people, the many people and so the people can get the advice, can give their advice to the government, so . . . like it mean, the . . . the people is the owner of the country and so we like the democracy. . . . the government should listen to the idea of demonstrators and because demonstrators they have the problem for living in the society, in the Khmer society and so, ah, the people have to, have to talk about this idea, about these problems to the people, to decide or discuss about problem of the people. But the demonstrators have to think about the safe and comfortable. . . . so the people should do, talk about the problem or the ideas to the government and the government can see the idea of the people, can discuss the problem of the demonstrators."[26]

"For me its good, ah, the democracy. The democracy mean the people, all the people . . . all the people in Cambodia [have a] say [in] democracy. Its not difficult we can take it easy and can go anywhere and haven't the . . . the war. Yeah don't have the war. . . . in Cambodia have money, have the pagoda, school, hospital and the people can go for a walk, can go to visit somewhere."[27]

"For me I think it is very important for people to demonstrate because what we have . . . what we want to say, its . . . we need democracy, and what I think democracy is . . . people is the boss before its, democracy. I think it mean, ah, people is the most important thing and so when people want protest something or demand something . . . the government should make a res . . . a resolution with the people. It is necessary in the Cambodia people, and the Cambodia need democracy. . . . the government should respect the law and also respected the people and what the people demands of what the people need . . . the government should show respect [for] the people and also the government should respect all, any kinds of law and regulation."[28]

"I think democracy is very necessary, it is very important for Cambodia and its people. We want the real democracy. I think it is important for Cambodia and for its people because . . . Cambodia people, they suffer the bad times, a long time ago . . . a long period of time, especially during, especially the Communist ideology . . . that leads to many people, Cambodia people killed and died and now we cannot yet find the people who committed the crime . . . the killing. Democracy is very important, its good and should for the Cambodian people because if this ideology is a practice, can lead, can make Cambodia people today . . . live with hope, because . . . democracy I think that all the . . . definition is that first . . . Cambodia people . . . when the country have democracy the leader, it mean that the leader is, they speak [to] the people and the leader think about the people's interests, thinking first [about] the people's interests. Secondly, the Cambodia, the people have the rights to say, to speak to the, the government. And thirdly and especially, the people have the rights free, rights to walk, to speak . . . to do their everyday life and, and to make the people love each other . . . no one can interfere or can take advantage on anybody, even the poor or the rich, everyone have equal rights, and respecting each other."[29]

"I think, yes the Cambodia needs the ideology that bring the people more . . . have more rights, they can say something . . . freely. Cambodia people don't need any Communist rule. . . . I think democracy is refer to a country that rule with . . . equal rights and people respect each other in term of their rights."[30]

"I think the Khmer people want democracy but sometimes they don't, they don't know they want, they don't know themselves they want that. But when we, when we talk about it, explain about democracy they, they want. So democracy I think, in my view is, first is the people run the country, listen to the people . . . to the voice of the people . . . and the voice of the people is the free voice, and also the voice of the people should be considered by the, by the leader of the nation. And, apart from that . . . about justice, social justice is playing the important role in democracy . . . So when we talk about justice, we talk about law and about legal system, about the court or the trial. So all people, all of that person they should, they should know about democracy, about the rights of the people, about the rights . . . the basic rights, is the rights of expression . . . so if there's no rights of, to expression, in the court maybe they have no right to expression in the court also . . . So if there are no rights in the court, no justice. When a soc . . . when one society, no justice . . . so the government of the society become disorder . . . no one, no . . . no one respect the law. So, the basic is, first the rights of the citizen and second, the legal system and the justice in the country . . . And the third one is the ability and the competencies of the leader of the country."[31]

Furthermore, you would be hard pressed to convince the 20,000 participants of the Democracy Square movement following the 1998 elections that democracy is not something they currently desire. Secondly, Peang-Meth's question is misplaced, as the more fitting query would be to ask why order and stability are privileged over unmediated interaction and democracy. The neoliberal answer, of course, is because the former pair helps to preserve the status quo of wealth and power. Indeed, when will we recognize that economic growth does not mean development?

Moreover, Peang-Meth takes a *strongly culturalist* position that has all the hallmarks of essentialism. In the course of one single paragraph, Peang-Meth (1997: 294) at first refers to Theravada Buddhism as having made the Khmer "placid, peaceful, tolerant, accepting, [and] respectful," all seemingly beneficial to democratic consensus, while then suggesting, "Compromise is . . . an alien concept" to the Khmer, meaning democracy is "inappropriate" for Cambodia. This stands in stark contrast to Neou and Gallup (1997: 290), who argue that Theravada Buddhism has moral precepts that "contain close parallels to international human rights standards" such as the emphasis on compassion, tolerance, and non-violence. Elsewhere, Peang-Meth's (1991) essentialist notions are even more pronounced, so much so that his article "Understanding the Khmer: Sociological-Cultural Observations" reads like a "how to" guide to the type of "othering" Edward Said (2003) denounces. Khmer people are generalized as "intransigent," "corrupt," "passive," and prone to laziness due to their supposed inclination for taking "action in spurts," while Cambodian political leadership is said to be "obsess[ed] with total control and absolute power" (Peang-Meth 1991: 447–49). This is again contradicted by Neou and Gallup (1997: 291), who maintain that "democratic elements [can be found] in indigenous Cambodian traditions that predate the modern era."

Either way, if there is one universal truth about culture, it is the certainty of change (Berman 1993, Clifford 1988; Gupta and Ferguson 1997), and thus Peang-Meth makes a profound mistake in connecting his generalizations back to the Angkorean era of the *Devarajas* (god-kings). He writes: "The Khmer carry with them an ingrained memory of their early leadership in the Southeast Asian region, their capability, even invincibility" thanks to their Angkorean heritage (Peang-Meth 1991: 447). If the severance from traditional modes of thought that occurred under the Khmer Rouge regime is not adequately convincing of a historical disconnection from the epoch of Angkor's *Devarajas*, then the notion that such "ingrained memory" is a re-appropriation of sorts should suffice in debunking such claims. This component of Cambodian identity was long forgotten by the Khmer themselves and only revived under French colonial rule, following the western "discovery" of Angkor Wat when "Cambodians were informed that their ancestors had built 'Angkor' (as they indeed had) and that at one time Cambodia dominated a large part of mainland Southeast Asia" (Chandler 1998b: 37). Nevertheless, falling prey to the same *"folie de grandeur"* to which Chandler (1998b) suggests many of Cambodia's leaders have succumbed, Peang-Meth (1991: 448) argues that modern Khmer people continue to "respect the social order of the *Devaraja's* universe, which has no place for complacency, accommodation, or conciliation." Geographer Audrey Kobayashi (1994: 77) warns of the folly in extending such essentialist forms of reason:

> essentialism carries the potential to create new forms of difference and division among those people it is meant to unite. Giving in to essentialism . . . has a . . . sinister political side, because it has the potential to be nothing but the reverse of historical forms of oppression through which racism and sexism became so powerful.

Perhaps Peang-Meth's intention is unity, as he himself is of Cambodian origin. However, his ethnicity does not excuse his pernicious characterization of the Khmer, as the claim for power in speaking for an entire people is an act of stereotyping that is no less insidious coming from "insiders" than those made by "outsiders" (Berman 1993).

Between beautification and the war on terror: Covert (re)productions of space and pretext as the new modes of control

Between 1999 and 2002, the RGC led by Hun Sen began to ease up on its overt domination of Cambodian public space, as authorities repeatedly turned a blind eye to most demonstrations held during these years (Hughes 2003b). This "retreat" from public space coincided with the modified public persona of Hun Sen, who no longer portrayed himself as the strongman of Cambodia (Osborne 2000). While this may appear to suggest that the CPP was beginning to conform to international pressure to respect the country's constitutional freedoms of expression and assembly, given their position of aid dependency (Osborne 2000), the reality of this response is very different. Peou's (2000) analysis provides one alternative interpretation, as he suggests that this development is better explained in terms of the CPP's renewed confidence following its 1998 election victory. The new coalition government was very much a one-sided affair, as the FUNCINPEC was an internally divided party due to both its near breakup in the wake of the 1997 coup, and the poor leadership skills of Prince Ranariddh (Hughes 2003b; Peou 2000; Roberts 2001). The nuisance of the Khmer Rouge had also evaporated following the defection of several high-ranking soldiers in 1997 and 1998 (Hughes 2003b; Peou 2000), and the insurgents disintegrated altogether following the death of Pol Pot in April 1998 (Sainsbury 1998). This meant the hegemony of the CPP was relatively stable. With elections not set to occur again until 2003, public opinion and particularly demonstrations appeared, at least outwardly, to be of little consequence to the dominant party. Peou's (2000) theory of secured hegemony is supported by a report issued by the International Crisis Group (2000), that observes a marked decline in violence directed toward opposition members in 1999. However, the International Crisis Group (2000: 15) also warned that,

> ... this should not lead observers to conclude the government or the CPP has qualitatively changed its ways. Rather, the reverse is true: with one party clearly in charge of the country – and in possession of most of the weapons – few are willing to mount challenges.

While overt violence against opposition elements may have decreased, the notion that few are willing to mount challenges is demonstrably erroneous.

Indeed, there has been a significant increase in the number of public protests in Phnom Penh since the 1998 election. In reference to the emergent trend of social mobilization in the public spaces of the capital, Hughes (2003b: 183) comments that "... the upsurge in protest over the past few years appears to be linked to the perception, on the part of a range of discontented groups in the city, that a space for public expression has emerged." Indeed, it would seem that through the threat of *violence from below*, or at least what "from above" has been a priori defined as illegitimate and threatening, put the RGC back on its heels and forced the government into the realization that it could no longer continue with such an overt strategy of spatial control. For the time being, in what was clearly a profound victory for the ongoing *process* of democracy, Lefebvre's notion of the "right to the city" had been won.

The lapse of overt CPP control over public space was, from the standpoint of absolute control, tactically risky. As the increasing frequency of demonstrations and protests in Phnom Penh following the 1998 elections suggest, this relaxation by the CPP allowed the democratic awakening fostered by the Democracy Square movement to grow considerably in the hearts and minds of Cambodians. Thus, although the Democracy Square movement may be viewed as unsuccessful in that authorities eventually dispersed it, the emerging protest trend is in fact indicative of the movement's success. Cambodians have clearly learned a number of valuable lessons from this movement. Most importantly, the public spectacle of this massive showing of solidarity allowed Cambodians to *take* the space necessary to rediscover themselves as both individuals and as an empowered collective. Thus, with this shared rediscovery of self that the Democracy Square movement inspired, some Cambodians have begun to recognize that they themselves are the true source of power in their society:

"I think [demonstrations] are a good way for Cambodian democracy because it can help people to speak their voice, to speak their ideas, yet before they don't have these kind of rights to say about what they want, what they [are] feeling, but right now [during demonstrations] we can say, so that is good."[32]

"For me I think if they demand something in a good way, [I] think it is good for them and I . . . I think that they do like this because they cannot do if they want demand something that they cannot get it. They cannot do something besides doing this kind of demonstration or protest because they don't have any other possible ways to do, and if they want to meet the, the people who responsible for this problem, the top leader, they cannot go to meet so they just only do this kind of . . . demonstration. So it can get the attention and [I] think they may see that people need this through demonstration. I think it is legitimate and should be legal because . . . I think that for example, they demand for their specific rights that, some leader that they don't provide them the rights so that they protest for this rights so I think it is a legal way for them to do. I think that for my idea, [I] believe in . . . [when] they demand to have, to ask for permission or they have for the rights to make a demonstration . . . sometimes they let us to have demonstration and sometimes they don't let us to have the demonstration. So if they, for me I think that if they give the rights or do not allow we still need to have demonstration even though they allow or not allow. For me I want them, the top leader in the government, to listen to what the people demand and protest, and also want them to think about this kind of thing that they raise and also take it to practice also."[33]

"[When] the people discuss [with] each other or the gather in the public space, it means they can speak about their ideas. It means, sometimes they can give advice to the government and sometimes the government can tell about the problems that they have . . . And sometimes it means we can show the experience of the people to the government, and the government to the people so I think its very good for demonstrations to make a meeting at the public spaces . . . and to [make] the gathering or to discuss about politics in the public spaces."[34]

"It is very important for democracy [for people to be able to protest in public space] because the democracy means they need the many idea of the people and [when people demonstrate] they think about the people as bigger than the government . . . and because the people can say everything, can speak altogether no problem."[35]

"In my point of view, I think that demonstrations in Cambodia, we have a clear law which state about this as well as in our constitution, we say that our country is a democracy and a multi-party system. So, in terms of this I think that people in Cambodia have the rights to speak or to demand or protest something that they feel that it is not good for them and so . . . if the people see that the government convicted something wrong and people say and tell them that it is wrong. But the government did not listen and the government did not follow the people. So one reason that [is] left for the people such as me is demonstration, so I decided to join many demonstrations."[36]

The CPP's response to this democratic reawakening has been to deny its existence.

The RGC has publicly tried to ignore demonstrations to the best of its ability, retreating from view when encountered by protesters and denying their calls for government accountability by simply not responding to demonstrators or their demands (Hughes 2003b). The public positioning of the RGC belies a covert strategy to reproduce Phnom Penh's public spaces, visually, administratively, and materially. The envisioned (re)production of space involves the expulsion of "unruly" elements of the population from the city altogether, and the replacement of unregulated squatter areas with both monuments to CPP power (Hughes 2003a; 2003b), and symbols of capitalist wealth such as modern office, apartment, and shopping complexes (Berthiaume and Nhem Chea Bunly 2005). Accordingly, as *The Cambodia Daily* newspaper headlines presented in Table 4.2 illustrate, forced evictions, although contested, have become common features of the collective lived experience of the

Table 4.2 Forced evictions

Headline	Date
Now Homeless, Villagers Remain in Bokor Park	15-21/11/2008
"Violent" Evictions Stir Controversy in Kampot	15-21/11/2008
City Inspects Renakse Armed Eviction Dispute	01-05/12/2008
Evicted Market Vendors Demonstrate at City Hall	15-19/12/2009
Battambang's Evicted Vendors Must Pay $2,400 for New Stalls	05-09/01/2009
Officials Forcibly Evict Dey Krahorm Holdouts	24-30/01/2009
Dey Krahorm Evictees Protest Outside City Hall	07-13/02/2009
Demolition of Rek Reay Begins Despite Protest	14-20/03/2009
French School Students Protest Housing Eviction	04-10/04/2009
Victims of Home Fires now Face Eviction	18-24/04/2009
Kratie Officials Start Removal of Homes on Land Concession	09-15/05/2009
No Money for Russei Keo Residents Facing Eviction	09-15/05/2009
Families Forced to Leave Borei Keila for Relocation Site	13-19/06/2009
Sek Sok Canal Expansion Starts, Remaining Houses to be Removed	13-19/06/2009
HIV/AIDS Families To Be Moved Shortly	13-19/06/2009
Borei Keila Families Begin Uneasy Settling at Toul Sambou	20-26/06/2009
After Eviction, Officials Back Away From Housing Guarantee	20-26/06/2009
Last of the Borei Keila HIV/AIDS Families to be Moved	20-26/06/2009
Compensation or Eviction for Group 78, City Says	04-10/07/2009
20 Borei Keila Families to be Relocated Next Week	04-10/07/2009
Group 78 Watches as Houses Are Demolished	11-17/07/2009
Group 78 Eviction Injunction Request Dismissed	11-17/07/2009
Soldier Alleges Home Burned Down By District Governor	11-17/07/2009
Bail Hearing Set for Two Men in Forced Eviction Case	08-14/08/2009
Eviction Notice Given to Boeng Kak Villagers	08-14/08/2009
Lake Residents Urged to Accept Compensation as Filing Persists	08-14/08/2009
Koh Kong Residents Trying to Fight Imminent Eviction	15-21/08/2009
80 Boeng Kak Families Prepare as Forced Eviction Looms	15-21/08/2009
Conditions Deteriorating for Squatters Evicted from Dey Krahorm	22-28/08/2009
Eviction of Boeng Kak's Village 1 Imminent, Authorities Say	29-04/09/2009
Most Villagers Accept Payout as Eviction Deadline Passes	29-04/09/2009
Families Call on Hun Sen to Stop Airport Area Evictions	29-04/09/2009
Victims of Forced Evictions Gather for Release of Report	05-11/09/2009
Group 78 Residents Still Awaiting Compensation	12-18/09/2009
Gov't Upholds Defense of Eviction Policies to UN	12-18/09/2009
Community B Residents Say Eviction Too Soon, Request Delay	19-25/09/2009
HIV Families Still Waiting for Apartments Promised by Gov't	19-25/09/2009
Dey Krahorm Families Face Eviction Again	03-09/10/2009
Homes Demolished to make way for Roundabout	09-16/10/2009
After Houses Torched, Villagers Seek Help in Capital	09-16/10/2009
Illegal Occupation Ruling to be Carried Out by K Kong Court	17-23/10/2009
O Meanchey Evictees Struggling With Illness and Food Shortages	17-23/10/2009
100 Police Visit Eviction Site as Deadline Passes	24-20/10/2009

Source: The Cambodia Daily: Weekly Review.

Cambodian poor. CPP municipal governor Chea Sophara, who in 2000 launched a beautification plan for the city, has spearheaded Phnom Penh's transformation (Hughes 2003a; Sodhy 2004). In Chea Sophara's view, squatter settlements are detrimental to Phnom Penh's social order, and their replacement with "parks full of flowers" marks "the turning of a new page towards a culture of peace and promotion of social morality," free from the "violence . . . that has created insecurity and turmoil in Cambodia for three decades" (quoted in Pen Khon 2000, 60). He also comments that squatter areas "are difficult to control and get access to. The area is like a barrier preventing fresh air from blowing into the city, instead of a foul stink," and they "badly damage the beauty and well-managed social order of the capital" (quoted in Pen Khon 2000, 62–63). That Chea Sophara was popular among the propertied class of Phnom Penh is unsurprising. His actions increased their land value while simultaneously, in a long tradition of capitalist exclusions, pushing the "unsightly" and supposedly "violence prone" poor from public view.

Pamela Sodhy (2004: 170), an apparent champion of the neoliberal "ordered" vision of public space, has a favorable view of the beautification scheme, calling Chea Sophara "a force for modernity in Cambodia." Indeed, Sodhy is absolutely correct in this assertion insofar as the beautification scheme cuts to the heart of modernization theory itself. Chea Sophara's visualization and administration of space is representative of a colonial-inspired attitude of seeking to recreate so-called "backward" people into "properly" behaved citizens, which is nothing short of an erosion of the ability of the poor to define and take care of their own lives (see Crush 1995; Escobar 1995; Leys 1996; Preston 1996; Rist 1997). Beautification is a "top-down" approach to further the neoliberal agenda done in the name of comfort, safety, and profit, where "political activity is replaced in spaces like the mall, festival marketplace, or redesigned park . . . by a highly commodified spectacle designed to sell either goods or the city as a whole" (Mitchell 2003b: 138–39, see also Crawford 1992; Zukin 1995). Thus, far from being concerned with the corporeal well-being of the citizenry, the beautification of Phnom Penh is little more than a sales pitch to would-be investors.

The rapid urbanization that resulted in the numerous squatter settlements found around Phnom Penh's perimeter represents one of the many undesired effects of free-market economics, and the CPP response to this problem should not be read as a manifestation of a supposed "cultural" proclivity for authoritarianism. Rather, it has everything to do with toeing the neoliberal line. The relationship between the RGC's authoritarian behavior and the neoliberal concern with "order" is clearly illustrated by the periodic roundup and exile of the homeless from the capital, Phnom Penh (see Botumroath Lebun 2004; Kuch Naren and Solana Pyne 2004a), as well as the tourist mecca of Siem Reap, home to Angkor Wat (see Thet Sambath 2004). Although denied by the authorities, homeless people, and particularly orphaned children, are regularly gathered up by the military and shipped by truck out to

the provinces, where they are dumped and told not to return to the city
(Botumroath Lebun 2004; Kuch Naren and Solana Pyne 2004a). The RGC's
roundup practice has become an ongoing routine, as most of those disposed
of eventually make their way back to Phnom Penh, which indicates that the
poor are willing to mount challenges against the authorities' visualizations,
materializations, and attempted administrations of city spaces, and in doing
so they are demanding their "right to the city." Of course, this resistance does
not go unnoticed by the RGC, and the criminalization of the poor is increasingly seen in Cambodia, where street people often complain of being arbitrar-
ily arrested and beaten by police for loitering (Reynolds and Yun Samean
2004a). The homeless have no private space to call their own, no sanctuary
to return to at the end of the day, and accordingly *violence from above* has
become yet one more of the many injustices that street people must negotiate
as they go about their daily lives.

Several members of the local NGO community I interviewed in 2007
conveyed disdain for the project of beatification, demonstrating an acute
awareness for its underlying capitalist objectives and spatialized strategies:

"Beautification, I can say it's actually just a term they [the Phnom Penh
municipal government] use so they can take the land from the people.
After that they will pass to private company, for example, maybe you
heard about the land just in front of Sam Rainsy Party [headquarters],
the building they are still constructing. So it was burned in 2001 or 2002
and that time it was burned to build public garden. So later they sold this
land to private company and build a lot of building over there. So beautification is just a shadow of development. They use this word and then
sell land to private company and private company can build many building. . . . I don't know their idea, they never talk about how development
can contribute to [improved] living condition. . . . So I think that this still
a big question for us, but the municipal [government] they don't care
about that, they [are] just thinking about how they can make their family
rich, nothing besides that."[37]

"The government is horrible because they need to be responsible [for
homeless people], but they aren't. Because in the strategy they said poverty reduction, when they do that [evict homeless people from Phnom
Penh parks] its against what they say. Some people have been living there
for a long time, and you have to ask the question, 'the city for who?'. The
city is for the people and you have to treat the [homeless] people as
our people, not just street people from outside the beautiful city. I think
the way that they [the municipal government] answer this [problem] is
not responsible, its going to cause the violence, a lot of violence will
happen."[38]

"At any cost, beautify the city at any cost, so this mean that they clear
away the people. But the duty, the obligation of the government is to find
the shelter for the poor. Why do we elect them? To solve all this kind of

problem! If they are the leader and they say 'Oh there are a lot of poor and I cannot find a way to take care of them', then go away, we don't need such a leader! It's easy to decline the responsibility, but they have to face this responsibility. Why are there a lot of poor? There is a reason, so find the reason and solve the reason! Forcing the poor from the city is not a way to solve the problem, by hiding this problem, because this case will go somewhere, it still exist in Cambodia. They get out of this place, and go to another place, but the case is still there. These people that they evict from Sambok Chab to go to Andong, they still here, they still human being, so they are still here. [There is a] lack of responsibility in dealing with this problem because of lack of political will, because they are incompetent, they are corrupted, and they don't care."[39]

By euphemizing the forced removal of poor people from the spaces of the capital city as beautification, the intent, as was recognized by these participants, is to obscure the ways in which the Phnom Penh municipal government is unable to cope with both the ongoing homelessness among many urban dwellers, and the large influxes of rural Cambodians who end up on the streets after migrating to seek employment in the capital when the jobs, by and large, simply do not exist. The logic of responsibility to the electorate is lost on a great many Cambodian officials, who instead concern themselves with shoring up as much capital for themselves and their immediate family as is possible through lucrative backdoor business deals. Contempt for beautification and its predilection for corruption was similarly expressed to me by opposition leader, Sam Rainsy:

"Yes, I share your view [on the imperative behind beatification as a means for domination of urban space and a stifling of democracy]. They want just to hide corruption and put forward projects such as beautification, but they can do things in different manners, why don't they build social housing for the poor? Why confiscate all the land and sell it to companies that can afford to pay millions of dollars? And it is the municipality who sells the land without any transparency. Most of the money lands in the pocket of small group, a small number of corrupt people. So this is a very specific approach that you cannot find in other countries. In Vietnam, they start to redistribute land and they punish whoever now is prosecuted for corruption. They get very severe sentences, including death penalty, but in Cambodia there is a total impunity for all kinds of criminals."[40]

What Rainsy ultimately describes is the "shadow state" activities of Cambodia's elites, which represents the paramount process through which neoliberalization has been internalized as a functioning logic of governance in the country.

Even individuals working within the IFIs expressed serious reservations with the beatification scheme, in what appears to be an implicit recognition that neoliberalization is not simply a matter of following donor prescriptions to the letter, but rather an articulation that results in hybridized and often unpredictable local forms of neoliberalism:

"I don't think that the municipality really cares about development. I think the motive is private interests, that of course coincide with their own interests for income from this. So beautification in their own terms, not in the [interest of the] urban poor. It's a cover, its an excuse to evict them I think. It's a private interest intermingled with the professional interests, using their personal position to intervene, you know?"[41]

"I am extremely sceptical of an argument that inequality in Phnom Penh has remained static, because if it has remained static it is probably because the court to a certain extent physically relocates poor out of the city. So to claim that you've reduced inequality by putting the poor in a half-nelson and moving them outside of city limits is not really most people's definition of poverty reduction. So what do I think of it? You can beautify a city without physically relocating the poor, I think yeah there is a genuine desire to make the city beautiful and modern and all the rest, but there is also an element, a very large element of self-interest involved in land management. . . . So I don't know how its going to stop. Do we need to get rid of the poor to beautify the city? No we don't, you know we could provide them with decent housing."[42]

In these responses we see how the local interpretation and application of neoliberal reforms are sharply criticized by those working within institutions that are known for being steadfast proponents of neoliberalization. The development discourse (in this case beautification) is challenged at the local scale as an obfuscating rhetoric for capitalist accumulation by Cambodian elites, which is clearly recognized as anathema to the notions of social justice these IFI employees surely espouse on a personal level. Yet their professional roles ensure that the level of critical reflection is almost never scaled-up to examine what development might then accordingly mean at the international level,[43] and how donor lending practices and conditionalities similarly promote and make possible accumulation by dispossession.

The contestation of public space between those who have been relegated to a life of abject poverty by way of their state's adherence to a market ideology that "squeezes" the poor, and the manifestation of authoritarian government responses concomitant to such neoliberal preoccupation can be seen in *The Cambodia Daily* newspaper headlines collected in Table 4.3. The government's unspoken policy of dealing with the homeless was very evident during my fieldwork in Cambodia. This was manifest both during and in the days leading up to the week-long Inter-Parliamentarian ASEAN summit held in Phnom Penh from 12 to 19 September 2004, as well as prior to the Cambodia Development Cooperation Forum (formerly called the annual Consultative Group meeting) from 19 to 20 June 2007. Along with banishing the homeless

Table 4.3 The battle of homelessness

Headline	Date
City Rounds Up Homeless, Again, for Festival	01-07/11/2008
Families Moved in 2001 Returning to City Center	24-30/01/2009
Poor Families Receive Homes From the King	31-06/01-02/2009
New Government Plan for Beggars Alarms Rights Groups	07-13/02/2009
Pagoda Stops Taking in Dying Homeless People	07-13/02/2009
Sex Workers, Homeless Swept From Daun Penh District	16-21/05/2009
UN, Rights Group Decry Sweep of Undesirables	23-29/05/2009
Authorities Continue Sweep of Undesirables	23-29/05/2009
Amid Criticism, Roundups of Homeless Continue	30-05/05-06/2009
Officials Defend Center Linked to Detentions	25-31/07/2009
Rights Group Accuses Gov't of Punishing Phnom Penh's Poor	25-31/07/2009
Controversial Social Affairs Shelter For the Homeless to Expand	25-31/07/2009
Gov't Undertaking Survey on Numbers of Homeless	01-07/08/2009
Homeless Villagers Forced to Leave Pagoda	09-16/10/2009
City Homeless Roundup To Intensify for Festival	17-23/10/2009

Source: The Cambodia Daily: Weekly Review.

from the capital's streets, the RGC maintained tight control of the city's public space by enforcing a strict social order during the days of the two meetings, forcing the removal of all visible signs of informal economic activity, such as street-stall fruit vendors and impromptu roadside gas stations.[44] More recently, following an 17 August 2009 Land Traffic Law directive from Interior Minister Sar Kheng, Phnom Penh municipal authorities began enforcing a complete ban on sidewalk vendors in the city (Chhay Channyda 2009). This was preceded in April 2009 by the utterly absurd, when a municipal directive was issued stating: "Phnom Penh City Hall has noticed that people using sidewalks and balconies as a place to dry clothes is disturbing public order, beauty and the environment in Phnom Penh. It is jeopardizing the dignity and honor of Khmer citizens, who used to be highly civilized" (Prak Chan Thul 2009). Presumably, the RGC has undertaken such measures to project to international patrons an image of Cambodia as a "modern" and "ordered" society, and hence an economically vigorous one. In the case of the ASEAN summit, the car bomb attack on the Australian Embassy in Jakarta on 9 September 2004 conveniently served as an ideal pretext for removing the marginalized from public space, as the RGC could cite "security precautions" to effectively silence those critical of the government's approach (Lor Chandara 2004).

Indeed, the RGC's tendency to suggest a concern with security as both a rationale and excuse for its own authoritarian behaviors has become commonplace in recent years. Kheang Un and Judy Ledgerwood (2002: 102) warn that there is "widespread concern that the government is using the global fear of terrorism, in the aftermath of the attacks on the United States, as a pretext to silence opposition parties." This became particularly manifest in 2000, when the CPP accused members of the SRP and FUNCINPEC of belonging to the Cambodian Freedom Fighters (CFF), an insurgent group led by Khmer-Americans based out of California (Marston 2002; Sodhy 2004). The group has vowed to take down the Hun Sen government and, as the year 2000 came to an end, Cambodia witnessed a rare showing of marked *violence from below* when the heavily armed CFF attacked government buildings in Phnom Penh (Hughes 2001a; Langran 2001; Marston 2002).

Although labeled as terrorists by the RGC, the CFF maintains it is a legitimate group with 500 members in California and 50,000 supporters in Cambodia (Sodhy 2004). However, many Cambodians are unconvinced of the group's legitimacy, and far from siding with the government, they believe the CPP staged the CFF attack to smoke out opposition to Hun Sen, as many FUNCINPEC and SRP members have been implicated in and arrested for the attacks (Marston 2002). Irene V. Langran (2001: 156) suggests that "while the insurgency was quickly subdued, it served as a reminder of the recent and fragile nature of Cambodia's democracy." The fact that the guise of terrorism can now be extended at will by the CPP to include any political movement that may challenge its authority has profoundly detrimental implications for Cambodian public space. Such use of subterfuge is a blatant attempt to restrict Mitchell's (1995: 115) notion of public space as "an unconstrained space within which political movements can organize and expand into wider arenas." As if the RGC's calls for an "orderly" and "stable" public space were not justified enough in the eyes of neoliberal donors, since "Without order [and stability], the argument goes, liberty is simply impossible. And that order must be explicitly geographic: it centers on the control of the streets and the question of just *who* has *the right to the city*" (Mitchell 2003b: 17), even some cynics within the international donor community would now be prone to accepting such claims in the post-9/11 world. Hence, "order" and "stability," conceived as such, represent unquestionable threats to the democratic ideal of public space.

Cambodia's intensifying centralization of power: Strengthening the bondage of patron–Client relations through market fundamentalism

The turn of the new millennium saw a "surge in vigilante justice, [and] the pervasiveness of corruption . . ." (Langran 2001: 156), including the continuance of the suspected involvement of police and soldiers in the kidnapping epidemic that enveloped Cambodia at the time (Bainbridge and Lon Nara 2002; Faulder 2000). Military forces and police have also been implicated in several extrajudicial killings, and criticized for failing to stop the lynching of criminal suspects (U.S. Department of State 2001). This trend has persisted as mob killings raged out of control in 2004, where the month of November alone saw five mob slayings (Yun Samean 2004b), which reflect a lack of faith in the judicial system as justice is sought through vigilantism. Indeed, a consistent refrain from participants involved in interviews I conducted from August to November 2004 was that police were generally far more concerned with rent-seeking activities than arresting violent criminals. These concerns seem well placed given that most incidents of mob violence effectively serve as a lesson in impunity, as perpetrators are rarely arrested in relation to mob slayings (Green 2002). The RGC has only worsened this tendency for vigilante justice by lending implicit support in creating the Peoples Protection Movement in 1999, a civilian militia used to combat street thefts and robberies (Bou Saroeun and Sainsbury 1999). In addition, electoral violence also returned in 2000, as the first homicide associated with the forthcoming commune elections of 2002 occurred on 3 June 2000. Pak Choeun, a recently nominated FUNCINPEC candidate, and his wife Doung Meas, were murdered by the chief of the local commune, who subsequently confessed to the killings because of the political competition the victim would pose in the upcoming election (U.S. Department of State 2001), a pattern that would continue as the election date approached.

Despite the CPP and FUNCINPEC's signing of an agreement to abstain from violence during the 2002 commune election campaign (Mockenhaupt 2001; Un and Ledgerwood 2002), political violence was once again a feature of the run-up to the February elections (Human Rights Watch 2002b). Human Rights Watch (2002a) indicates more than 267 cases of alleged violence and intimidation were documented from 1 January 2001 through 5 January 2002, including harassment, threats, arbitrary arrest and detention, restriction of assembly, property violations, destruction of party signboards, and numerous violent acts, including 14 confirmed murders. The campaign was also tainted, like the previous national elections, by widespread allegations of CPP vote buying, confiscation of voter cards, and coerced loyalty oaths, as well as unequal access to the media (Human Rights Watch 2002b). Much of the violence is said to have been directed by commune chiefs who control the local militia and police, and intended to send a message to villagers that if they vote the "wrong way," their security could not be guaranteed (Human Rights Watch 2002a). The situation was particularly acute in Kompong Cham province, which serves as the base for the Royal Cambodian Armed Forces' Military Region 2, where soldiers were "repeatedly implicated in serious human rights violations, from extortion and armed robbery to assault, rape, illegal detention, and murder" (Human Rights Watch 2002b: 7). However, as sordid as this picture is, it represents an improvement as "the [commune] elections came off relatively smoothly" compared to the 1993 and 1998 elections (Un and Ledgerwood 2003: 114), and generally Cambodians went to the polls feeling confident that violence would not mar the actual election day (Slocomb 2004).

Bankrolled by international donors, the stated goal of the commune elections was decentralization, or a shifting of power to the local level. While couched in the language of greater democracy, from a cynical perspective donor support for the election can be interpreted as another facet of the neoliberal prescription of "rolling back" the state. Nevertheless, the commune elections of 2002 did not transform the centralized control of power and patron–client links remained firmly entrenched (Slocomb 2004; Un and Ledgerwood 2003), nor did the commune elections of 2007 offer any substantive change. As the discussion below will reveal, this is to be expected. Margaret Slocomb (2004: 465–66) contends that Cambodian political power has become more centralized over the last twenty years, and far from reversing this trend she argues the idea that commune chiefs might now "claim their newly 'decentralized' authority back from 'the top' is almost inconceivable within Cambodian political culture." However, such *culturalist* explanations appear misplaced given Slocomb's recognition that a centralization of power has occurred only in the last twenty years, that is, those years in which Cambodia has become increasingly integrated into the global capitalist system. Indeed, according to Scott and Kerkvliet (1977), certain political conditions such as marked inequalities of wealth, status, and power, and the absence or inability of impersonal guarantees, kinship units, and villages to promote the security of person and property or advancement, serve to reinforce and promote patron–clientelism. Thus, the centralization of power occurring in Cambodia by way of strengthened patron–client bonds cannot be explained as exclusively cultural. Rather, it is a social reality that is founded on inequality, one that has only been exacerbated by the transition to free-market economics. As Giles Mohan (2000: 89) explains,

> The neoliberal agenda is, by its very nature, highly centralised because it seeks to free markets which are viewed as ubiquitous and spaceless, unlike state apparatuses which are place-bound and spatially uneven. In this way deregulation of markets entails the re-regulation of political space and this leans towards authoritarianism. This then precludes any real redistribution of social welfare which increases social and regional polarization in countries whose space economy is already skewed towards relatively immobile primary products.

Thus, Mohan sheds some light on the Global South's ever-present urban bias.

While most scholars of Cambodia are very much aware of such a bias in the country, and "rural development is on everybody's lips in Cambodia, . . . the heavy concentration of economic growth around Phnom Penh has not been broken" (Ovesen, Trankell, and Ojendall 1996: 25). This suggests a fundamental misunderstanding of the origins of urban–rural disparity among some Cambodian scholars such as Kao Kim Hourn (1998: 195), who while acknowledging urban bias as a "potentially damaging situation," still look favorably and uncritically upon the role of the IFIs and the entire neoliberal model in general. Kao Kim Hourn (1998: 193) comments: "the IMF and World Bank have played an important role in supporting macroeconomic stability through various economic strategies and the implementation of structural adjustment programs. This type of support generates a favourable investment for investors . . . enabling the private sector to become the engine of growth and development." Thus, as an individual who has clearly succumbed to the monolithic "cult of growth," Kao Kim Hourn espouses neoliberalization as the order of the day without reflecting on its role as the primary suspect in the creation of urban–rural disparity. The free-market economic system that has exacerbated urban–rural inequality is more than "potentially damaging," it is empathically destructive to the majority of the country's primarily rural population. Perhaps the "potentiality" for damage that Kao Kim Hourn refers to is meant for the incumbent regime, as the growing animosity among rural citizens may boil over into mass resistance and *violence from below* to overthrow the highly inegalitarian status quo. As Michael Doyle (1998: 90) notes, urban–rural inequality has continued to heighten since the UNTAC period, "engendering rural anger with ominous overtones." Indeed, in my conversations with Cambodians during my fieldwork in 2004 and again in 2006–7, some individuals expressed that they felt something "big" was coming in terms of civil disobedience and mass resistance "from below."[45]

Returning to patron–clientelism, if one is content to make *culturalist* arguments about this phenomenon, then why is there an insistence among scholars of this persuasion to relate their observations and base their hypotheses only on the last 10,000 years of human history while ignoring the 200,000 years prior to this? If we were to dig even deeper into the murk and mire of the historical past, one would uncover a global human condition free from any such patron–client relations, as it was only after the agricultural revolution 10,000 years ago that human societies left the egalitarian democracy of small tribal bands to till the soil for what would eventually become stratified kingdoms and empires. With this transformation and its concomitant assignment of new and specialized social roles, inequalities of wealth, status, and power were able to flourish, where patron–client bonds became a dialectic method of negotiating inequality for both the peasantry and the elite. Clients sought, and continue to seek today, inclusion in the limiting and oppressive system of patron–clientelism to build personal security and enhance their own chance of survival and advancement (Scott and Kerkvliet 1977). On the other hand, the patron enjoys the relationship because it entrenches her or his own position *vis-à-vis* the client, allowing her or his exploitation to continue in an "agreed to" fashion.

Far from being a cultural reality among certain populations, the bonds of patron–clientelism is a post-agricultural revolution reality for the entire human race, equally visible in the corporate office buildings of the Global North as it is in the villages of the Global South. Furthermore, capitalism, as the ultimate realization of a societal stratification set in motion by the agricultural revolution, is an unforgiving economic system, and the patron–client relation provides a "backdoor" or alternative means to negotiate this system. It seems only fitting that the more an economic system is premised upon inequalities and against collectivism, the more frightening insecurity becomes, so that individuals will be encouraged by their own fears to seek unique ways to negotiate this system. Those in control of the economic system are only too happy to exploit such vulnerability as the patron–client bond acts to perpetuate and ensconce their privileged position. This view is corroborated by Ovesen, Trankell, and Ojendall (1996: 54) who argue that the "promotion of economic, social and political equality" along with the "creation of kinship and village solidarity" offer a "recipe for dismantling or diffusing of patron-client relationships;" however, "Unfortunately, the combination of privatization of land, [and] economic liberalization (capitalism) . . . do not seem conducive to the attainment of these goals." Indeed, the deepening centralization of power and the continuing penchant for patron–clientelism in post-transitional Cambodia is not born of a supposed cultural aberration. Rather, such phenomena are more accurately related to ongoing neoliberal reforms.

With the new millennium, international donors began to increase pressure on the Cambodian government to promote policies of reform. The May 2000 meeting of the Consultative Group of international donors generated a working group for public administration reform, with a focus on promoting "good governance" (Hughes 2003b; Peou 2000). With reference to the CGM's recommendations, Hughes (2003b) acknowledges that the proposed reforms of the judiciary, natural resource management, anti-corruption, and military demobilization would be met with significant local resistance. However, Hughes (2003b: 53) at that time had clearly internalized the neoliberal rhetoric:

> State reforms advocated by international interveners reflect a concern to rationalize and legalize the extractive and repressive activities of the state, and to leaven them with ideas of free-market sustainable development, which will generate profits that can trickle down to the poor. At present, international aid constitutes half of the Cambodian state budget. However, Cambodia's economic destiny ultimately depends, not upon aid, but upon free-market trade. To facilitate this, Cambodia's donors have called for the state to reform, shedding workers, demobilizing soldiers, promoting the judiciary as a guarantor of property rights and contractual obligations, extracting higher levels of tax, and putting more revenue from extractive industries through the books of the Ministry of Finance and Economics. These policies amount to an institutionalization of the repressive and extractive capacities of the state – capacities that are at present mediated through personal self interest in a context of patrimonial protection. Such an institutionalization would improve efficiency, accountability and transparency in the name of good governance.[46]

Hughes (2003b: 53) is also cognizant that the current Hun Sen government cannot afford to reject the donors' reform package outright, but suggests that there is "unlikely to be significant movement on it, because of the political economy of state cohesion." Hughes is right on the mark that Hun Sen is unable to reject donor demands. However, in terms of "significant movement" on neoliberal reforms, this sentiment is very debatable, and it depends on what one believes to be the fundamental objective of such reforms. If one accepts the rhetoric of bilateral and multilateral donors at face value without recognizing concerns of human rights and democracy as mostly lip service, then it is clear that Hun Sen has not moved. Yet, if one dissects the concept of "good governance" to reveal its intent of promoting corporate interests, then Hun Sen has made good on his promise to free up Cambodia's markets.

Indeed, the privatization of government assets and public space more generally is a prevalent feature of the current Hun Sen government (discussed below). Although Hun Sen has his share of critics in the west, one has to wonder why his government's proclivity for authoritarianism is often met with indifference. A prime example of this is the tepid response from some bilateral donors following the March 2005 slaying of five villagers in Poipet by police. The killings came after an incident of apparent land grabbing by village chief Tin On, who claimed that the villager's land belonged to him after word began circulating in 2001 that the property value was rising (Berthiaume and Prak Chan Thul 2005). In fact, many donors including the WB declined to comment when questioned about the incident (Thet Sambath and Shaw 2005), revealing an obvious hypocrisy. It is a common practice to criticize Global South leaders when their authoritarianism has an inclination toward shoring up state or partisan power, such as during episodes of electoral violence. However, silence becomes golden at the international level when authoritarian behavior relates to the interests of global capital and the neoliberal doctrine, in this case the marketization of communal land.

Subverting public trust: Rampant privatization and the renewed crackdown on demonstrations

The CPP's overt control of public space returned in 2003, as the year began with mob chaos in the streets of Phnom Penh. The violence erupted on 29 January 2003, when rumors began to circulate that Suwanan Khongying, a Thai actress who was also popular in Cambodia, had allegedly claimed on Thai radio that Angkor Wat rightfully belonged to the Thai people and should be repatriated to Thailand (ADHOC 2004; Albritton 2004). It was also rumored that she said she would rather be reincarnated as a dog than as a Cambodian (Post Staff 2003; Tin Maung Maung Than 2004). Some Cambodians responded to the claim by launching a public protest in front of the Thai Embassy, which ended with the embassy burned to the ground, and the subsequent looting of several Thai-owned businesses located in the capital (Albritton 2004; Penh Post 2003). The violence that erupted in Phnom Penh can be understood in terms of the profound role Angkor Wat plays in contemporary Cambodian identity, through Cambodia's historical geography of vulnerability stemming from centuries of conflict with hostile neighbors and foreign aggressors since the decline of the Angkorean era, and via the discursive construction of Thai "Otherness" (Hinton 2006).

While law enforcement was conspicuously absent for hours as the protest raged in front of the Thai Embassy (Tin Maung Maung Than 2004), the government response since has been to crack down on virtually every protest or demonstration in the name of "order" and "stability" (ADHOC 2004). In a letter dated 8 April 2005, the Ministry of Interior, the ministry responsible for granting licenses to hold public demonstrations, responded publicly to its ban on virtually all public demonstrations over the previous two years. Interior spokesperson, Khieu Sopheak, used the letter to respond directly to criticisms by union leaders and human rights groups that the RGC has refused to grant permits for all demonstrations held since the anti-Thai riots and has used violence against those that do arise:

> Organizers did not fill out forms or abide by the Law in Demonstrations, and some demonstrations did not notify the authorities or authorities could not give permission. . . . Participants always caused serious impacts to security and public order, which create opportunity for gangs, and other offenders to steal, snatch or commit other acts which cause damage to public and private property
>
> (quoted in Pin Sisovann 2005: np).

Kieu Sopheak continued by blasting human rights workers and the critical reports they have written in response to the government ban stating: "[They] earn for their boss only, not for the interests of the Cambodian people. Their job is to criticize . . . if they do not write such reports their work would be finished" (quoted in Pin Sisovann 2005: np).

This response appears to be little more than a pretext to strip people of their constitutional rights, most prominently freedom of assembly, via the denial of access to public space. Indeed, if "The Cambodian people are the masters of their own country" and "All powers belong to the people," as Article 51 of the Cambodian constitution suggests (Jennar 1995: 16), then the RGC's banning of public protests, an activity that manifests people's empowerment, is emphatically a denial of such rights. Moreover, there is some evidence that the anti-Thai riots may have been fomented by CPP elements to serve as a pretext for the RGC's renewed crackdown on public space. The rumors concerning Suwanan Khongying's supposed accusations, which have never been substantiated, first surfaced in the pro-CPP newspaper *Rasmei Angkor* (Light of Angkor) on 18 January 2003 (Albritton 2004; Tin Maung Maung Than 2004). Hun Sen appears to have inflamed the incident by declaring the Thai movie star to be "not even worth a clump of grass at Angkor Wat" during the inauguration of a new school in Kompong Cham province just two days before the riot in Phnom Penh erupted (Tin Maung Maung Than 2004: 82). Finally, the "Pagoda Boys" (Pagoda Children, Intelligentsia and Student Association), a pro-CPP group consisting of former monks who are often used to "counterattack" public demonstrations, were identified by a confidential US State Department report as the leaders of the anti-Thai riots (Vong Sokheng 2003a).

Speculation aside, the clampdown on public space is undeniable and has been tenacious. Table 4.4, which contains headlines collected from *The Cambodia Daily*, illustrates a protracted campaign by the RGC to deny freedom of assembly, subvert the potential for the emergence of *spaces for representation*, and thereby challenge the Cambodian desire of *democracy as public space*. The National Assembly's approval of the final articles of the controversial Law on Nonviolent Demonstrations on 21 October 2009 represents the culmination of the government's efforts to strip away the Cambodian people's constitutional freedoms of assembly and expression. The new law

Table 4.4 Freedom of assembly under fire

Headline	Date
Adhoc: Protesters Fear Post-Rally Blacklist	01-07/11/2008
Village Chief Accused of Intimidation	24-30/11/2008
Workers Nearly Stopped From Marching in Siem Reap	08-12/12/2008
Rights March Nixed By City, Group Says	08-12/12/2008
Activists Given Sentences in Eviction Case	14-20/02/2009
Protesting K Cham Villagers Face Road Blockages	04-10/04/2009
Gov't Tells Workers to Eschew May Day Parades and Protests	25-01/04-05/2009
Barred Protest to Coincide with Thai PM Visit	06-12/06/2009
CCGR Cancels Forum After Losing Lake Venue	06-12/06/2009
National Assembly to Review Demonstration Draft Law	06-12/06/2009
Guesthouse Told It Needs Official OK Top Host CCHR Meeting	06-12/06/2009
Wat Lanka Monks Prevent Prayers for Burma's Aung San Suu Kyi	20-26/06/2009
Ministry Defends New law Limiting Demonstration Numbers	27-03/06-07/2009
Gov't Denies Rights Forum for Boeng Kak Residents	04-10/07/2009
Police Block CCU Members' Preah Vihear Protest	11-17/07/2009
CCU Is Denied Request to Protest Thai Troops	11-17/07/2009
Police Looking To Arrest More Poipet Protestors	25-31/07/2009
26 Charged With Incitement After Poipet Protest	25-31/07/2009
Police Break Up Post-Trial SRP Protest March	01-07/08/2009
Students Stopped From Entering Nat'l Assembly	01-07/08/2009
Boeng Kak Protest Canceled Because of Police Presence	15-21/08/2009
Riot Police Sent To Preah Vihear Ahead of Protest	12-18/09/2009
Parliament's Closed Door Shut Democracy Out, Opposition Says	12-18/09/2009
Protesters Prevented from Reaching Preah Vihear	19-25/09/2009
Police, Officials Block Route in Medical Student Protest	19-25/09/2009
Debate Opens on Law Restricting Protests	09-16/10/2009
National Assembly Passes Demonstration Law	17-23/10/2009
Most Articles in Demonstration Law Approved	17-23/10/2009
Sam Rainsy Leads Fiery Assembly Debate Against Protest Law	17-23/10/2009
Protest To Halt Seafront Kampot Development Broken Up by Police	24-30/10/2009
Officials Stifling Opposition to Kampot Project, Villagers Say	24-30/10/2009

Source: The Cambodia Daily: Weekly Review.

restricts the size of protests to 200 people and bans any gathering inside or outside of factories and government buildings, citing public order and national security as its principal concerns (Meas Sokchea 2009a). Many Cambodians I interviewed did not believe the rhetoric of the "ordered" view of public space, expressing disdain for both the government and the armed forces for stopping demonstrations:

> "For me I feel very painful and angry to the police and the armed forces who, who do something that only serve their leader. They are not afraid to fight or kill the demonstrators. They're not serving the people, they're serving their leader, their group leader."[47]

> "I think they are wrong, they should not do like this [stop demonstrations] because their duty is to prevent people from committing any bad thing . . . their duty is [to provide] security to demonstrators . . . if they disperse demonstrators, that may lead to violence, some people may get killed, some people may get angry. . . ."[48]

> "For me I feel upset and angry for the policemen who stop the demonstration . . . demonstrator because I want them to make a demonstration in order to decrease the gas . . . the prices so that I can earn more money."[49]

> "During the demonstrate the government use the . . . police or army to suppress all the people of demonstrate. This is the problem that the students or the teacher at all of the University, they feel very angry, they feel 'why the government do this, this is not, not very good'. . . . So I feel sad. This is unfair, not justice, why to do that? Khmer the same, why have to fight people? They should not fight them but do by peace. . . . And the government should answer and to tell them why . . . okay . . . democratic country, democracy, why do they blind or block all the things that happen at the [demonstration], don't let the people know why, so otherwise people want to know why. They wait for government to answer, what's happened? And please tell, why. Okay, sometimes we wait, wait, wait, but [the] government never tell or announcement on TV or on radio, no . . . so otherwise the newspaper they always write why, why, why? . . . Well, the government, they also say we will stop the demonstrate because we want to keep the situation normal, we know what they're gonna say. The people will demonstrate because they do in the peace, okay, it not relative to the violence or fighting, but the many feel, no, during the demonstration surely you will do that violence. So they take this reason and then they come and then they suppress the group of the person that [demonstrate]. Actually, government should protect all the demonstrator. They should allow them and protect them and then let them to share their requests, okay?"[50]

> "I think about this and get very angry to the police that disperse the demonstrators . . . I am very angry to them, to the police, army that stop and disperse to the demonstrators because the people, they want to

get something to go down [like the gas prices, and] to have the democracy so when the police stop like this, [it's] not good, it's very unfair."[51]

"For me its, its the peoples' right, that the police or . . . do the wrongful against the law and because the police, they know the constitution and they know the rights of the people . . . stipulated in the constitution. So when they do that I think they are acting against the rights of the people . . . against the constitution. . . . They should allow. I think that that's good . . . to keep the demonstrator safe to protest and to protect from disturb them . . . that is the duty of the police."[52]

"It's not suitable for the police to come to disperse, to hit, [and] to break up the demonstrations and protests. Difficult, because when the people to do like this, they need to complain, solve the problem [so they] make the demonstration. It's not good for the police come to disperse, or stop, or and break up the demonstration and protests."[53]

"I feel angry to the police because the police hit the people, some people they don't know anything [about their rights], so the police they hit [and] use violence against the people. It's the police duty to protect the people or don't use violence [against] the people, only protect the people and allow the people to do the demonstration."[54]

"I am worried that when they [are] doing the demonstrations, and the policeman and the security they come to do, to have a political violence to the demonstrators, and for me, I want the policemen to help the demonstrators instead of using the political violence toward the demonstrator."[55]

With this renewed crackdown on demonstrations came an intensification of Chea Sophara's beautification plan.

This was immediately evident when I arrived back in Phnom Penh for the first time in two years in June of 2004 to begin fieldwork for this project. A number of changes had occurred to "beautify" the city, most noticeably a general cleaning up of the recreational waterfront area where the Bassac, Tonle Sap, and Mekong Rivers meet, and the beginning stages of the "revitalization" of Hun Sen Park, which is located next to Independence Monument in central Phnom Penh. Over the course of the next several months, I watched as Hun Sen Park was transformed from an empty and unmanaged field where the homeless often gathered, to a symbol of urban wealth frequented by Cambodia's middle and upper class. Grass, shrubs, and trees were planted throughout the grounds, and an elaborate brick and stone walkway was laid down around the perimeter of the new park. While this appeared to be a positive development, as people began using the park for all sorts of recreational activities, the unrestricted usage of this space soon became highly regulated. It was not long before signs, along with armed police officers, were stationed in the park instructing visitors on its "proper" usage, such as not walking on the grass, sitting only on benches, and not riding bicycles on the pathways. On one occasion, I watched as a police officer told an elderly homeless couple that they were not welcome in the park, and needed to leave immediately.[56]

Upon returning to Cambodia for more fieldwork in November 2006, I witnessed even further intensification of the beautification project as the area adjacent to Democracy Square, where homeless people had a tendency to congregate, was now in the process of "revitalization." Large piles of dirt were present on the site, apparently for the purpose of upgrading the grounds. I interviewed several people living in the park and they had very different ideas about the purpose of the dirt and the implications that the beautification project would soon have for their desire and ability to remain in the park:

> "They want to renew the garden here so they put lots of dirt. They would like to move us out, they don't want us to live here. I don't know where I will go if they come and force us to go to the place where they want us, I just go because I have nowhere else to go. And if I don't like it there I will escape and come back here again. If the police try to hit me if I come back, then let it be. If the police not control and not walk around here then no problem, but when they come over here I run. . . . I am afraid to live here, I am afraid of the police, but I don't know what else to do. I don't know why they want to make the park beautiful. I think instead of making the park nice, they should spend the money to help the people who live here, but the government doesn't care about us, they just want to get rid of us. They just care about the garden, not about people. They just want the tourists to come here, and to make a nice place for the rich people who have free time. They spend the money for the rich people, but for the poor people they don't care to help us. The police just make us go from here, and collect our things and burn them. They take our carts and break it, and then take our things. This is stealing but they don't care. Maybe the karma from the Buddha will get them in the next life. I am upset and angry but I don't know what to do."[57]

> "They put all the dirt here because they are making a garden. Hun Sen wants a new garden. . . . When they make a garden here, they will make me move out. I have nowhere else to stay [starts crying]. If I had a home, I would go home. That's why I stay here in the park, and I am sad that they will make me leave here. Normally the police try to make this place clean and nice so people like me cannot live here, they do not allow. They want to make it nice for the rich people and the tourists."[58]

> "The dirt piles are to make a new garden, and it makes it difficult for us to live here because they leave it for a long time before they start work. I think they make like this to try and make us leave here. This is the way they want, but if we try to against to disagree, we will be hit by the police or the guards who control the park. I don't know why they make us leave, because the tourist not complain, the rich people not complain, they just sometimes share the money with us. We try to talk about this to the police too, but they don't care, they just say 'Here is the garden, not the

shelter for the poor people'. But if I try to talk back something or stay here, I will be hit. They can try to force us to leave, but I will keep coming back."[59]

"They will make the park new here and then they will ask us all to leave. We know they want us to leave because they want the park to be clean, and if we live here it is not clean for them, that's how I know. In Hun Sen Park they did the same thing, when they made that park nice the other year, they not allow the poor people to go there anymore. They will make here new, and make the titles on the ground to make it new for the tourist people, and people from the city to come and sit and talking. If police come and see our cloths hung up to dry, they will collect them and burn them up because it not look nice. This has happened to me before in this park. The police come and if they see clothes they just burn it. The police always come to make problems for us here."[60]

These comments demonstrate how such exercises in spatial control impact the subjectivities of homeless people by making them feel as though they are dirty and repulsive contradictions to the cleanliness desired for these spaces, which clearly excludes their presence in the park.

Even more troubling than the confiscation and burning of their personal articles by police, were their revelations concerning their internment into what effectively amounts to concentration camps for the poor:

"About five months ago they catch me and take me to Chom Chao center, they force us to go there. They take everyone here and lock us there for three months and then release us. To poop, pee, and drink, there is only one place inside. It is really dirty and smelly. I have only been out for two months now, and I don't want to go back. I don't know why they can keep us there, its not fair. I was there for only one day and I already want to run out. After three months we come back here, but if the police come and see us still here, they will take us to that place again. The guards have sticks, and if I try to run out they will hit me with the stick. If they take us there and we try to disagree to go they would hit. They treat us like criminals, that place is worse than jail. The jail has the food, something to eat, has the uniform, jail is better than there. . . . If the people get sick, they don't take us to see doctor, no one takes care of us there. I know the guards rape the woman there too, they try not to let us see this, but we all know it happens."[61]

"They need to make a new garden, and if you don't go, they will come and catch us and take us to Chom Chao center. They have taken me there one time already. While I stayed in that place, I was pregnant and my husband tried to find good food for me, but I could not eat something inside there because it is so dirty. . . . In that place [Chom Chao center] they lock us in, they lock all of us in there to live in the sewage water, and its dripping everywhere on me, like on my leg and makes me dirty and sick. The last time I was there was about five months ago. They don't say anything to us, they just come and collect us into the truck and make us go there. If we try to stay here and say we don't want to go, they force us. They grab my arm, or my clothes and force me into the truck. The last time I was sleeping, and my child too and they didn't come and try talking or anything, they just come and carry us and throw us in the truck like this. They do not talk or say anything, and if we do not go, we will be hit. And if we have something like blanket, or mattress, or something I own, they will collect it and not give it back. They won't ever give back. They take all that to burn it, not to give back. When they take me there, they grab me and check me, and if you have something like money they will take it and keep it, not give back they steal from us."[62]

"One time they take me to the Chom Chao center, they force me to go, but only one time for me. It's really dirty there and someone hit me when I was there. The guard that controls the people there, he attacked me. He hit me because I am against them and talk bad to them, so they hit me and take me outside, and let me free like this. They lock the people inside. They are afraid that someone will escape from there and come here [to the park] again, so they lock inside so they can't come here. I wonder why they come and take us there and lock us in. I think maybe its because we live in the park, and just don't want us here. . . . The police force us to go, they grab you like this and say 'Go to the truck'. If we try to run away they will kill us, they will hit until die. This case has happened a lot, where the people try to run so the police catch them and hit them until die. They kill many this way. They die a lot, so I never know when it will happen again. And if the lady try to escape from the Chom Chao center, the guard will rape her until she die like this. There were seven guards and they [gang] raped the lady and she die. They did not kill her, but they rape her a long time, and hitting her like this, and then she die[d later]."[63]

"Before the police come and collect the people and put them in a truck and make us all leave this place. But for four or five months already, they have not been here to make the people leave. They collect us and take us to the place for people like us, they call it Chom Chao center. They collect us and just drop us there. . . . its not a good place. They make us just eat there, piss there, and poop there, all in the same place. The Chom Chao center, they collect all the homeless people to put there and they kept me there for about 12 days. And the food and water, and shelter is very dirty so it make my children sick with disease. My children get diarrhoea all day, so they told us to leave after 12 days. They let us go out. It is really bad in the center, do many things like pee and poop, and even water, they don't have any clean water for us to drink. It is more difficult than jail. The police say they just collect some men who are the robbers and the people who are drunk or sniff glue to go to the jail, but really they collect all. I live in this area too and they collect everyone here and take us away.

That place is very difficult, that's why I always try to find a way out but they lock us inside and we cannot leave."[64]

Although Chom Chao center is euphemized by RGC officials as a rehabilitation center or shelter for poor people to help them get back on their feet, the participants shed a very different light on this picture. These testimonies reveal the extent of the depravity that Cambodian officials are willing to stoop to in seeing their beautification agenda pushed through. The desire to provide a sanitized image of a "developed" capital city to tourists and other visitors clearly takes precedence over any concerted effort to address poverty. Instead, spatial fixes such as exile and imprisonment of the homeless are used to reproduce Phnom Penh as an attractive space not only for tourism, but equally for capital investment by lending the appearance of an effective and orderly municipal government.

One human rights worker I interviewed was acutely aware of the CPP's covert strategy to transform this *representational space* from a potential *space for representation* to a *representation of space* through the project of beautification:

"If they [the CPP] want to allow the people to demonstrate they should let the place [Hun Sen Park] be free . . . but they don't . . . there should not be a garden in that place. . . . Before there was no garden, so the people can be free [to demonstrate]. Now there are plenty of gardens with grass and flowers, so it is difficult for people to gather."[65]

Indeed, like nearby Democracy Square, Hun Sen Park has become a heavily contested space, whereby the beautification of this park is symbolic of the RGC's desire to impose an "ordered" view of Phnom Penh's public space, leaving the contending vision of unmediated interaction as unwelcome in the spaces of the park. However, the RGC's (re)production of space in Hun Sen Park is not as absolute as the park's moniker would suggest, as many have resisted this "garden scheme" by holding demonstrations in the park in direct defiance of the government's visualization and attempted administration of this space. On the morning of 19 September 2004, I visited Hun Sen Park following an announcement in *The Cambodia Daily*, a few days earlier, that a demonstration against the high price of gasoline would be taking place near Independence Monument (Yun Samean 2004a). When I arrived at 8:00am, approximately 20 demonstrators sat and stood quietly in the park holding signs. A few military police officers were already on the scene when I arrived, although at this point they had not yet taken any action, other than issuing orders through a loudspeaker for the protesters to leave. A very small crowd had assembled to watch from across the street, but traffic remained undisturbed at this point. About two minutes after I arrived, one police officer began confiscating the signs from protesters. The protesters did not resist the officer who took their signs, but they did stand their ground and refused to leave the park. At approximately 8:10am, a truck with several more army personnel arrived followed closely by another truck carrying about 50 plainclothes police officers. The use of plainclothes officers became increasingly common in 2004, and is used as a tactic to avoid the unwanted publicity that has arisen in relation to heightened police violence (Yun Samean 2004c). The arrival of the extra soldiers and police was announced by flashing lights and sirens, which caused the crowd of onlookers to grow considerably larger, and traffic stopped at this point. This force of about 75 police proceeded to push, punch, and kick the protesters, while several of the soldiers who were armed with batons, freely wielded these weapons against the demonstrators, which included two visibly pregnant women.[66]

However, officials vehemently refute such accusations. Ouch Sokhon, deputy police chief of Chamkar Mon district, denied that police used force to halt the protest in Hun Sen Park, and claimed that those who were seen beating the protesters were not plainclothes police but ordinary citizens who did not want the demonstrations to occur. He further said police merely detained the protesters to "educate" them not to hold any demonstrations because "They provoked disorder in the city, they think only of their interests" (quoted in Yun Samean 2004d: 13). Although evidently false in this instance, the claim that demonstrations cause disorder is a consistent refrain from the RGC. The only apparent "disorder" was the disruption of traffic, which would not have occurred had the police not interfered with the demonstration. Moreover, the RGC's defence of breaking up demonstrations in an effort to secure "order" and "stability" in the city unmistakably falls in line with the neoliberal vision, echoing the denial of protester rights in other world cities such as Quebec, Seattle, Cancun, and Genoa.

Although some of the Cambodians I interviewed had internalized the idea that stopping demonstrations was necessary to avoid violence, most recognized that the violence related to public protest in Cambodia had a "top-down" trajectory:

> "For me, I, I think that political [violence] is . . . for example, the high officials, high ranking officials do something bad to the . . . poor people that do something, that commit the right thing, and they, the political violence is usually come from the high officials, high ranking officials towards the poor people[and] uneducated people."[67]
>
> "I think if they stop the demonstration . . . sometimes they have the violence, like a fight, fighting or sometimes shoot . . . I don't like about this, and like if they, this stuff is okay if we just talk don't have violence, I think its better that way. I hear all the time when have demonstrations usually have, usually have violence. Because usually the demonstrations are have violence but usually the police because the police have the guns or sticks so they have violence to the demonstrators. . . . The police make violence about it. Yeah, the demonstrations just say about something, just talk about something but they don't want to have the violence by the

police . . . they want to stop, they want them to stop so sometimes they have violence to the demonstrators."[68]

"Political violence, I think they . . . they have victim and perpetrator. So in case of incident that, ah, the perpetrator belong to the government official and the victim is ordinary people, or political supporter . . . something like this. I call political violence."[69]

"I think it is from the above, and it's from the, I think it's from the people who commit the bad thing, the . . . the dictator, from the dictator to . . . the democratic people. For me I think it happen through the police of the dictator and it sometimes leads to killing. And one more thing is, which is very popular in a lot of case, happens through secret thing that they committed secretly which they cannot show who is who. Yeah it conspire something that no . . . to kill, no one know that who kill, who is behind this killing."[70]

As protests in Democracy Square have increasingly come under siege by authorities, demonstrators have often shifted the location of their resistance, where increasingly Hun Sen Park has become the space of choice. The RGC has adopted a similar strategy, and in at least partial response to the growing associations of place at Democracy Square, the National Assembly was recently relocated away from this heavily contested space. Although lacking the same "a-where-ness" as Democracy Square in Cambodian's collective *geography of identity*, Hun Sen Park is still an ideal location for protest, as it too has a spatial orientation rich with symbolic allusions to power. Hun Sen Park is about one kilometer south of Democracy Square in central Phnom Penh, bordering Independence Monument to the west, and Hun Sen's house, Wat Botum-Vadei, and the Cambodian-Vietnamese friendship monument to the north. The significance of the spatial proximity to power was demonstrated by the recent self-immolation of a Buddhist monk in an area of the park located directly in front of Hun Sen's residence, which suggests the suicide was an act of resistance directed at Cambodia's leader (Berthiaume et al. 2004). The RGC's attempt to dismantle Phnom Penh's protest geography by the movement of the National Assembly has been pre-empted by the new *geography of resistance* emerging in Hun Sen Park, as the location for the new parliament buildings ironically border the park to the southeast.

The assault on Cambodia's public space is also reflected in the RGC's increasing internalization of neoliberal ideals such as privatization, which have previously come packaged as part of the country's SAPs/PRGFs. A recent example is the privatization of fishing lots in 2000, a move that represents a particular concern to Cambodians, as fish is both a staple food, and a primary source of income for many families. This reform sparked several days of protest by anglers who were denied access to these lots (Langran 2001). The RGC effectively privatized the National Highway system in 2001, and has since publicly defended a move by private company, AZ Investment Co. Ltd., who in December 2004 announced it would start charging tolls on

Cambodia's busiest highway Route 4 (Kay Kimsong 2004). The RGC has also defended the uprooting of households located along Cambodia's major routes so that roadways can be widened, a process which displaced residents frequently refer to as involving intimidation and lacking adequate compensation (Purtill 2004). This situation has prompted a number of public protests and clashes with police between both taxi drivers, who regularly use the highways to make a living, and the families who have had their land appropriated without proper compensation and respect for the land law (Wasson and Pin Sisovann 2005).

In January 2003, Hun Sen issued the order for all agricultural public enterprises to be privatized by 2006, including seven state-owned rubber plantations, a fish export company, and a fertilizer company. This move allowed the RGC to qualify for a US$35 million agricultural sector loan from the Asian Development Bank (ADB), where the foremost conditionality was divestment of these state enterprises (Green 2003; Weinberger 2003). Cambodian ministries have increasingly become involved in "land swapping" deals, whereby the prime locations of ministry office buildings in central Phnom Penh are traded for privately held land on the outskirts of the city (Lor Chandara and Phann Ana 2005). On 11 March 2005, the *Cambodia Daily* announced that the RCG was privatizing the country's postal and telephone services (Kay Kimsong and Wasson 2005), and on 13 April 2005, in what was to many Cambodians the ultimate sacrilege, it was finally revealed that the genocide memorial site *Choeung Ek* (the Killing Fields Monument) was leased to the Japanese government for 30 years (Kuch Naren 2005a). The deal was kept secret from the public, until general manager of the memorial site, Neang Say, blew the whistle on the deal commenting: "I want the world to know that Cambodia has become a place where they use the bones of the dead to make business" (quoted in Doyle 2005: np). The dead are not alone in their marketization, as the sick have also fallen prey to neoliberalization.

The neoliberal "roll-back" of civil service salaries, as discussed above, has fostered conditions of extensive rent-seeking, to which the health care system is not immune, and as a result, medical care has become increasingly privatized. In 1997 the Ministry of Health introduced a user fee system "since all tiers of the health care system are plagued by staff absenteeism, extortion of fees, substandard or dangerous care, and an incapacity to meet demand" (Gollogly 2002: 796). This has resulted in an extreme disparity of care, as in many hospitals large percentages of the user fees have been used as staff incentives, resulting in the inevitable tendency for public hospitals to secretly implement schemes that exempt the poor from receiving care.[71] One participant I interviewed in 2007 was particularly impacted by the disparities of the Cambodian health care system through the death of a family member:

> "Health is ok for the rich people, like they can afford to see the doctor, but it's a problem for the poor because every time, they have to like pay. So they have to find money, like sell their land, and if no money or land,

just depend on . . . like we gonna die. . . . The doctors will not want to cure the people, like the poor people without money. The treatment always goes only to the rich people. . . . I understand that medical clinic set up like the business, like they need to get money so that is fair, because its like a business organization or business firm, so its ok for when we have to visit the clinic to have to pay, but for the poor normally they cannot afford to pay them so we have to go to the public hospital, but they never give good service to the people who have no money. Because they know all the people who go to the public hospital poor, like the poor people, so they just don't want. They not treat them well, that's the problem. It's like discrimination between the doctor and the poor. So for the people who have serious sickness, sometimes they die because service not provide on time . . . some public hospital ask [for] money from the people, but some place they might respect the rules. But like my wife, she had the very serious sickness, and when we go to the hospital, when she go there the nurse and the staff ask for 5000 riel for the service, like when my wife is on the table, cuz she cannot walk so must have someone to carry her to the urgent room. So they ask me to pay to carry her on. And my wife, she die from ovary sickness, like ovary cancer. She die three months ago already because the hospital would not help her because we don't have enough money for the operation. Because it costs thousands of dollars not riel for the operation, so I could not afford and she die."[72]

The participant exemplifies acquiescence to an unjust two-tiered system that privileges the lives of those who are able to pay. Although there is an implicit acknowledgment of the unfairness to poor people like himself, and his wife ultimately died as a result of his inability to pay for her care, neoliberalism's market logic is internalized and the commodification of life and death is deemed acceptable on the grounds of health care operating on a business model. Under such market fundamentalism the poor have effectively been abandoned by the state, as they are left to bear the extraordinary burden of health care alone, a condition that has only exacerbated landlessness. As the poor resort to desperate measures to receive medical attention, such as the sale of the land to pay for health care, their marginalization is likewise only deepened.

Privatization is an inherently undemocratic endeavor, insofar as those spaces and enterprises that were formally public and controlled by and for the common good are removed from this domain. It places these spaces in the hands of the privileged elite minority who are then empowered by law, and often backed by armed forces, to determine how these spaces are materialized and administered, which in turn manipulates how citizens come to visualize these spaces. That is, people come to accept, sometimes through coercion, that they should now pay a private company to provide goods and services that formerly belonged to and were controlled by the public, for the benefit of the public. Thus, privatization comes with fences, both material and virtual, built around services and goods that were formerly available to the public as provisions of the state. Schools and hospitals, once considered as necessary for community cohesion and well-being, are for all intents and purposes locked to those individuals who cannot afford to pay the user fees, thereby condemning them to sickness and ignorance. Privatization also breeds corruption via "shadow state" politics, as the incumbent elite increasingly manipulate their capacity as gatekeepers in self-serving ways. The above examples clearly illustrate how privatization in Cambodia has come in the form of non-accountability to citizens, with little to no regard for the impacts on society as a whole, and in particular on the poor. In Cambodia, the idea that free-market mechanisms will allow poverty to alleviate itself has been proven incorrect, as the "trickle-down effect" has not borne fruit.

From deadlock to death threats: Economic liberalization and its menace to labor, land, and life

National elections were also once again held in 2003 and again in 2008. The UN, the European Union, and other international observers noted some progress in the country, reporting that these two election campaigns were relatively free from violence and corruption in comparison to previous ones (ADHOC 2004; Albritton 2004; European Union Election Observation Mission 2008). Nonetheless, a number of political killings marked the lead-up to the 2003 election, most notably the February murders of FUNCINPEC senior member and advisor to Prince Ranariddh, Om Radsady (Sullivan 2005; Vong Sokheng 2003b), and the Venerable Sam Bun Thoeun, a senior monk based in Oudong, who was opposed to the CPP's ban on monks' voting (Human Rights Watch 2003b). Human Rights Watch (2003a) reported that while overt political violence was not as evident, more sophisticated forms of intimidation and coerced party membership replaced it. Village and commune chiefs, most of whom are members of the ruling CPP, threatened opposition party supporters with violence, expulsion from their villages, and denial of access to community resources such as rice distributions (Human Rights Watch 2003a; 2003b). Similarly, the 2008 elections were tainted by the murder of opposition journalist Khim Sambo and his son Khat Sarinpheata on 11 July 2008, just two weeks prior to voting day (Human Rights Watch 2008).

The 2003 and 2008 national elections themselves once again ended in the need for a coalition government, as no single party managed to secure two-thirds of the vote. In the 2003 campaign the CPP was placed first in capturing 47.3 percent of the vote, the SRP rose to second place with 21.9 percent, while FUNCINPEC continued to slide, with only 20.7 percent of the vote (Albritton 2004). Voter turnout, while still high, dropped from previous elections to 81.5 percent reflecting "creeping voter apathy, and the active rejection of the major parties by an electorate – especially in the countryside – that has observed little or no improvement in the standards of living over the decade since the 1993 elections" (Sullivan 2005: 133–34). The results of the 2008 elections saw the CPP further consolidate its control over the national legislature in a victory that saw it capture 58.1 percent of the popular vote. The SRP was placed second with 21.9 percent, while FUNCINPEC, splintered by ongoing internal strife and leadership incompetence, had an abysmal fourth-place finish with 5.1 percent, behind the newly formed Human Rights Party, which captured 6.6 percent of the vote to finish third (National Election Committee 2008). The CPP's grip on power was even tighter than the election results would appear to demonstrate, as Cambodia's proportional representation system is based upon multi-member provincial constituencies, which gives a significant advantage to the largest parties. As a result the CPP was awarded a total of 90 out of 123 National Assembly seats, representing a considerable increase from 73 in the last parliamentary term (Hughes 2009a).

Perhaps somewhat predictably, the 2003 election outcome resulted in yet another stalemate when, immediately following the announcement of the results, both FUNCINPEC and SRP once again refused to join a government with Hun Sen at the helm (Albritton 2004). The two opposition parties formed the "Alliance of Democrats" with the express purpose of rejecting the election results, claiming irregularities and NEC bias (ADHOC 2004; Sullivan 2005). The deadlock lasted a total of 11 months before finally being resolved in July 2004 (Reynolds and Yun Samean 2004b; Vong Sokheng and Wood 2004). The SRP was once again left out of the official government, as in the end FUNCINPEC broke off the "Alliance of Democrats" and joined the CPP in forming a new coalition government. Ranariddh claimed that his deal with Hun Sen saved Cambodia from factional violence: "Hun Sen and I had to solve a problem and if we made the wrong decision, the Khmer nation would have become bloody with [violence] more serious than the factional fighting on July 5 [and] 6 1997" (quoted in Cochrane, Hunt, and Vong Sokheng 2004). Sam Rainsy dismissed Ranariddh's claim, and suggested the real reason for the coalition was Ranariddh's acceptance of a US$50 million bribe offered by the CPP and pro-CPP businesspersons (Cochrane, Hunt, and Vong Sokheng 2004). The claim prompted Ranariddh to file a lawsuit against Rainsy and lead a movement to have the SRP leader stripped of his parliamentary immunity so that he could be prosecuted for defamation (Cochrane, Rith, and Vong Sokheng 2004; Yun Samean 2004e). This bid met with success in February 2005 when in a closed-door session the National Assembly voted in favor of revoking Rainsy's immunity (Yun Samean and Pin Sisovann 2005). Following the decision Sam Rainsy fled the country, and he was tried in absentia on 22 December 2005. The court sentenced him to 18 months in prison and ordered him to pay around US$14,000 in fines and compensation (Vong Sokheng and McDermid 2005). On 5 February 2006, Rainsy received a Royal Pardon by King Norodom Sihamoni at Hun Sen's request after the prime minister received a formal apology from the exiled opposition leader for linking him to the 1997 grenade attack (Yun Samean and Kvasager 2006).

These legal proceedings set a precedent that continues to shape the

Cambodian political scene as lawsuits filed by high-ranking government officials, particularly with respect to defamation and disinformation, have become commonplace in recent years (Human Rights Watch 2009). As Table 4.5 illustrates, the government's campaign to stifle public criticism through legal means has reached a fever pitch. The most high-profile defamation suit since the Sam Rainsy proceedings is a case involving Hun Sen and SRP parliamentarian, Mu Sochua, who filed a defamation suite against the Prime Minister in early 2009, over comments he allegedly made during a nationally broadcast speech. Although this case was quickly dismissed, Hun Sen filed his own defamation suit against Mu Sochua, suggesting that by attempting to sue him for defamation, she had in fact defamed him. The absurdity of this countersuit is perhaps obvious to all but the Cambodian court, which found Mu Sochua guilty, to which the National Assembly swiftly responded by stripping her of her parliamentary immunity. Women's groups organized protests, which saw substantial numbers gather in the streets of Phnom Penh

Table 4.5 The legal chokehold on public opinion and information

Headline	Date
Hun Sen Accuses Global Witness of Defaming Gov't	21-27/02/2009
Court Seeks To Lift Immunity From SRP Chief	21-27/02/2009
PM, Mu Sochua Sue Each Other For Defamation	25-01/04-05/2009
Prime Minister Sues Mu Sochua's Attorney	25-01/04-05/2009
Gov't Files Disinformation Suit After Light Installation Criticism	30-05/05-06/2009
SRP Lawmaker To Answer Defamation Claims	30-05/05-06/2009
NGO Head Sues Newspaper Publisher for Defamation	30-05/05-06/2009
Rights Worker Summoned in Takeo Disinformation Case	06-12/06/2009
Mu Sochua's Suit Against PM Dismissed	06-12/06/2009
PM Defends Spate of Disinformation Suits	13-19/06/2009
Bar Association Votes to Summon Mu Sochua's Counsel	13-19/06/2009
UN Human Rights Body Slams Lawsuits Aimed at Gov't Critics	13-19/06/2009
Sok An Defends Angkor Libel Lawsuit	20-26/06/2009
Court Clerk Threatens To Sue Accusers	20-26/06/2009
Vote Strips Immunity of Mu Sochua, Ho Vann	20-26/06/2009
Court Jails and Fines Editor for Disinformation	27-03/06-07/2009
Hun Sen Drops Suit Against Mu Sochua's Lawyer After Apology	04-10/07/2009
Court Date Set for Hun Sen's Defamation Suit	04-10/07/2009
Criticism of Lights Gets Man 2 Years	11-17/07/2009
Ho Vann Will Not Return Home For His Defamation Hearing	11-17/07/2009
Two Pro-Gov't Newspapers Avoid Lawsuits by Apologizing	11-17/07/2009
Groups, Pols Criticize Disinformation Sentence	11-17/07/2009
Shooting the Messenger–Defamation Charge for Daily Reporter	11-17/07/2009
Mu Sochua Stands Trial For Defamation	25-31/07/2009
Mu Sochua Convicted, Fined $4,100	01-07/08/2009
Hun Sen Brags of Court Victory, Scoffs at Plaintiff	08-14/08/2009
Takeo Court Questions Reporter, Activists Over Disinformation	26-02/09-10/2009
Mu Sochua's Defamation Conviction Upheld by Appeal Court	24-20/10/2009

Source: The Cambodia Daily: Weekly Review.

to support the beleaguered politician, but Hun Sen remained defiant, boasting: "If you want to play legal games, I will also play legal games . . . You wouldn't be able to run, all of you would be arrested. . . . External groups, please listen closely . . . If you do not sue me, then I will not file a countersuit" (Meas Sokchea 2009b). The capstone to this silencing crusade came in October 2009, when the government rushed through 87 penal code articles pertaining to criminal incitement and insult to state authorities in a sweeping bid to further insulate government officials from public criticism. The articles define incitement in terms of speech, writings, and drawings in public spaces (Khy Sovuthy 2009).

It is precisely this sort of ongoing intimidation of opponents and brazen arrogance that led the SRP to contest the irregularities of the July 2008 election. The country held its collective breath fearing a repeat of the prolonged period of uncertainty following the 2003 elections, and the new Cambodian parliament convened quickly on 24 September 2008. The fact that the CPP once again won both the 2003 and 2008 elections is indicative of the one-party state that economic liberalism has helped to create by way of the continuing prevalence of patron–client relations, which, as discussed above, are reinforced by unfettered marketization. The potential to undo the bondage of patron–clientelism has not been helped by economic liberalism. Rather, the poor in Cambodia continue to face the same precarious situation that they were in prior to UNTAC, and in many cases they are worse off as neoliberalization has unleashed a plague of social and environmental ills upon Cambodia, including rampant deforestation, prostitution, and human trafficking, and an epidemic of land grabbing and landlessness. It is no small wonder that the recent Cambodia National Youth Risk Behavior Survey conducted by the Education Ministry reported that many of Cambodia's youth feel worried and hopeless about their lives, contemplate suicide, engage in risky sexual activity, suffer from domestic violence, and survive on two meals a day (Shaw 2005). These are symptoms of the poverty, unemployment, and low standards of living wrought by neoliberal reforms. However, in the neoliberal style of defending the market at all cost, while ignoring the collective voice of the people, Hun Sen maintains, "We have to realise that the government is in a development phase. People have to make sacrifices" (quoted in Berthiaume and Phann Ana 2005b). Of course, the problem is that while the elites may easily weather these sacrifices via a manipulation of their role as gatekeepers into the politics of the "shadow state," that is, by way of corruption, the burden of "sacrifice" that rests on the poor is far too much to bear.

Development in the "top-down" neoliberal context is not so much a case of people *needing* to make sacrifices, as it is people actually *being* sacrificed to the market. Thus, marketization has become the new *modus operandi* of tyranny as money becomes the focal point of empowerment, a commodity that is in very short supply for the poor. In the face of such dejection, such as that expressed by Cambodia's youth, where economic liberalization has been a lesson in disempowerment, democracy in Cambodia has been reduced to an electoral process. Indeed, in Melanie Beresford's (2005: 136) estimation this is all democracy has ever been in Cambodia, since the focus of the UNTAC was "on establishing the institutional shell of a democracy – periodic elections, administration reform, and dispute resolution via recourse to the law and judiciary – rather than supporting an indigenous democratic movement that has genuine control over the policy agenda." Thus, as Giles Mohan (2000: 91) argues, "Democratization is promoted as a way of weakening the excesses of the 'Leviathan' state because it transfers power to civil society." This is hardly a democratic outcome, since as Chapter 2 has shown, civil society weakens the state by empowering the market, which subsequently disempowers those segments of society that are already marginalized and empowers the elite class who come to control the state themselves. At the same time, the realm of civil society is regulated by the state, a condition that affords little opportunity for critical public spaces to emerge. In short, civil society is simply another form of "top-down" politics, with little prospect for empowering people to a position where "pressure from below" can be applied via non-violent means. Thus, the *taking* of public space, which often involves *violence from below*, becomes the only viable method of empowerment.

In spite of the crackdown, the production of Phnom Penh's public space is continually challenged "from below." The active and organized attempt to *take* a space in which individuals can represent themselves and assert rights is particularly evident in Cambodia's labor movement. Worker strikes have become a common feature of Phnom Penh's protest landscape. However, organized labor represents a strong challenge to neoliberalization, and a disincentive to footloose corporations who actively seek non-unionized locations in which to do business. Thus, the RGC's authoritarian response of *violence from above* in dealing with labor strikes must be read as a course of action that attempts to secure the neoliberal agenda of keeping business opportunities as open as possible, and not as a manifestation of Khmer culture. The willingness to challenge employers, and the state's market fundamentalist-inspired authoritarian response, is immediately evident in newspaper headlines gleaned from *The Cambodia Daily*, which are presented in Table 4.6. However, as some of the headlines indicate, such challenges are not without extreme risk to participants, and the response of *violence from above* acts as a strong deterrent to future mobilization:

> "For me I feel shocked and scared when I saw the army to go to disperse the workers when they are on strike . . . sometimes they fight the worker, and that I see some . . . on the strike near my factory. For my factory, we haven't had this kind of fighting or shooting but there is a factory nearby my factory that used the, policemen to fight and shoot . . . policemen and the worker fight each other and shoot one worker died. So I feel scared."[73]

> "For myself I don't have suffer from any political violence, also my family [never suffers], but for my friend, I used to have friend that suffer

Table 4.6 Unionization and the contestation over labor exploitation

Headline	Date
Decision Final On Rubber Despite Protest	01-07/11/2008
21,000 Cambodian Kids Toil in Domestic Labor	08-14/11/2008
Solidarity Groups' End Likely Near	08-14/11/2008
R'kiri Officials Confirm Order to Vacate Rubber Plantations	01-05/12/2008
Deaths Prove More Construction Workers at Risk	08-12/12/2008
Low Pay Threatens Education Quality: Teachers	15-19/12/2008
Union Asks Ministry to Pay Prey Veng Teachers	15-19/12/2008
Dispute Brews Between Rubber Workers and New Land Owner	22-28/12/2008
Rubber Plantation Solidarity Group Plan Last Ditch Protest	05-09/01/2009
Kandal Garment Workers' Protest Over Bonuses Turns Ugly	17-23/01/2009
More than 400 Factory Workers Protest Over Layoffs	24-30/01/2009
Ratanakkiri Provincial Authority Puts End to Solidarity Groups	14-20/02/2009
Labor Leaders Angry About Proposed Law Amendments	21-27/02/2009
Trade Unions Reiterate Labor Law Concerns	28-06/02-03/2009
Proposed Labor Law Changes Cause Outcry From Unions	14-20/03/2009
Palin RCAF Soldiers Complain About Unusual Salary Reduction	28-03/03-04/2009
Several Thousand Gather for Labor Day Protest	02-08/05/2009
Garment Workers, Police Clash in Kompong Speu	16-21/05/2009
Investigations Into Labor Murders Have Been Inadequate, UN Says	20-26/06/2009
Chances Slim for Garment Worker Wage Increase	04-10/07/2009
B Meanchey Veterans Protest Missing Pensions	08-14/08/2009
Union Leader Chea Mony Faces New Lawsuit	15-21/08/2009
Hundreds Jobless After Factory Owners Abandon Business	15-21/08/2009
Mass Fainting at Garment Factory Blamed on Ramadan	29-04/09/2009
Second Mass-Fainting at Factory Blamed on Ventilation	05-11/09/2009
Teachers to Rally for 150 Percent Wage Increase Next Month	12-18/09/2009
Despite Gov't Promise, Some 600 Court Clerks Without Pay Raise	03-09/10/2009
Garment Workers Stitched Up Over Expected Layoffs	03-09/10/2009
Workers Protest in Front of Labor Ministry	09-16/10/2009
Torture Case Shine Light on World of Child Servants	17-23/10/2009
Questions Persist in Case of Abused Child Servant	17-23/10/2009
Laid-Off Garment Workers March in Front of Hun Sen's House	17-23/10/2009

Source: The Cambodia Daily: Weekly Review.

from political violence in 1998, they used to be, I, I saw police fight my friend and also use water to spray my, my friend in 1998 at Democracy Square. I saw by, from my eyes. . . . When after I see I feel scare, I afraid that it happen to me, to my family, so that I dare not to do like them, like my friend. It doesn't effect me much because I only see them from my eyes about the political violence but I feel, next time, if it [a big demonstration like the Democracy Square movement in 1998] happen, I still can go to see, just see, because I, I can not join them."[74]

Several participants also revealed that *violence from above* fosters a constriction of public space in Cambodia insofar as the fear instilled from experiences of violence results in either the reticence of personal expression, or imposes boundaries on how they negotiate space in their everyday lives:

"Some day when the . . . around [the] election [time], I went to visit my cousin at his home village. I saw about the, maybe the another party, another party made the people, the normal people, they fight each other about the party, which party . . . ah, which people love another party and another people love another party, so [they] fight each other and cut each other. . . . Yeah I saw them fighting. I saw them fight until die, kill, someone die. When I saw about this, I have feel . . . afraid about this. So I don't want to talk about my ideas."[75]

"I see it [violence] by myself when I travel on the road for some time. Around the factories area. Garment factories area. I see kill . . . something, someone . . . I saw the dead body. I feel scared so I can't, I don't want to stay at that place and don't want to go to come to the other factory, just stay in Phnom Penh. I don't go there anymore. . . ."[76]

"I not remember all what, what case that happen and just remember some like he was killed by someone, shot, not sure who is, who is the killer and I just heard about people talking about [who] he is, he is the political activist of Sam Rainsy and he, he was pass away by people kill him. And I heard from the other sources the information talk that this not related to political violence . . . just related to . . . personal problems. This make me still afraid . . . still afraid to talk, to talk about political party about the party what I, what I like. [Scared because if I talk, someone] Will try to kill me."[77]

However, for other participants the desire for democracy was so strong, that they placed it before their own physical safety:

"I think it is a big issues in Cambodia, a serious [issue]. I think nowadays the . . . political violence it seems to be . . . habit, usual thing, that make the Cambodia people to lose their instinct, . . . no one have a confidence and to who and who [in each other], and if they lead to this kind of situation, I think it may lead to destroy the whole Cambodia. And I think it's the political violence in Phnom Penh is more serious than the countryside. The countryside also have, but mostly the people dare not to speak so that they, they . . . the political violence is less than in Phnom Penh. I never effect and suffer from any political violence but I used to be told by some people that I shouldn't, should not be . . . show off . . . especially they saw me walking by the, the demonstration and walking with the with . . . some top leader so they just want to remind me, they told me not to show off more. And my family also never affected [by] any political violence, my friends as well but I used to know someone, some student that, used to belong, used to be victim by, by political motivated violence but now he's disappear. For me, I'm not afraid anything, I do not scare, in my view, point of view. I think that if I want to do something if I think that it is correct, I will do it, I know nothing can change my mind, even during the demonstration . . . the policeman . . . shot, shot one people and died in front of me, I also not scared."[78]

"Well, people because of that . . . politic violence so make the people they feel scared, especially the old people in the province it change . . . change people like, 'oh why should I get this problem'. But you want to do this, and then they kill now. [But for me], because my freedom, I'm not scared. You can kill, kill me, kill me just in the body or mind, like talking about my thinking, [but] like here [puts hand over heart] you cannot kill."[79]

The implication of this finding is that although *violence from above* is an impediment to the furtherance of the notion of *democracy as public space*, public space, as the *process* we know it to be, will continue to be contested by those social actors who are selflessly motivated by a fierce desire for social justice.

The most insidious act of *violence from above* in response to the labor movement to date was perpetrated against one such social actor with the January 2004 murder of SRP activist and respected union leader Chea Vichea (Post Staff 2004; Yun Samean and Wency Leung 2005b). As co-founder of Free Trade Union of Workers of the Kingdom of Cambodia (FTU), Chea Vichea had long been a target of threats and violence. He was among the injured in the 1997 grenade attack on the KNP (later the SRP) in Democracy Square, a security guard beat him during a protest outside a factory in 2002, and in 2003 he received a death threat in the form of a text message on his mobile phone, which police refused to investigate after determining the message came from a high-ranking government official (Post Staff 2004; Yun Samean and Wency Leung 2005b). Since his murder in 2004, Chea Vichea's wife and children have received a number of menacing phone calls, and have since fled Cambodia with the help of the UN High Commissioner for Refugees, receiving asylum in Finland (Yun Samean 2005b). Although two individuals were arrested for the crime, many Cambodians, including Chea Vichea's family, believe the accused are merely scapegoats who are being used to fend off criticism of Cambodia's tendency for impunity because the murder was so high-profile and received a significant amount of attention from the international media.[80] The suspects themselves maintain their innocence, claiming that authorities beat them mercilessly until they confessed to the murder (Cochrane and Cheang Sokha 2004). Although the killing of Chea Vichea along with the murder of another FTU leader, Ros Sovannareth, in May 2004 has created a state of fear among workers (Yun Samean and Wency Leung 2005a), the response to Chea Vichea's murder was overwhelming, as 15,000 people, mostly garment factory workers, marched through Phnom Penh on the day of the funeral (Beresford 2005; Post Staff 2004).

This massive show of solidarity could not have come at a worse time for

Cambodian elites, who were on the eve of witnessing the country's ascension to the World Trade Organization (WTO) in October 2004, which they viewed as the key to preserving Cambodia's position in the global garment trade (Beresford 2005: 134). Intensifying neoliberalization, illustrated by the strong desire to join the WTO among Cambodian elites, requires that workers do not assert their rights so that capital investment may be attracted, and the RGC's campaign of fear and suppression of public protests has clearly been ineffective given the determined frequency of continuing worker strikes. Thus, in spite of WTO ascendancy, the response from garment factory owners has been a number of closures and significant layoffs, as 25,000 workers lost their jobs between September 2004 and January 2005 (Yun Samean and Wency Leung 2005a). Exploited workers who reaffirm their rights and practice democracy should not be blamed for the garment industry closures and layoffs. Instead, the very mobility of capital that comes concomitant to a globalized economy is at fault. Moreover, the reaction to unionization by way of closures and layoffs has created what can only be seen as an impending social disaster. The garment industry spurred rapid urbanization in the 1990s, as many young women, the primary demographic hired by the industry, made their way to Phnom Penh to find work in factories. Not only have these young women become accustomed to urban life and thus will be reluctant to return to the village, but for most, their families back home rely on monthly payments to supplement their livelihoods. The closures and layoffs mean that these young women must find other means to secure an income. Some will undoubtedly be absorbed into "formal" economy activities such as selling fruit and working in the service industry. However, for thousands of others, the neoliberal maxim of "leaving things to the market" means that they will effectively be forced into the "informal" economy, which in the Cambodian context often means the violent life of the sex trade (International Textile, Garment, and Leather Workers' Federation 2005).

Another clear example of the violence that neoliberalization provokes is the preponderance of land grabbing in Cambodia, which can be seen in *The Cambodia Daily* newspaper headlines collected in Table 4.7. In their annual publication, *Human Rights Situation Report*, ADHOC (2004: 31), a French acronym for the Cambodian Human Rights and Development Association, reported that "Land rights violations committed against the poor were a serious concern," after having investigated 148 cases of land disputes involving almost five thousand families in 2003. Cases of land grabbing are by definition a violent endeavor, as was clearly illustrated by the November 2004 grenade attack on a group of villagers protesting a 300,000 hectare land concession granted to the Pheapimex corporation in 2001. Pheapimex began logging the site in 2004 to make way for a eucalyptus plantation on forested land that villagers claim they have been using communally for generations and is essential to the livelihood of their community (Yun Samean and Reynolds 2004; Vong Sokheng and Cochrane 2004). Although no one was killed in the attack, three protesters suffered serious shrapnel wounds, while

Table 4.7 The struggle for land

Headline	Date
30-Centimeter Land Dispute Leads to 3 Deaths	01-07/11/2008
Keat Kolney's Firm Takes Offensive on R'kiri Land	01-07/11/2008
Court Criticized for Pressuring Detainees Over Land Dispute	01-07/11/2008
RCAF General Detained in Alleged Land Grab	01-07/11/2008
Villagers Take Official Hostage in Land Dispute	15-21/11/2008
Kampot Villagers Given Ultimatum: Leave or Face Legal Action	24-30/11/2008
Kratie Villagers Guard Leaders, Fearing Arrests	01-05/12/2008
Canadia Bank President Rejects Land-Grabbing Accusations	15-19/12/2008
Rich Using Courts Against Villagers in Land Disputes: Adhoc	15-19/12/2008
After Violent Land Clashes, Situation Still Tense in Mondolkiri	22-28/12/2008
Privatizing Boeng Kak Lake Was Illegal: Report	22-28/12/2008
Kandal Families Say Company Bulldozing Farms	29-02/12-01/2008-09
Villagers, Reporter Jailed over Siem Reap Dispute	29-02/12-01/2008-09
Police, Officials Burn More Than 100 Homes in Land Dispute	17-23/01/2009
B Meanchey Families Protest Alleged Railroad Encroachment	31-06/01-02/2009
More Than 1,000 File Complaint in Land Dispute	31-06/01-02/2009
Siem Reap Land Dispute Leads to Detentions	07-13/02/2009
Soldiers in B Meanchey Accused of Land-Grabbing	07-13/02/2009
Villagers Pressed To Drop Keat Kolney Land Suit	21-27/02/2009
Violence Avoided – For Now – in Kratie Province Land Dispute	28-06/02-03/2009
Rights Group Finds Unlawful Action by Police in Land Dispute	21-27/03/2009
Villagers in Land Dispute Report Attack by Guard	28-03/03-04/2009
Villagers Claim Senior Official Grabbed Land	18-24/04/2009
B'bang Land Dispute Fueling Poverty, Officials Say	09-15/05/2009
Villagers Allegedly Abduct Siem Reap Commune Official	09-15/05/2009
Teachers Union Files Complaint Over Land Grab	16-21/05/2009
Licadho Report Denounces an "Epidemic of Land-Grabbing"	06-12/06/2009
Oddar Meanchey Villagers in Land Dispute With RCAF Unit	20-26/06/2009
7 Summoned For Questioning in Land Dispute	27-03/06-07/2009
Government Unfazed by Criticism Over Land Rights Policies	18-24/07/2009
B Meanchey Court Charges 31 For Illegal Land Sale, Protests	25-31/07/2009
Gov't Orders Koh Kong Villagers To Register Land	01-07/08/2009
300 Reps Expected to Attend Land Dispute Protest	08-14/08/2009
Boeng Kak Residents Keep Up Peaceful Protest	15-21/08/2009
Kompong Speu Villagers Protest Sale of Local Land	22-28/08/2009
Villager Representatives Given $450 to End Role in Dispute	05-11/09/2009
Land Dispute Victims Bring Attention to Plight	12-18/09/2009
Villagers Representative in Land Dispute Summoned for Incitement	12-18/09/2009
3 Jailed, 1 Summoned to Court in Ongoing K Chhang Land Dispute	19-25/09/2009
Farmers Ask Gov't to Intervene in Land Dispute with CPP Senator	26-02/09-10/2009
Local Official Downplays Food Shortage in B'bang Land Dispute	26-02/09-10/2009
Villagers Block Trucks in Development Protest	03-09/10/2009
Angkor Sugar Land Dispute Leaves Sour Taste For Villagers	03-09/10/2009
Draft Law Empowering Gov't To Confiscate Property Approved	09-16/10/2009
Land Dispute Villagers Get Ministry Runaround	17-23/10/2009
Siem Reap Provincial Court Hears Deadly Land Dispute Case	17-23/10/2009
7 Released 2 Jailed in Chi Kreng Dispute	24-30/10/2009
Villagers in Koh Kong Land Dispute Appeal to King, Hun Sen	24-30/20/2009

Source: The Cambodia Daily: Weekly Review.

five others sustained minor injuries. Villagers were very clear in identifying Pheapimex as being behind the attack in an effort to intimidate protesters into leaving the site. However, police refused to entertain the idea of intimidation as a motive for the attack, and instead accused the protesters themselves of throwing the grenade in an effort to frame Pheapimex and tarnish its image (Yun Samean and Reynolds 2004). Villagers who attempted to travel to Pursat city in order to protest in front of the provincial government buildings were prevented from doing so as police constructed a roadblock to intervene. The RGC's initial response was to ask that Pheapimex cease operations; however, this request had little sincerity or staying power as the company resumed its activities unimpeded mere days after the RGC's order to stop and logging activity continues unabated at the time of this writing (see Kuch Naren and Solana Pyne 2004b).

In cases such as this, villagers have little hope, as their claim to the land is based on usage alone, not on their permanent occupancy. However, even in urban areas where occupancy of land is clear, the poor have little hope as the law favors those with land deeds that supposedly prove ownership over those who physically occupy a space. Rather than regard the urban poor as victims of the strains resultant from the exacerbation of urbanization under neoliberal reforms, the law considers squatter settlements illegal, and thus criminalizes the poor (Rumdoul 1997). Hence, the law is often used a vehicle for elite privilege and power, a situation made even worse by the pervasive corruption of the Cambodian judiciary and the current trend of buying justice in Cambodia. Furthermore, although Article 44 of the Cambodian constitution asserts, "The right to confiscate possessions from any person shall be exercised only in the public interest as provided under law and shall require fair and just compensation in advance" (Jennar 1995: 15), fair and just compensation is rarely forthcoming. Evicted families often complain that they will receive nothing at all if they do not agree to a minimal payment for their land or exchange it for a parcel of land with negligible value, lacking appropriate amenities and infrastructure on the outskirts of the city.[81] Those who try to resist are met with *violence from above*, which increasingly comes in the form of bulldozing homes whether there are occupants inside or not (see Neubauer and Pin Sisovann 2005; Saing Soenthrith 2004).

The case of Group 78 is particularly demonstrative of the insolence Cambodian officials display with respect to the existing land law. Until recently Group 78 was a community of about 146 families that had made their homes near the Phnom Penh riverfront since 1983. Unlike most evicted peoples in Cambodia, approximately 53 of Group 78's families possessed formal documentation demonstrating their entitlement to the land. While many Group 78 residents did not possess such legal proof, they nonetheless had a legal right to the land because their status had gone uncontested for more than five years, which under Cambodia's existing land laws bestowed ownership upon them.[82] In 2006, following the successful eviction of the neighboring Sambok Chab community, Group 78 residents were given eviction notices that indicated Phnom Penh City Hall needed the land for their beautification project to develop the image of the city. According to Community Spokesperson, Lim Sambo, residents were offered US$600 per family to vacate at that time, even though it was well known that the land was worth considerably more than this.[83] The community responded by enlisting the services of a group of student architects to design a plan for the site that would allow for such beautification in the form of new apartment buildings for the residents. If "development" in the sense of improving people's lives was really the motivation here, then the municipality should have been pleased with such initiative because, as Huy Rumdoul (1997: 62) argues, "Inhabiting adequate housing can in no way be considered a privilege, but is tantamount to being human and living a full and dignified life." However, this was not the sense of "development" City Hall had in mind, and they quickly changed their story suggesting the land belonged to a private company that wanted to proceed with commercial developments on the site.

Since the eviction notice was first served, many Group 78 residents agreed to marginal offers of compensation and left the site. But some families, particularly those with documentation, simply refused to be bullied. An independent property valuation conducted by Bonna Realty Group confirmed that the 260-meter-by-45-meter plot of land was worth more than US$15 million, or about US$1,300 per square metre (Post Staff 2009). Knowing the value of the land, the municipality changed their story several more times over the course of a three-year-long coercion campaign, suggesting that they planned to widen the road in order to construct a new bridge, that the residents' homes were impeding an important water project development, and that the land simply belonged to the state.[84] Despite their best efforts, which included numerous public appeals for help and an obstinate refusal to vacate their land, on 17 July 2009, the remaining handful of determined families were each promised US$20,000, an amount that was quickly reduced to US$8,000 after army personal began disassembling their homes while negotiations continued (Thittara and Shay 2009). As the basic right to housing is stolen from the poor in the name of "development" and "beautification," although ultimately unsuccessful in their bid, the residents of Group 78 nonetheless demonstrate how a growing number of Cambodians are willing to stand in the face of oppression and battle for their rights. Continued solidarity, the *taking* of public space via protest, and outright refusal of capitalist development agendas together represent the way forward for the poor in their effort to democratize Cambodia and secure their right to conduct meaningful lives.

This view stands in sharp contrast to Caroline Hughes's (2003b: 5) argument that, economic development constitutes the link between the emergence of the ability to provide pressure for democratization "from below" and the mobilization of economic resources by non-state actors, where "These resources may be used to force the state to concede terrain – public forums, free media – in which public political debate can take place." She further contends that the experience of Cambodia has shown that there are no "shortcuts to democracy in an environment of severe material dearth" (Hughes 2003b: 220). In other words, Hughes's argument here is that economic development, by way of economic liberalism, must precede democracy. This contradicts the view of democracy as both the primary end and as the principal means of development, a conclusion shared by Joakim Ojendal (1996) in his analysis of Cambodia. In this view, development consists of the removal of various types of "unfreedoms" that leave people with little choice and insignificant opportunities to exercise their reasoned agency, which contrasts with narrower views of development, such as identifying development with the rise in personal incomes. In this light, Hughes's denigration of "shortcuts to democracy" reveals an incongruity in her argument, since she is well aware of the importance of participatory politics, so much so that she in fact argues that the very future of Cambodian democracy rests in the hands of urban protest movements.

Furthermore, Hughes (2003b) maintains that in rural Cambodia the "political terrain remains monopolized by partisan state authorities." Moving beyond this terrain and into a plural sphere of political action requires the confidence to reject co-option into state structures of patronage, which Hughes (2003b) argues can only be achieved via access to resources independent of such co-option, that is, through free-market economics. According to Hughes, such conditions are increasingly being met in the city, while in the countryside the majority of voters remain trapped in patron–client relations and subject to the monopolization of public activities by the partisan state. She states: "The move to the free market, so successful in shoring up state power in rural areas, had a contradictory effect on state control over urban loyalties and urban political action" (Hughes 2003b: 175). In other words, Hughes contends that economic liberalism has opened space in the city for political contestation precisely because it has allowed citizens access to resources outside of the state. Whereas in the periphery, the liberalization of the economy has not been as far-reaching, and a public space in Cambodia's rural areas will not be opened so long as the "material dearth" of the countryside remains unaddressed. Hughes (2003b) implies that the power of the free market has not permeated deeply enough into rural Cambodia, and only its further unfolding will free rural Cambodians from the bondage of oppressive patron–client relations. Rather than challenging the wisdom of the economic system, she calls for not only more of the same, but also its intensification. Given her recognition of the problems privatization has caused for the poor and marginalized in Cambodia, this is an odd conclusion to make. Perhaps critical reflection on this point goes some way to explaining why Hughes's arguments have done a complete turnaround, since her most recent book, as was mentioned in the introductory chapter, is now very critical of neoliberalism (see Hughes 2009b).

Table 4.8 illustrates how Cambodian landscapes of protest now include a diverse range of social actors comprising both urban and rural constituents,

Table 4.8 Landscapes of protest

Headline	Date
200 Protest as ADB Completes Rice Donations	01-07/11/2008
Phsar Thmei Vendors Protest Outside PM's Home	01-07/11/2008
Siem Reap Demonstration Seeks Release of Four in Land Dispute	01-07/11/2008
Phnom Penh Villagers Protest Against Electricity Middleman	15-21/11/2008
In Koh Kong, 400 Protest Human Trafficking	24-30/11/2008
Students Protest Altered Admission Regulations	24-30/11/2008
Market Vendors Rally Against Rising Electricity Costs, Fees	24-30/11/2008
Vendors Continue Protest Over Sidewalk Sales Ban	01-05/12/2008
Kratie Protesters Say Developer Destroyed Graveyards, Farms	01-05/12/2008
Rights Group to March in Parade Today	08-12/12/2008
Fearing Representatives' Arrest, Kratie Villagers Rally at Court	08-12/12/2008
Minority Villagers Stage Protest About Destroyed Kratie Graves	29-02/12-01/ 2008-09
Siem Reap Protest Calls for Release of Detainees	17-23/01/2009
Dey Krahorm Families Protest, Demand $20,000	31-06/01-02/2009
Olympic Market Vendors Rally Outside PM's Home Over Rent	07-13/02/2009
B'bang Villagers Protest Land-Dispute Sentences	21-27/02/2009
City Residents Protest Fencing-In of Rek Reay	07-13/03/2009
Communities Rally Against Forced Evictions	07-13/03/2009
Banteay Meanchey Villagers Protest RCAF Claims on Land	14-20/03/2009
Minority Villagers Protest Outside International Donor Meeting	25-01/04-05/2009
Students Join Rek Reay Families For Protest at Canadia Bank HQ	25-01/04-05/2009
Villagers Protest for Abbot's Removal, Officials Say	02-08/05/2009
P Vihear Villagers Protest Relocation Plans	02-08/05/2009
Protesters Greet Opening of Asean-EU Summit Meeting	23-29/05/2009
Prey Veng Villagers Protest After Company Backs Out on Promise	23-29/05/2009
Villagers Demonstrate Against Filling in of Field for Airport	06-12/06/2009
200 R'kiri Villagers Protest Over Disputed Land	20-26/06/2009
Vendors at Borei Keila Protest Planned Market, Bar Officials	27-03/06-07/2009
Prey Veng Villagers End 2-Day Electricity Protest	11-17/07/2009
CCU Marks Anniversary of P Vihear Standoff With Protest	11-17/07/2009
Takeo Vendors Protest Cost of Stalls in Renovated Market	25-31/07/2009
Poipet Villagers Protest After Ruling in Land Dispute Case	01-07/08/2009
Complaints Filed for 11,923 Families in Protest	08-14/08/2009
Leaflets Scattered in Capital Take Aim at Hun Sen	15-21/08/2009
500 Gather at Preah Sihanouk Office to Protest Moto Fines	15-21/08/2009
Residents Protest Looming Eviction of Boeng Kak Community	15-21/08/2009
Stung Treng Students Who Failed Exam Protest Results	22-28/08/2009
Siem Reap Tuk–Tuk, Moto-Taxi Drivers Protest Registration Costs	22-28/08/2009
Failed Medical Students Protest Against Exam Results	12-18/09/2009
About 240 Cycle for Peace Through Capital	19-25/09/2009
Villagers Protest at Justice After Letters Go Unanswered	26-02/09-10/2009
Demonstrators Gather to Protest The Filling of Boeng Kak Lake	03-09/10/2009
O Meanchey Villagers to Protest over Eviction	09-16/10/2009
100 Rally at Wat Phnom for Climate Change Awareness	17-23/10/2009
Hun Sen's House Sees Another Protest From Homeowners	17-23/10/2009
100 in Kampot Protest Vietnamese Fishing in Cambodian Waters	17-23/10/2009
Group Gathers at Premier's Home to Protest Roundabout Eviction	17-13/10/2009
70 Villagers Protest Kampot Project at Hun Sen's Takhmau Home	24-30/10/2009

Source: The Cambodia Daily: Weekly Review.

contesting a vast array of perceived injustices. Thus, the idea of protest has spatially diffused into Cambodia's periphery, where public demonstrations are quickly becoming an embedded feature of the country's rural *geography of resistance*. Indeed, the day after finishing my last interview for fieldwork undertaken in 2004, and after repeatedly hearing from participants in Pursat that protests had never occurred in their province, a protest erupted along the riverfront in Pursat city. I spoke at length with a local English-speaking bystander, who expressed amazement at the actions of the demonstrators:

> Does Pursat have many demonstrations?
> "No this is the first time. Normally we do not have demonstrations in Pursat. We cannot dare to say, we can only keep in our minds. If you dare to say, you will be put in prison or killed. Can only see and know, but cannot say."
> Was this the very first demonstration in Pursat then?
> "Yes, normally you cannot talk out loud like this, because you do not know who is listening. Sometimes there are spies, so we have to be very careful."[85]

Four days after this, on 15 November 2004, Pursat province saw its second demonstration in the town of Krakor. This was the aforementioned Pheapimex protest. In the years since 2004, both rural and urban protests have reached a fever pitch, much to the chagrin of the RGC which continues to use a variety of legal implements and spatial subterfuge to dissuade, intimidate, and deny protest movements. What we can learn from the Cambodian example is that sustained contestation is essential to winning the "right to the city," which in turn will procure the right to the nation and deepen democracy. The emergent protest geography that has swept over Cambodia in the last few years indicates that both urban and rural Cambodians have clearly taken this cue.

Conclusion

Although the fact that Cambodians are now more than ever willing to mount challenges and demand the accountability of the government is clearly a positive development on the country's road to deeper democracy, the *disquieting nexus* between violence and democracy is sure to become increasingly manifest. In other words, before things get better in Cambodia, they are bound to get worse in terms of the proliferation of violence. The denial of public space that has previously been largely successful for the RGC in terms of keeping the Cambodian population submissive is now clearly beginning to wear thin. It is the poor who are asked to weather the storm of hardship that invariably accompanies neoliberalization, and the frustrations of the poor are slowly beginning to boil over. As the pressure on the poor continues to mount, latent dissatisfactions are transformed into manifest assertions whenever

Cambodians demand greater democracy by making their protests seen and heard in the spaces of the public. The most common response from the RGC to public displays of solidarity and demands for representation has been the use of *violence from above*, which is effected in the name of "order" and "stability."

With all this dogmatic promotion of and focus on "order," "stability," and "security" we might rightly ask what exactly it is that the neoliberal doctrine is seeking "order," "stability," and "security" from? The experiences of Cambodia suggest a clear answer. It appears that first and foremost the discourse of "order" is little more than propaganda, chosen for its honorific connotations in an effort to mystify the population into believing that those who impose "order" have the best interests of the public in mind. For its part, "stability" is used to indicate a solid foundation from which Cambodian development is meant to proceed, and indeed this is the case as it is not the "stability" of individual Cambodian lives that is at stake. Rather, "stability" in Cambodia's developmental terms means market stability, which is made possible through trenchant neoliberal reforms. The reality of the application of these discourses is that they act as little more than a fortification against the development of deeper democracy. This assertion is supported by the continual suppression of democratic expressions such as public protests in the name of "order" and "stability," and also by the observation that "security" is used to protect those with power from the marginalized segments of society by denying them any participatory capacity through the spatial control of their daily activities, which subsequently denies the poor a voice. The marginalized are further robbed of their collective and individual voices by laws that protect property over people, as these laws serve to criminalize those on the bottom of the capitalist hierarchy. Thus, those victims of the very system that oppresses them into poverty who might risk stealing a loaf of bread so as to not go hungry, defecate in a park because the "public" washrooms of private businesses are for paying customers only, or squat on the margins of the city because they have nothing left but fear, emptiness, and despair in their home villages, are misconstrued as menacing threats to society. "Order," "stability," and "security" as conceived under neoliberalism mean a preservation of the status quo, a safeguarding of elite privilege, and the conservation of the global hierarchy of wealth. This stands diametrically opposed to democracy, which is at once a dream of egalitarianism and a forever protean process that is meant to be messy so that all members of a society can be equally seen and heard.

Chapter 4 has shown that the denial of democracy in Cambodia is fundamentally a spatial endeavor. This is unsurprising once we recognize, as many Cambodians are beginning to discover for themselves, that public space is paramount to the constitution, affirmation, and execution of power. This relationship becomes considerably more lucid if we read "power" for "resistance" in Steve Pile's (1997: 3, emphasis added) maxim: "resistance is understood where it takes *place*, and not through *abstract theories* which outline the insidious mechanisms, strategies, and technologies of domination." Power then should be understood in spatial terms where its circulation in society is facilitated, to a significant extent, through public engagements. The circulation of power is always contested, and unfortunately there are occasions, like in contemporary Cambodia, where and when access to public space becomes so repressed, subverted, and constricted as to render it virtually nonexistent as a democratic ideal. It is in such conditions that violence lamentably takes on an inevitable character. Neoliberalization in Cambodia exacerbates this situation through its *tout court* acceptance of "order," "stability," and "security" discourses, which in turn legitimizes *violence from above* in the form of authoritarian responses. The purpose is the smooth flow of capital, but at the same time citizens' rights are delegitimized and eroded. In a context where for almost two decades the equality of democracy has been promised, and instead we have seen an ever-increasing gap between rich and poor, existing dissatisfactions may threaten to erupt into *violence from below* in Cambodia, the potential of which should not be underestimated. In contemporary Cambodia, although still somewhat rare, expressions of *violence from below* can be understood as representative of an insurrection against the dogged tyranny of the existing neoliberal order. The conundrum of this situation is that while violence is never an option for democracy as it undermines its fundamental character of equality by reconstituting hierarchy through its expression, it is difficult not to see some emancipatory potential in *violence from below* as it paradoxically marks the first steps toward greater democratic empowerment. This is not an argument in favor of violence, but a recognition of the frustrations and difficult choices Cambodians face as their experiences of neoliberalization come up against and confound their desire for democracy.

5 Conclusion

Sowing the seeds of a new revolution?

Seeing that the wood is rotten, do not yet sit down.

– Cambodian proverb.

Long-time Cambodia observer Milton Osborne (2000) has noted that in recent years the US has shown acceptance of the political status quo in Cambodia by way of expressing little interest in criticizing the government in Phnom Penh. Indeed, the US is not alone in its apathetic attitude toward the political situation in Cambodia, as virtually the entire donor community has been ambivalent toward substantive democratic reform in the country. Such indifference and contradiction have been repeatedly conveyed by bilateral and multilateral donors throughout Cambodia's transitional period and continues up to the present day. This is exemplified most clearly by the following four factors. First, is the UNTAC's failure to implement its primary mandate of creating a "neutral political environment," leaving the CPP in a militarily powerful position that allowed Hun Sen to contravene the election results and force his way into a co-prime ministerial position. Second, is the failure to seriously investigate and hold accountable those responsible for the March 1997 grenade attack against members of the KNP. Third, is the questionable haste in declaring the 1998 elections "free and fair" despite the dubious neutrality of the NEC based on their refusal to hear hundreds of voter complaints of violence and intimidation, and the massive protest movement that erupted in Phnom Penh in the days following the announcement of the election results. Finally, and most overtly, international indifference is illustrated by the universal refusal of donors to label the "events" of 5–6 July 1997 as a coup d'état. Thus, aside from the frequently repeated mantra that Cambodia's political parties should respect the principles of "good governance," the donor community has maintained an unspoken policy of looking the other way whenever democracy is flouted in the country.

To date, Hun Sen's government stands apart in having weathered the lion's share of the blame for setbacks to Cambodian democracy. The International Crisis Group (2000: 34) offers a typical assessment shared by many donors in concluding: "the RGC's commitment to [democratic] reform is disingenuous."

Others have argued from a decidedly *culturalist* position, contending that democracy has not come to Cambodia because Khmer culture is premised on a supposedly intrinsic resistance to power sharing, and is accordingly " 'violent" and "absolutist." However, there is no credibility to such arguments, as they are essentialist in nature, recapitulate notions of "scientific racism" that predominated during the colonial era, and very often simply toe the "Asian values" line. In short, *culturalist* accounts serve to demonize Cambodian culture and thus a priori Cambodian people themselves. This outcome does not assist us in advancing our understanding of contemporary political developments in the country, nor is it supportive of the intense desire many Cambodians have for democracy. Nevertheless, this is not to say that Hun Sen's regime has no culpability for the dearth of democracy in Cambodia, as his government certainly has a lot to answer for. Rather, it is simply a contention that we can find answers for his government's authoritarian behavior in systems that do not imply there is something inherently "wrong" with the Cambodian people. Indeed, as Dylan Hendrickson (2001) maintains, there is ample evidence that external agencies are equally to blame for Cambodia's failure to consolidate democracy, having downplayed the impact global economic forces would have on institutional reforms.

Those who focus their criticisms exclusively on the Hun Sen regime fail to understand that Cambodia's transition was not intended to be a singular one. That is, alongside a transition to democracy, the goals of the UNTAC were to transform Cambodia from a state of war to conditions of peace, and from a command economy to a free-market economic system. It is the third facet of this "triple transition" that I have singled out as being the most deleterious to the prospect of democracy consolidating in post-war Cambodia. Democracy has been defined in this book as a participatory *process* that is vital to the project of development insofar as democracy constitutes both the primary means and principal end of development (Sen 1999a). However, the neoliberal agenda follows its own "development discourse," and far from championing democracy through the concept of "good governance," neoliberalization in the Cambodian context actually stands in irreconcilable contradiction to democracy. The concept of "governance" sets a free-market economy as a requisite and inalienable condition for democracy. However, this pre-determination of the economic model, which was imposed "from above" via the PPA and the UNTAC mission by the donor community removes the element of choice and the concomitant collective participatory involvement necessary to make such a choice, both of which are fundamental to the *process* of democracy.

Moreover, the relationship between democracy and capitalism we so often hear about is nothing if not ambiguous, as the competition inherent to the capitalist system promotes social and economic inequalities, which are inseparable from their political counterpart. The CPP negotiated Cambodia's transition with its powerful political position intact, and was subsequently able to utilize its authority to informally control Cambodian markets so as to enhance their social status and enrich their economic standing. That is, by assimilating the neoliberal doctrine, the CPP was able to amass an inordinate amount of wealth by twisting IFI and donor interests into instruments of power via the politics of the "shadow state." In contrast to the neoliberal agenda of "rolling back" social welfare provisions and "rolling out" new regulatory reforms that work in concert to weaken the state, a strong and democratic government that is capable of being accountable to its citizens is needed so that the pilfering and pillage of the "shadow state" does not come to represent the *modus operandi* of economic activity. This is a concern shared by Hendrickson (2001: 104), who states:

> Cambodia today is integrated into the global economy, though not in a manner that has allowed it to protect itself from the most harmful effects . . . In the absence of a strong regulatory framework, there is a risk that Cambodia will continue to attract investors more concerned with pillaging its resources than strengthening the productive base of the economy. In these circumstances, the short-term benefits of further integration into the global economy may be limited to a relatively narrow group of political, military and economic elites.

It is not surprising that "Democracy, as practised in contemporary Southeast Asia, is often perceived as a form of government dominated and manipulated by the rich and powerful . . ." (Vatikiotis 1996: 92), as this is precisely what democracy has become in Cambodia via its linkage to neoliberalism.

The application of "good governance" to the country has reduced Cambodian democracy to electoralism, an arrangement that has been rejected by this study as being only superficially democratic whereby the potential to influence policy and practice has not been forthcoming. Far from being a symptom of a cultural characteristic, as some Cambodian observers such as David Roberts (2001) would have us believe, such lack of democratic accountability is an outcome of a state weakened by neoliberal reforms. The capitalist global economic order envisaged by neoliberal ideology demands the emancipation of market forces from political control, and through the promotion of SAPs/PRGFs, the IFIs have been able to realize this goal. While "shadow state" responses are perhaps an unforeseen consequence of neoliberalism's articulation with existing political economic realities, the ultimate goal of weakening Global South governments so that the market may reign supreme has nevertheless been achieved. Cambodia, as representative of a state weakened by a variety of regulatory reforms that have eliminated social protections and commodified commonly held assets, is unable to respond to the demands of its citizens in a constructive and democratic manner. Instead, the Cambodian state resorts to authoritarian measures, principally manifested as violence, which "became a modality of power and economic accumulation, effectively manipulated by the country's political elites and economic entrepreneurs and fuelled by rampant marketization"

(Hendrickson 2001: 102). Thus, *violence from above* is employed to maintain the "order" that both the free-market economic system and the government's own position of hegemony rest upon, meaning the rhetoric of "order" and "stability" is a language shared by the IFIs, bilateral donors, and indigenous elites alike.

A geographical analysis of Cambodian public space has exposed the rhetoric of "order" and "stability," commonly presumed as worthwhile and honorific goals that serve the interest of the populace, as in fact subversive to the interests of democracy. Mitchell (2003b: 129) reminds us that "Public space is the product of competing ideologies about what constitutes space – order and control or free, and perhaps dangerous, interaction." This interpretation corresponds with Lefebvre's (1991) theory on the production of space, where the "ordered" view is captured in the concept of *representations of space*, or how space is visualized and administered by the government, and Lefebvre's notion of *representational space* which is analogous to the view of public space that espouses unmediated interaction, or how space is actually materialized by members of society. This distinction is important in that it appreciates the difference between an "official" and "unofficial" status of public space. That is, we are able to recognize that public space is fundamentally both a social construction and a site of contestation. Public space, like democracy itself, is a perpetually variable *process*, and is given life only through the ongoing action of struggle. Accordingly, in this study I have forwarded the idea of *democracy as public space* as an alternative to the "top down" mode of development that is epitomized by the neoliberal order. *Democracy as public space* represents the opportunity to allow the development agenda to be set "from below," giving people a participatory stake in society, and thereby putting power back in their collective hands where it rightfully belongs.

Empowering the people themselves entails the simultaneous disempowerment of those who currently occupy a privileged position in society, and as such powerful elites will try to impede any movement toward a "from below" vision of democracy and development. Such obstruction efforts apply equally to indigenous and extraneous elites. Those from within the country have an obvious and direct stake in wanting to maintain their hegemony, while those from outside are interested in preserving a political and socioeconomic hierarchy at the national level, as power for the few rather than for all represents the best way to avoid any interference with the market. In fact, the only way a capitalist free-market system can successfully operate is through a hierarchical socioeconomic and political system, since notions of egalitarianism that form the basis of democracy stand diametrically opposed to the competitiveness of capitalism.

Public space, or at least the view that envisions it as the very site of democracy, is thus the antithesis of the neoliberal order, and it is for this reason that neoliberal reforms are so concerned with privatization schemes. Public property, services, and goods, and more generally public space itself, are beyond the penetration and scope of the market, and only by privatizing them can they become "ordered" and subjected to the control of market forces. This also explains why the RGC's crackdown on public space, which this study has shown to be a predominant feature throughout the transitional period, has not received the ire and scorn of bilateral and multilateral donors. The donor community, firmly entrenched in the market fundamentalist camp as they are, view the authoritarian action taken by Hun Sen and the CPP as conducive to maintaining their own interests, although this of course remains unspoken and hidden behind the rhetoric of both "good governance" and the need for "order" and "stability."

The denial of public space in Cambodia, effected through *violence from above* and predicated on the need to maintain "stability," is really just a method of controlling the content of debate without having to acknowledge that this is what is in fact being done. Such refusal is an act of silencing that strips people of their right to representation and voice, and is an affront to the Cambodian peoples' collective expression of democratic desire and material need. Moreover, the control of public space in the name of "order" and as a preventive measure against the manifestation of violence must assume that all protest is an inherently violent and riotous act (Mitchell 2003a). This in turn presupposes the Cambodian people who would dare to demonstrate for a social, economic, or political cause as being guilty of a "crime" they have not committed, much less even had the opportunity to do so. This flips the constitutionally enshrined provision of the Cambodian law on its head, whereby guilt is now assumed, while innocence must be proven.

While protest is at times accompanied by *violence from below*, this is certainly not always or necessarily the case. However, when the state shows a clear and defiant position of not listening to the demands of the people it is meant to represent, or is unable to respond to such demands, that is, it exhibits all the telltale characteristics of a state weakened by neoliberal reforms, then *violence from below* is almost certain to erupt as the frustrations of the general populace begin to boil over. This is a notion corroborated by James C. Davies (1973: 63), who argues that

> . . . we must recognize a common ingredient in all such violent activity: the profound frustration among people whose position in society has been subordinate with respect to the satisfaction of their need for power, their need to *control* the satisfaction of all their needs. This is to say that in any political protest movement its participants demand political influence, political power. . . . They will want to be part of the policy process as it affects them.

There are times, such as the French and American revolutions, when the alienating political structures of the day have been transformed through violence, and by means of such action, the democratic potential of the system was able to grow. As Mitchell (2003b: 230–31, original emphasis) states: "The only way to transform, and even to overthrow, the *order* – and hence the interests encapsulated in that order – has been to defy that order, to break laws, to act without proper decorum." Nevertheless, the reader should not be misled into believing that I am championing violence in the name of democracy. Explanation does not equal justification, and indeed the relationship between democracy and violence is morally ambiguous at the best of times. Thus, the *disquieting nexus* that exists between democracy and violence is always also an *irreconcilable schism* because while violent contestation may procure "the right to the city," and ultimately the right to the nation, it also comes contemporaneous with an impossible brutality that places societies dangerously close to the edge of the abyss. Violence begets violence. This simple idiom always remains true, regardless of whether violence was originally manifested in the name of social justice, or as an act of abhorrence.

Iadicola and Shupe (2003) persuasively argue that violence is more likely to occur in the context of hierarchical structures, where greater inequality translates into higher levels of violence. Indeed, this correlation between violence and inequality is what we have witnessed in Cambodia's UNTAC and post-transition years. During the UNTAC mission, Cambodia was once again, after nearly 15 years of isolation, brought full force into the global economic hierarchy in 1991 by way of neoliberal reforms and the opening of its markets. As Cambodia became increasingly economically liberal throughout the 1990s, violence did not wane. Instead, the country "experienced an upsurge in crime and internal disorder" (Hendrickson 2001), a pattern that has continued into the new millennium. This rise in *violence from below* in post-transitional Cambodia is representative of the social discontent the predominantly poor population have with their growing marginalization, where such anger is inevitably manifested against the government, as this is the institution that is supposed to represent and facilitate their interests. However, although perhaps often unknowingly, the frustrations Cambodians are currently experiencing run much deeper than with the government, and are in fact latent dissatisfactions with neoliberalism itself. The increasing gap between rich and poor and the concurrent disempowerment of the majority of Cambodians is an outcome of the population having been subjected to an economic system they had no part in choosing. Thus, free-market capitalism is a reality that has been vehemently contested by poor, marginalized, and propertyless Cambodians who have attempted to insert their voices into the "development" policies and practices that are effectively destroying their lives.

Effectively, neoliberalization in the Cambodia represents a powder keg waiting to explode, where ongoing violent dispossessions may prove to be the trigger (Cheang Sokha 2007; 2006). This is something Prime Minster Hun Sen himself has recognized, as he frequently addresses the Cambodian media with paranoid invocations of his firm grip on political and military power (Saing Soenthrith and Yun Samean 2004; Koh Santepheap 2008), and even more tellingly, he has warned the nation of an impending "farmers revolution" should the land-grabbing issue not be moderated (Kuch Naren 2005b). This led to a declaration of "war on land-grabbing" in March 2007 (Barton 2007; Yun Samean 2007), which symbolically demonstrated his concern, not for the people of Cambodia, but for his own position of power (Vong Sokheng 2005). Yet in spite of such shrewd observations, Hun Sen's unremitting lack of modesty frequently gets the better of him. In March 2009, the Economist Intelligence Unit, a British think tank and branch of the *Economist Magazine*, released a report that ranked Cambodia as one of the top five countries in the world at risk for major political unrest in the current global economic climate. Cambodia tied with Sudan for fourth, placing it just behind the top three countries, Zimbabwe, Chad, and the Democratic Republic of Congo respectively, but ahead of Afghanistan and Iraq, which were placed sixth and seventh. Cambodia scored 8 out of a possible 10 on the group's political instability index, which uses 15 measures including income, inequality, corruption, factionalism, regime type, and unemployment to rate the likelihood of mass revolt (Economist Intelligence Unit 2009). Hun Sen dismissed the report outright, publicly laughing at Cambodia having been ranked higher than Iraq and Afghanistan and thumbing his nose at the looming economic crisis and global recession (Yun Samean and Neou Vannarin 2009).

Such insolence is at odds with the simmering resentment for Hun Sen and the arrogance of his government. In the first half of 2009, several people linked to the Cambodian Freedom Fighters were arrested and charged with establishing a new anti-government group, called the "Tiger Head Movement." The group, which includes several former Royal Cambodian Armed Forces intelligence officers and the former police chief of Mondolkiri province, is thought to be behind the July 2007 attempt to blow up the Cambodian-Vietnamese Friendship monument in Phnom Penh, and and several of these individuals were arrested and charged with planting bombs near the Defense Ministry and a CPP-affiliated TV station in January 2009 (Prak Chan Thul and Eang Mengleng 2009; Saing Soenthrith 2009). Yet the slight that these formerly well-connected, high-ranking officials must have felt in legitimizing their call to arms surely pales in comparison to the humiliation and degradation experienced by a disaffected population increasingly characterized by their shared dispossession. Given the historical pattern of financial crises as an catalyst for the further accumulation and consolidation of capital among the wealthy class (Harvey 2005), Hun Sen's snickering in the face of a major financial crisis seems perverse. At the time of this writing the full effect of the strains imposed on Cambodian livelihoods by the global economic recession are still unfolding, but many Cambodians will surely find themselves in an even more precarious position than they were before the crisis hit. The possibility therefore exists that the final joke may very well be on Hun Sen and his neoliberal order.

The circumstances of a hierarchical system that presents itself as monolithic and functions to marginalize the majority of the population to the benefit and reward of the very few, eventually giving rise to widespread social discontent, frustration, anger, and ultimately revolution, should sound familiar to the reader as this very scenario has already been played out in Cambodian history. In 1975, the Khmer Rouge seized the wheel of time and brought Cambodian back to "Year Zero," ousting not only the government, but also the social and economic institutions and systems along with it. The communist movement in Cambodia was much more than an isolated group of revolutionaries, and by the time the Khmer Rouge captured control of the state, their cause had become an extremely popular indigenous movement. However, while inequality causes violence, as Cambodia witnessed firsthand during the colonial and postcolonial era in the run-up to the Khmer Rouge regime, violence has a "reciprocity of reinforcement" (Iadicola and Shupe 2003: 375), meaning violence also causes inequality. Thus, while the Khmer Rouge were initially motivated by a desire to transform Cambodia from the unjust and hierarchical structures that dominated Cambodian society prior to their seizure of state power, the *violence from below* that was exhorted to overthrow this system functioned to corrupt and pervert the movement. Ultimately, the Khmer Rouge simply recreated the inequality and hierarchy they had initially set out to replace.

Unfortunately, the Achilles' heel of humankind seems to be our adverse tendency to refuse to learn from history. Indeed, Pamela Sodhy (2004: 171), an ardent enthusiast for the modernization school of thought, admonishes contemporary Cambodians, suggesting that in order for the country to "develop," Cambodia must "shed its victim mentality." Although she recognizes that Cambodia has a history of subjugation, Sodhy does not acknowledge the current neoliberal order as another "turn in the history of servitude" (Gray 1998: 208), where the market itself has replaced Angkorean kings, French colonizers, Cold War bombardiers, and genocidal Communists, as Cambodia's newest tyrant. Indeed, it is hard for victims to dispose of such a "mentality," when they are still being victimized. Nonetheless, Sodhy's advice to the Cambodian people is ill-considered. While members of the current Cambodian government may be too wrapped up in enjoying the ride of wealth that neoliberalization has taken them on, and simultaneously blinded by notions of "there is no alternative," the Cambodian people themselves have indeed started to move on. Cambodians are not content to be thought of as hapless victims, or to have their agency to take control over their own lives reduced to mere handouts from well-meaning foreign development agencies. Rather, some Cambodians are beginning to remember themselves as the true source of power in their society. This rediscovery has come about via the *taking* of space through protest and the internalization of the idea of *democracy as public space*. Indeed, democracy ". . . if necessarily buttressed by checks and balances to protect weaker groups, offers one of the few means of reconciliation" (Pinkney 1994: 37).

While the *taking* of public space is a necessary component of democracy, this process is not necessarily democratic. The idea of a *disquieting nexus* between democracy and violence reminds us that public space is inherently dangerous, where the continual threat of both *violence from above* and *violence from below* means that public space always entails risks. Public space is thus an enigma, because while it represents the crucible of democracy, the crucible itself is necessarily and perpetually fractured, where such ruptures are actually symbolic of democracy's functioning. As Mitchell (2003b: 234) contends, "The ideal of an unmediated space can never be met – nor can the ideal of a fully controlled space in which the public basks in the splendor of spectacle but is never at any sort of 'risk'." This contradiction of public space corresponds with the two contrasting utopian visions David Harvey (2000) sets out in *Spaces of Hope*.

First, Harvey (2000: 160) identifies "utopias of spatial form," which are the traditional utopias that follow Thomas Moore's original vision in functioning as "isolated, coherently organized, and largely closed-space econom[ies] ... [where] the internal spatial ordering ... strictly regulates a stabilized and unchanging social process." That is, "utopias of spatial form" are predicated on the longing for an idealised future (often rooted in nostalgia for an idealized past), where "the temporality of the social process, the dialectics of social change – real history – are excluded, while social stability is assured by a fixed spatial form" (Harvey 2000: 160). The dimension of time, along with its concomitant social, political, cultural, and economic processes are discarded in such a vision, as the fixity and order of the spatialized utopian present is seen to no longer require any such changes that these processes offer. Everything is currently as it should be. Mitchell (2003b) recognizes the dream of a perfectly secure city and risk-free public space as just this sort of utopia, while in the historical context of Cambodia, the Khmer Rouge's Democratic Kampuchea (DK) represents another.

The second type of utopian vision is expressed purely in temporal terms in what Harvey (2000) calls "utopias of social process." Here, utopias "are literally bound to no place whatsoever and are typically specified outside the constraints of spatiality altogether. The qualities of space and place are totally ignored" (Harvey 2000: 174). Harvey (2000) identifies neoliberalism as one such utopia, where we are repeatedly told if we just "leave things to the market," then all will be right, fair, and just in this world. According to Mitchell (2003b) the same form of utopia is to be found in the dream of a fully democratic and inclusive public space. However, Harvey (2000: 179) reminds us of the chimerical quality that underlies all utopian ideals: "In exactly the same way that materializations of spatial utopias run afoul of the particularities of the temporal process mobilized to produce them, so the utopianism of process runs afoul of the spatial framings and the particularities of place constructions necessary to its materialization."

Thus, we have a dialectic, where each form of utopia ignores a central component of the other, but is ultimately forced to deal with this negligence once it is put into practice. This is precisely why the Khmer Rouge's utopian dreams of DK and now neoliberalism's perfect market have both failed in

Cambodia. Each has had to contend with this dialectic, and in confronting time and space respectively, a perversion has occurred. The Khmer Rouge tried to negate all manner of temporality in bringing Cambodia back to "Year Zero," where all Khmer citizens were envisaged to interact as equals free from the hierarchies of the colonial era.[1] However, as mentioned above, the violent social processes used to create DK also worked to deprave it once this "utopia of social process" was materialized. In addition, not all Cambodians entered DK as equals, and *Angkar* (the Organization), comprising those who spearheaded the revolution, soon emerged as the facilitator of all social processes to make certain that equality prevailed. This "forced equality" simply fostered a new hierarchy with *Angkar* at its apex, and required the same panopticism that is central to all "utopias of spatial form" in ensuring that the "imaginative free play" of individuals was adequately controlled so that an alternative to the Khmer Rouge's utopian scheme was not materialized (Harvey 2000: 163). Thus, an epidemic of paranoia was unleashed in DK that eventually uprooted the regime, but not before 1.5 million "enemies of the revolution" were killed along the way. On the other hand, neoliberalization has failed in modern Cambodia for the opposite reason. This "utopia of social process" has been upset not by time like DK, but by "its manner of spatialization" (Harvey 2000: 179), insofar as investment in infrastructures always generates geographical biases and uneven geographical developments. That the idea of the perfect market is broken upon the rock of geography is incontrovertible; the evidence of this is all around us in landscapes of poverty and inequality that are reflected through escalating violence. From Phnom Penh's "squatter" encampments to what was for many years my own backyard of Vancouver's notorious Lower Eastside, we only need open our eyes to see it. Thus, the rhetoric of "stability" and "order" is one of two weapons in the neoliberal arsenal that is used to mitigate the frustration and anger that grow out of such geographical bias. Should certain individuals or groups see through this propaganda, neoliberalism does not retract itself from using the only other weapon at its disposal: violence. However, the failures of DK and the free market in Cambodia do not mean that we should abandon utopian thought altogether. Indeed, yearning for a better social condition penetrates to the very core of the human experience, and without such dreams, we would ultimately lose our humanity. Thus, while utopia may be impossible, the ongoing struggle toward it is not (Mitchell 2003b).

Metaphorically, the aphorism that opens this conclusion ("seeing that the wood is rotten, do not yet sit down") refers to inspecting things that look suspicious. To understand why democracy has failed to consolidate in post-UNTAC Cambodia, we must ultimately realize that the free-market economic system currently practiced in Cambodia is suspect. Not until we fix the "rotting wood" that is the current globalized free-market system, will democracy in Cambodia finally be able to "sit down." This recognition and repair requires the articulation of alternative utopian visions. Herein rests the major contribution of this book: the acknowledgment that the struggle for social justice, the battle for "the right to the city," and the contestation of public space mark the first steps in deposing the neoliberal order, not only in Cambodia, but across the globe. In Cambodia, these challenges represent the cry "from below" that the market has failed, that the Cambodian people have had enough poverty, labor exploitation, dispossession, hunger, disease, and unemployment, and that the market has not brought deliverance as has been promised by neoliberal ideology, but has instead meant only more strife and increased violence. The contestation of public space is a move toward the collective empowerment of the people themselves, through which they will together seek to carve out and establish new kinds of "stability" and "order," built not on the fears of the rich, "but on the needs of the poorest and most marginalized residents" (Mitchell 2003b: 9). It is to this conception of "order" and "stability" that this study has shown the Cambodian people to be deeply committed, and it is this vision that they will continue to struggle toward as their own utopian ideal, their own *democracy as public space*:

> "Even though every time when we do the demonstration, we are hit, [RGC] crackdown, and we are killed by the army . . . our people still do the demonstration. That is our hope is, that in the future we will win, we will get our demands."[2]

Notes

Chapter 1

1 The overseas, weekly review edition of *The Cambodia Daily* was used for the survey, which unfortunately does not specify the exact dates of the assembled articles.

Chapter 2

1 The bourgeoisie is conspicuously almost absent in much of the Global South, a condition that is reflective of the extreme disparity of wealth in these societies, and indicative of the abysmal failure that contemporary "development" has come to represent.
2 Some would recognize the insertion of "governance" and "rulers" into our definition as effectively taking power out of the hands of the people, and thus we no longer have a democracy in its truest or most "radical" sense. However, without these insertions (i.e. some form of representation) it remains unclear as to how democracy could be institutionalized, as no such theory yet exists. See Lummis (1996) for a convincing example of the argument for "radical democracy," complete with a lack of institutional proposals, as democratization is precisely what is at stake.
3 Following the work of Edward Said (2003), I reject the merit of such designations as "west" and "east" with regard to civilization as products of the discourse of Orientalism. However, while acknowledging the problems inherent to such categorizations, this study utilizes the language of this dichotomous construct as an heuristic device for the sake of academic inquiry and common understanding. The labels "Third World" and "Global South" are also recognized as clearly problematical inasmuch as they represent residual categories to the "First World" and the "Global North" respectively. The First World/Global North is further conceptualized as a synonym for the "west" under the terms of the Orientalist "east"/"west" dichotomy.
4 Samuel P. Huntington is no stranger to "cultural" controversy as his "the clash of civilization" thesis is a *strongly culturalist* reformulation of Orientalist geopolitics that characterizes Confucian-Islamic Asia as a civilizational threat to the Judeo-Christian western sphere (see Huntington 1993b).
5 Philippe Le Billon 2002 provides a detailed analysis of how elites have accomplished this reshaping in the Cambodian context via forest exploitation and the instrumentalization of disorder and violence, primarily through patronage networks, as a mode of control for accessing forests.
6 At present, to accept the following characterizations of civil societies, despite being a matter of concern, means that there is not a diversion from the book's

major thesis. Alleviating all anxiety concerning civil society is impossible without enlarging the argument beyond a reasonable length. For comprehensive accounts of civil society's origins and contested meanings see Cohen and Arato (1992); Edwards (2004); Mercer (2002); Wiarda (2003).

7   The elision between space and place is purposeful. Held within the discourses they deploy, space and place are typically thought to counterpose as there exists an implicit imagination of different theoretical "levels": space as the abstract versus the everydayness of place. Massey (2005: 6) asks what if we refuse this distinction, "between place (as meaningful, lived and everyday) and space (as what? the outside? the abstract? the meaning*less*)?" She encourages us to view space as simultaneity of stories-so-far, and place as collections of these stories, articulations within the wider power-geometries of space.

8   Identity formation also occurs in semi-public and private spaces, as well as subaltern counterpublic spaces, where subordinated groups formulate oppositional interpretations of their identities by circulating counter-discourses (Fraser 1990).

9   It is imperative to recognize the violent legal geographies of property rights that constitute private space. The property system entails violent "acts" of dispossession at its founding moment, as well as enduring violent "deeds" – which need not be physicalized to be operative, as self-policing becomes reflexive – that (re)enforce the exclusionary basis of private property (Blomley 2000; 2003).

10 The notion that public space might ever be unmediated is chimerical. All spaces are socially regulated, if not by explicit rules then by competitive regulation. This, however, does not mean that the utopian ideal of unmediated space should not be aspired to (Harvey 2000), because while unscripted public space is fantasy, it is precisely the chaos, openness, and uncertainty embodied in space and place that makes them potentially democratic crucibles. The challenge is to treat them this way, as instituting democratic spaces requires that exclusions be foregrounded and made visible so that they can be contested (Massey 2005).

11 In fact, the original and primary purpose of the modern police force was (and still is) to protect private property and thus maintain the interests of the landowning elite (Tilly 2003).

12 Cambodia's "Democracy Square" has a moniker which intends to mimic Tiananmen Square's associations of place.

13 In the political fallout since 11 September 2001 (hereinafter 9/11), the tendency to confuse explanation with advocation has unfortunately become more frequent. Likewise the reader would be mistaken to interpret my arguments as a celebration of violence or its sanction when expressed in certain forms or under particular circumstances. All violence is deplorable. I simply wish to acknowledge how subordinate groups will at times use violence in their attempts at democratic empowerment. Accordingly, democratization should not be viewed as a social or political panacea. Democracy still comes with its own frailties, where the occasional tendency for violence, just as lamentable when expressed from below as it is in all its forms, can be understood as one such weakness.

14 The nexus between capital and state proposed by Yeung (1998) alerts us to the idea that violence may have a corporate logic is actually nothing new. The very notion that violence may be "monopolized" reveals a capitalist character.

15 The collective "right to the city" becomes even more important to Global South peoples when we consider that modern development policies and practices are rapidly driving up the rate of urbanization.

16 This reading corresponds with the Marxian political economy critique that neoliberalism is an elite-driven project (Duménil and Lévy 2004; Harvey 2005).

17 Le Vine, like many scholars, refers to this situation as a "culture of violence." However, as the preceding discussion has shown, not only is "culture" thinly defined in this view (i.e. as any learned behavior), but it also focuses blame on the

"culture," and accordingly the people themselves rather than on the structural socioeconomic and political context. Accordingly, within this view there is an implicit supposition of cultural inferiority, one that at base recapitulates racist modes of thought. Thus, it is best to accept the predicament Le Vine describes only for what it is, learned behavior, and leave it at that.

Chapter 3

1 The name "Democratic Kampuchea" serves as an example of the misappropriated use of the word democracy as discussed in Chapter 2. Even the most perverted conception of this word would not be appropriate to describe the reality of the abysmal tyranny of the DK regime.

2 This is a common phrase used by Cambodians to signify the agony of the Khmer Rouge period in which every day of survival was counted.

3 For example, Minister of Economy and Finance, Keat Chhon, was educated at the National Institute of Nuclear Science and Technology in Saclay, France, and Minister of International Cooperation and Foreign Affairs, Hor Namhong, studied at the University of Paris.

4 Participant Observation, July 2002, June 2004 – December 2004, November 2006 – August 2007, June 2009, Cambodia. Rural areas are the traditional powerbase of the CPP party, and accordingly this feature of the landscape may be read as an indication of CPP popularity. However, it is also undeniably a spatial strategy employed to assert CPP dominance, as many Cambodians have informed me that opposition party signboards are frequently removed and subject to vandalism by elements loyal to the CPP.

5 My deficiencies in the Khmer language required that I have a native Khmer speaker present with me during all interviews, except for those conducted in English. Four different individuals provided translation for this study. Those interviews that were conducted in English without the aid of a translator are noted as such. On all occasions, I have presented the participants words exactly as they were spoken to me, either by the participants themselves, or by the translator present at the interview. Thus, grammatical errors have been preserved throughout.

6 Interview, International NGO Worker, Female, Age 45, 9 Nov. 2004, Pursat Province, conducted in English.

7 Interview, Cook, Female, Age 33, 17 Sept. 2004, Phnom Penh.

8 Interview, Nurse, Age 38, 8 Nov. 2004, Pursat Province.

9 Interview, Market Stall Owner, Age 49, 6 Nov. 2004, Pursat Province.

10 Interview, High School Teacher, Age 25, 6 Nov. 2004, Pursat Province.

11 Interview, Local NGO Worker, Female, Age 22, 7 Nov. 2004, Pursat Province.

12 Nonetheless, Ranariddh was made the "official" leader of the country, as he was designated First Prime Minister, while Hun Sen became Second Prime Minister.

13 Interview, Hotel Desk Clerk, Male, Age 26, 21 Sept. 2004, Phnom Penh.

14 Interview, Local NGO Worker, Male, Age 41, 8 Nov. 2004, Pursat Province.

15 Interview, Monk, Male, Age 33, 28 Sept. 2004, Phnom Penh.

16 Interview, Monk, Male, Age 27, 3 Nov. 2004, Pursat Province, conducted in English.

17 Interview, Homemaker, Female, Age 48, 22 Aug. 2004, Phnom Penh.

18 Interview, Human Rights Worker, Male, Age 60, 28 Sept. 2004, Phnom Penh, conducted in English.

19 Interview, Market Stall Owner, Female, Age 49, 7 Nov. 2004, Pursat Province.

20 The "re" prefixes used here are intended to destabilize the Orientalist view that democracy is somehow a "western" concept. Instead, I seek to acknowledge democracy as the universal arrangement of pre-modern peoples who organized themselves into small groups of hunter-gatherers long before Athens "discovered"

democracy and transformed its content. This view has become increasingly mainstream within anthropology.

21 The claim that economic inequality has increased only in post-transition Cambodia is supported by the rise in value of the country's Gini coefficient. The Gini coefficient is a number between 0 and 100, where 0 corresponds with perfect equality (where everyone has the same income) and 100 corresponds with perfect inequality (where one person has all the income, and everyone else has zero income). Prior to the UNTAC mission in 1990, Cambodia's Gini coefficient was 41.6. This value has continued to rise in post-transition Cambodia, where 2004 represents the highest recorded value to date at 46.3 (World Bank 2004). In terms of poverty, Ear (2006) notes a "lack of robustness" in IFI data on poverty in the context of Cambodia. The World Bank (2006) recently reported a considerable 12 percentage point decrease in poverty over the previous decade based on household consumption data collected in 2004. However, the Bank recalculated the national poverty rate in 1993/94 from 39 percent to 47 percent using a flawed backward projection that incorrectly assumed non-Khmer Rouge-controlled areas were richer than Khmer Rouge-controlled zones, the latter of which are well documented to have been thinly populated and heavily endowed with natural resources that facilitated a booming illegal cross-border trade, particularly in timber, due to the areas' proximity to Thailand (see Le Billon 2000). Thus, instead of reporting a minimal decline in poverty from 39 percent to 35 percent during the 1993–2004 period, the Bank claimed that poverty dropped from 47 percent to 35 percent. Moreover, Ear (2006) points out that if the 2004 national poverty line (1,826 riels or US$0.45 per person per day) is increased by only 10 percent, or 183 riels (US$0.045), the national poverty rate jumps 6.6 percentage points from 35 percent to 41.6 percent.

22 Interview, Motorbike Taxi Driver, Male Age 25, 18 Sept. 2004, Phnom Penh.

23 Interview, High School Teacher, Male, Age 25, 6 Nov. 2004, Pursat Province.

24 Interview, Market Stall Owner, Female, Age 29, 20 Sept. 2004, Phnom Penh.

25 Interview, University Student, Male Age 25, 16 Sept. 2004, Phnom Penh, conducted in English.

26 Interview, Hotel Desk Clerk, Male, Age 26, 21 Sept. 2004, Phnom Penh.

27 Interview, Government Civil Service Worker, Age 48, 22 Aug. 2004, Phnom Penh.

28 It should also be noted that the amount of aid actually dispersed to a recipient country rarely equals the amount pledged by donors. John Marston (2002) cites the Cambodian Development Resource Institute which suggests that Cambodia typically receives approximately 60 percent of the amount pledged each year. In this regard, 1997 may be viewed as a good year for Cambodia's aid market, as the actual disbursement figure nears 79 percent of the total pledged amount.

Chapter 4

1 Interview, Government Civil Service Worker, Male, Age 48, 22 Aug. 2004, Phnom Penh.

2 Interview, High School Teacher, Male, Age 25, 6 Nov. 2004, Pursat Province.

3 Interview, Motorbike Taxi Driver, Male, Age 26, 3 Nov. 2004, Pursat Province.

4 Interview, International NGO Worker, Female, Age 45, 9 Nov. 2004, Pursat Province, conducted in English.

5 Interview, Motorbike Taxi Driver, Male, Age 26, 3 Nov. 2004, Pursat Province.

6 Interview, Khmer Language Teacher, Female, Age 25, 12 Sept. 2004, Phnom Penh, conducted in English.

7 Interview, Elementary School Teacher, Female, Age 21, 7 Nov. 2004, Pursat Province.

8 Interview, Monk, Male, Age 27, 3 Nov. 2004, Pursat Province, conducted in English.

9 Interview, Government Civil Service Worker, Male, Age 48, 22 Aug. 2004, Phnom Penh.

10 Interview, International NGO Worker, Female, Age 52, 8 Nov. 2004, Pursat Province.

11 Interview, Local NGO Worker, Age 41, 8 Nov. 2004, Pursat Province.

12 Interview, University Student, Age 25, 16 Sept. 2004, Phnom Penh, conducted in English.

13 Interview, Homemaker, Female, Age 48, 22 Aug. 2004, Phnom Penh.

14 Interview, Market Stall Owner, Age 29, 20 Sept. 2004, Phnom Penh.

15 Interview, International NGO Worker, Female, Age 45, 9 Nov. 2004, Pursat Province, conducted in English.

16 Interview, Garment Factory Worker, Female, Age 24, 18 Sept. 2004, Phnom Penh.

17 Interview, Market Stall Owner, Female, Age 49, 7 Nov. 2004, Pursat Province.

18 Interview, Monk, Male, Age 33, 28 Sept. 2004, Phnom Penh.

19 Interview, Homemaker, Female, Age 48, 22 Aug. 2004, Phnom Penh.

20 Interview, Craftsperson, Male, Age 28, 4 Nov. 2004, Pursat Province.

21 Interview, Small Business Owner, Male, Age 47, 23 Sept. 2004, Phnom Penh.

22 On the importance of recognizing poverty and inequality, along with their parallel geographies of violence, as outcomes of neoliberalization, see Springer (2008).

23 Any claim that the CPP was "popular" at this time should immediately be dismissed as fanciful and unfounded. For example, David Roberts (2001: 187) strains his credibility when he alleges: "The external perception of the CPP and Hun Sen was that they were unpopular. This is clearly at odds with the vote outcome." In contrast to the assertion that "The dominant CPP won a majority of the votes" (Roberts 2001: 183), the reality was the CPP had not won a majority, rather it won only 42.4 percent. Furthermore, the findings of a Canadian assessment mission to Cambodia, dispatched prior to the 1998 elections, indicated that Hun Sen's lack of popularity was very apparent (Bosley, Owen, and Armstrong 1997), a position the subsequent protests clearly corroborate.

24 Interview, Small Business Owner, Male, Age 47, 23 Sept. 2004, Phnom Penh.

25 Interview, International NGO Worker, Female, Age 45, 9 Nov. 2004, Pursat Province, conducted in English.

26 Interview, Monk, Male, Age 27, 3 Nov. 2004, Pursat Province, conducted in English.

27 Interview, Cook, Female, Age 38, 6 Nov. 2004, Pursat Province.

28 Interview, Hotel Desk Clerk, Male, Age 26, 21 Sept. 2004, Phnom Penh.

29 Interview, Small Business Owner, Male, Age 47, 23 Sept. 2004, Phnom Penh.

30 Interview, Widowed Homemaker and Street Stall Vendor, Female, Age 48, 7 Oct. 2004, Phnom Penh.

31 Interview, Human Rights Worker, Male, Age 60, 28 Sept. 2004, Phnom Penh, conducted in English.

32 Interview, Garment Factory Worker, Female, Age 24, 18 Sept. 2004, Phnom Penh.

33 Interview, Market Stall Owner, Female, Age 29, 20 Sept. 2004, Phnom Penh.

34 Interview, Monk, Male, Age 27, 3 Nov. 2004, Pursat Province, conducted in English.

35 Interview, High School Teacher, Male, Age 25, 6 Nov. 2004, Pursat Province.

36 Interview, Small Business Owner, Male, Age 47, 23 Sept. 2004, Phnom Penh.

37 Interview, Phann Sithan, Secretariat Officer, Housing Rights Task Force, Male, 9 July 2007, Phnom Penh, conducted in English.

38 Interview, Chhith Sam Ath, Executive Director, NGO Forum On Cambodia, Male, 3 July 2007, Phnom Penh, conducted in English.

39 Interview, Kek Galabru, President, LICADHO, Female, 6 July 2007, Phnom Penh, conducted in English.
40 Interview, Sam Rainsy, Opposition Leader, Sam Rainsy Party, Male, 19 July 2007, Phnom Penh, conducted in English.
41 Interview, Anonymous, Program Officer, Asian Development Bank, Male, 3 August 2007, Phnom Penh, conducted in English.
42 Interview, Anonymous, Senior Poverty Specialist, World Bank, Male, 6 August 2007, Phnom Penh, conducted in English.
43 Of course Joseph Stiglitz, former chief economist of the World Bank, represents a notable exception.
44 Participant Observation, 12–19 September 2004, and 19–20 June 2007, Phnom Penh.
45 Interviews, Homemaker, Female, Age 48, 22 Aug. 2004, Phnom Penh; International NGO Worker, Female, Age 45, 9 Nov. 2004, Pursat Province; Small Business Owner, Male, Age 47, 23 Sept. 2004, Phnom Penh; Security Guard Male, Age 26, 20 April 2007, Phnom Penh. Group 78 Community Representative, Lim Sambo, Male, Age 52, 7 June 2007, Phnom Penh.
46 As mentioned in the introduction, Hughes's position has done a 180 degree turn and she now positions herself as a critic of neoliberalism and the "good governance" agenda in Cambodia.
47 Interview, Market Stall Owner, Female, Age 29, 20 Sept. 2004, Phnom Penh.
48 Interview, Monk, Male, Age 33, 28 Sept. 2004, Phnom Penh.
49 Interview, Motorbike Taxi Driver, Male, Age 30, 18 Sept. 2004, Phnom Penh.
50 Interview, University Student, Male, Age 25, 16 Sept. 2004, Phnom Penh, conducted in English.
51 Interview, Vegetable Seller, Female, Age 30, 3 Nov. 2004, Pursat Province.
52 Interview, Human Rights Worker, Male, Age 60, 28 Sept. 2004, Phnom Penh, conducted in English.
53 Interview, Market Stall Owner, Female, Age 49, 7 Nov. 2004, Pursat Province.
54 Interview, Nurse, Female, Age 38, 8 Nov. 2004, Pursat Province.
55 Interview, Cook, Female, Age 33, 17 Sept. 2004, Phnom Penh.
56 Participant Observation, 10 Oct. 2004, Phnom Penh.
57 Interview, Homeless, Male, Age 34, 15 June 2007, Phnom Penh.
58 Interview, Homeless, Female, Age 38, 15 June 2007, Phnom Penh.
59 Interview, Homeless, Male, Age 36, 15 June 2007, Phnom Penh.
60 Interview, Homeless, Female, Age 53, 15 June 2007, Phnom Penh.
61 Interview, Homeless, Male, Age 34, 15 June 2007, Phnom Penh.
62 Interview, Homeless, Female, Age 38, 15 June 2007, Phnom Penh.
63 Interview, Homeless, Male, Age 36, 15 June 2007, Phnom Penh.
64 Interview, Homeless, Female, Age 53, 15 June 2007, Phnom Penh.
65 Interview, Human Rights Worker, Male, Age 60, 28 Sept. 2004, Phnom Penh, conducted in English.
66 Participant Observation, 19 September 2004, Phnom Penh.
67 Interview, Cook, Female, Age 33, 17 Sept. 2004, Phnom Penh.
68 Interview, Khmer Language Teacher, Female, Age 25, 12 Sept. 2004, Phnom Penh, conducted in English.
69 Interview, Human Rights Worker, Male, Age 60, 28 Sept. 2004, Phnom Penh, conducted in English.
70 Interview, Market Stall Owner, Female, Age 29, 20 Sept. 2004, Phnom Penh.
71 Interview, Nurse, Female, Age 38, 5 June 2007, Phnom Penh.
72 Interview, Construction Worker, Male, Age 45, 27 April 2007, Phnom Penh.
73 Interview, Garment Factory Worker, Female, Age 24, 18 Sept. 2004, Phnom Penh.
74 Interview, Street Stall Vendor, Female, Age 40, 17 Sept. 2004, Phnom Penh.
75 Interview, Waitress, Female, Age 24, 5 Nov. 2004, Pursat Province.

76 Interview, Motorbike Taxi Driver, Male, Age 30, 18 Sept. 2004, Phnom Penh.
77 Interview, Local NGO Worker, Male, Age 41, 8 Nov. 2004, Pursat Province.
78 Interview, Small Business Owner, Male, Age 47, 23 Sept. 2004, Phnom Penh.
79 Interview, University Student, Male, Age 25, 16 Sept. 2004, Phnom Penh, conducted in English.
80 Interview, Chea Mony, President, Free Trade Union of Workers of the Kingdom of Cambodia, Male, 10 July 2007, Phnom Penh.
81 Interview, Photographer, Male, Age 30, 11 June 2007, Andong; Interview, Housewife, Female, Age 55, 11 June 2007, Andong; Interview, Fruit Seller, Female, Age 40, 11 June 2007, Andong; Interview, Construction Worker, Female, Age 48, 11 June 2007, Andong; Interview, Retired Teacher, Male, Age 70, 11 June 2007, Andong.
82 Interview, Noun Sokchea, Group 78 Lawyer, Community Legal Education Center, Female, 27 June 2007, Phnom Penh, conducted in English.
83 Interview, Lim Sambo, Group 78 Community Representative, Male, 7 June 2007, Phnom Penh
84 Interview, Noun Sokchea, Group 78 Lawyer, Community Legal Education Center, Female, 27 June 2007, Phnom Penh, conducted in English.
85 Informal Conversation, Demonstration Bystander, Male, Age Unknown (Approximately early 50s), 11 Nov. 2004, Pursat Province, conducted in English.

Chapter 5

1 Indeed, hierarchy in Cambodia has deeper roots than the colonial era, and while the Angkorean epoch serves as a most obvious candidate, the nostalgia of the Khmer Rouge precluded them from recognizing this aspect of Angkor. The Khmer Rouge's vision of utopia placed Angkor at the centre of a bountiful Garden of Eden that they ultimately sought to recreate.
2 Interview, Small Business Owner, Male, Age 47, 23 Sept. 2004, Phnom Penh.

Bibliography

Abrahamsen, R. (2000) *Disciplining Democracy: Development Discourse and Good Governance in Africa*, New York: Zed Books.

Abu-Ghazzeh, T. M. (1996) "Reclaiming public space: The ecology of neighbourhood urban spaces in the town of Abu-Nuseir, Jordan," *Landscape and Urban Planning*, 36: 197–216.

Abu-Lughod, L. (1991) "Writing against culture," in R. Fox (ed.) *Recapturing Anthropology*, Santa Fe, NM: School of American Research, pp. 137–62.

Adewumi, F. (1996) "The violence and poverty of structural adjustment in Africa," in A. Louw, and S. Bekker (eds.) *Cities Under Siege: Urban Violence in South, Central and West Africa*, Durban: Indicator Press, pp. 21–30.

ADHOC. (2004) *Human Rights Situation Report 2003*, Report (February), Phnom Penh: The Cambodian Human Rights and Development Association.

Agacinski, S. (2001) "Stages of democracy," in M. Henaff, and T. B. Strong (eds.) *Public Space and Democracy*, Minneapolis, MN: University of Minnesota Press.

Ake, C. (1993) "Rethinking African democracy," in L. Diamond, and M. F. Plattner (eds.) *The Global Resurgence of Democracy*, Baltimore: MD: Johns Hopkins University Press, pp. 129–43.

Albritton, R. (2004) "Cambodia in 2003: On the road to democratic consolidation," *Asian Survey* 44: 102–9.

Amnesty International. (1997) *Cambodia: Escaping the Killing Fields?* News Brief (27 October). Available HTTP: <http://www.amnesty.org/en/library/info/ASA23/038/1997> (accessed 4 November 2009).

Anderson, B. (1991) *Imagined Communities: Reflections on the Origin and Spread of Nationalism*, 2nd edn, New York, NY: Verso.

Apter, D. (1997) *The Legitimization of Violence*, London: Macmillan Press Ltd.

Arat, Z. F. (1991) *Democracy and Human Rights in Developing Countries*, Boulder, CO: Lynne Rienner Publishers, Inc.

Arefi, M., and W. R. Meyers. (2003) "What is public about public space: The case of Visakhapatnam, India," *Cities*, 20: 331–39.

Arendt, H. (1958) *The Human Condition*, Chicago, IL: University of Chicago Press.

Ashley, D. (1996) "The nature and causes of human rights violations in Battambang province," in S. Heder, and J. Ledgerwood (eds.) *Propaganda, Politics, and Violence in Cambodia: Democratic Transition Under United Nations Peace-Keeping*, Armonk: M.E. Sharpe, Inc., pp. 159–82.

—— (1998a) "Between war and peace: Cambodia in 1991–98," in D. Hendrickson (ed.) *Safeguarding Peace: Cambodia's Constitutional Challenge*, Accord: An international review of peace initiatives, London: Conciliation Resources, pp. 20–29.

—— (1998b) "The failure of conflict resolution in Cambodia: Causes and lessons," in F. Z. Brown, and D. G. Timberman (eds.) Cambodia *and the International Community: The Quest for Peace, Development, and Democracy*, New York, NY: Asia Society, pp. 49–78.

Asia Foundation. (2003) *Democracy in Cambodia 2003: A Survey of the Cambodian Electorate*, The Asia Foundation (16 May). Accessed HTTP: <http://asiafoundation.org/pdf/DemocracyinCambodia.pdf> (accessed 4 November 2009).

Atkinson, R. (2003) "Domestication by cappuccino or a revenge on public space? Control and empowerment in the management of public spaces," *Urban Studies*, 40.9: 1829–43.

Auyero, J. (2000) "The hyper-shantytown: neo-liberal violence(s) in the Argentine slum," *Ehtnography*, 1: 93–116.

Ayres, D. M. (2000) *Anatomy of a Crisis: Education, Development, and the State in Cambodia, 1953–1998*, Honolulu, HI: University of Hawai'i Press.

Babb, J. G. D., and G. W. Steuber. (1998) "UN operations in Cambodia: A second 'decent interval'," in J. T. Fishel (ed.) *"The Savage Wars of Peace": Toward a New Paradigm of Peace Operations*, Boulder, CO: Westview Press, pp. 91–112.

Baber, Z. (2002) "Engendering or endangering democracy? The Internet civil society and the public sphere," *Asian Journal of Social Science*, 30: 287–303.

Bainbridge, B., and Lon Nara. (2002) "Kidnapping spectre haunts Cambodian parents," *Phnom Penh Post*, (8–21 November). Available HTTP: <http://www.phnompenhpost.com> (accessed 4 November 2009).

Banerjee, T. (2001) "The future of public space," *Journal of the American Planning Association*, 67: 9–24.

Banister, J., and E. P. Johnson. (1993) "After the nightmare: The population of Cambodia," in B. Kiernan (ed.) *Genocide and Democracy in Cambodia: The Khmer Rouge, the United Nations and the International Community*, New Haven, CT: Yale University Southeast Asian Studies, pp. 65–140.

Bar-On, B. (2002) *The Subject of Violence: Arendtean Exercises in Understanding*, New York, NY: Rowman and Littlefield Publishers, Inc.

Barton, C. (2007) "Rhetoric vs reality: Touch talk little comfort in Andong," *Phnom Penh Post* (May 4–17): 3.

Becker, E. (1998) *When the War Was Over: Cambodia and the Khmer Rouge Revolution*, 2nd edn, New York, NY: PublicAffairs.

Bell, D. A. (1996) "The East Asian challenge to human rights: Reflections on an East West Dialogue," *Human Rights Quarterly*, 18: 641–67.

Bell, D. A., and K. Jayasuriya. (1995) "Understanding illiberal democracy: A framework," in D. A. Bell, D. Brown, K. Jayasuriya, and D. M. Jones (eds.) *Towards Illiberal Democracy in Pacific Asia*, New York, NY: St. Martin's Press, pp. 1–16.

Benson, P., E. F. Fischer, and K. Thomas. (2008) "Resocializing suffering: Neoliberalism, accusation, and the sociopolitical context of Guatemala's new violence," *Latin American Perspectives*, 35: 38–58.

Beresford, M. (2005) "Cambodia in 2004: An artificial democratization process," *Asian Survey*, 45: 134–39.

Berger, M. T. (2000) "Up from neoliberalism: Free-market mythologies and the coming crisis in global capitalism," *Third World Quarterly*, 20: 453–63.

Berman, B. (1993) "The politics of culture: Part three; Kosher Szechuan," *The Whig-Standard Magazine* (23 January): 8–10.

Berthiaume, L., Phann Ana. (2005a) "Court drops grenade attack case against PM," *The Cambodia Daily* (20 January): 15.

—— (2005b) "Families facing eviction told development requires 'sacrifices'." *The Cambodia Daily* (2 April): 3.

Berthiaume, L., Phann Ana, Prack Chan Thul, Saing Soenthrith, Kuch Naren, and W. Shaw. (2004) "Man ignites self near PM's house," *The Cambodia Daily* (18 November): 1–2.

Berthiaume, L., and Nhem Chea Bunly. (2005) "Mall planned on Tonle Bassac commune site," *The Cambodia Daily* (25 January): 12.

Berthiaume, L., and Prak Chan Thul. (2005) "Villagers say police forces shot to kill," *The Cambodia Daily* (23 March): 1–2.

Bill, J. A. (1973) "Political violence and political change: A conceptual commentary," in H. Hirsch, and D. C. Perry (eds.) *Violence as Politics: A Series of Original Essays*, New York, NY: Harper and Row Publishers, pp. 220–31.

Bit, S. (1991) *The Warrior Heritage: A Psychological Perspective of Cambodian Trauma*, El Cerrito, CA: Seanglim Bit.

Bjornlund, E. (2001) "Democracy Inc.," *The Wilson Quarterly*, 25: 18–24.

Bjornlund, E., and J. Course. (1998) *The Continuing Crisis in Cambodia: Obstacles to Democratic Elections*, Report (30 January), Washington, DC: International Republican Institute and National Democratic Institute for International Affairs.

Blomley, N. (2000) " 'Acts,' 'deeds' and the violences of property," *Historical Geography*, 28: 86–107.

—— (2003) "Law, property, and the geography of violence: The frontier, the survey, and the grid," *Annals of the Association of American Geographers*, 93: 121–41.

Blum, W. (1998) *Killing Hope: U.S. Military and CIA Interventions since World War II*, Montreal: Black Rose.

Bondi, L. (1996) "Gender, class, and urban space: Public and private space in contemporary urban landscapes," *Urban Geography*, 17: 160–85.

Bondi, L., and M. Domosh. (1998) "On the contours of public space: A tale of three women," *Antipode* 30: 270–89.

Borras, S., and E. Ross. (2007) "Land rights, conflict, and violence amid neo-liberal globalization," *Peace Review: A Journal of Social Justice* 19: 1–4.

Bosley, J., S. Owen, and G. Armstrong. (1997) *Program Assessment Mission to Cambodia*, Final Report (September), Ottawa: Parliamentary Centre.

Botumroath Lebun. (2004) "Rights groups protest illegal round-ups of city homeless," *The Cambodia Daily* (22 November): 17.

Bou Saroeun. (1998) "Casualty figures fluid as violence continues," *Phnom Penh Post*, Special Edition (12–17 September): 4.

Bou Saroeun, and P. Sainsbury. (1999) "Militias bring spectre of lynch mobs," *Phnom Penh Post* (17–30 September): 4.

Bourgois, P. (2001) "The power of violence in war and peace: post-Cold War lessons from El Salvador," *Ethnography*, 2: 5–34.

Boutros-Ghali, B. (1995) *The United Nations and Cambodia 1991–1995*, New York, NY: United Nations Department of Public Information.

Boyer, M. C. (1992) "Cities for sale: Merchandising history at South Street Seaport", in M. Sorkin (ed.) *Variations on a Theme Park: The New American City*, New York, NY: Hill and Wang, pp. 181–204.

Brenner, N., and N. Theodore. (2002) "Cities and the geographies of 'actually existing neoliberalism'," *Antipode*, 34: 349–79.

Brown, F. (1992) "Cambodia in 1991: An uncertain peace," *Asian Survey*, 32: 88–96.

—— (1993) "Cambodia in 1992: Peace at peril," *Asian Survey*, 33: 83–90.

Brown, F., and D. G. Timberman. (1998) "Peace, development, and democracy in Cambodia: Shattered hopes," in F. Z. Brown, and D. G. Timberman (eds.) *Cambodia and the International Community: The Quest for Peace, Development, and Democracy*, New York: Asia Society, pp. 13–32.

Brown, M., and J. J. Zasloff. (1998) *Cambodia Confounds the Peacemakers 1979–1998*, Ithaca, NY: Cornell University Press.

Burk, A. L. (2003) "Private griefs, public places," *Political Geography*, 22: 317–33.

Calhoun, C. (1998) "Community without propinquity revisited: Communication technology and the transformation of the urban public sphere," *Social Inquiry*, 68: 373–97.

Cammack, P. (1997) *Capitalism and Democracy in the Third World: The Doctrine for Political Development*, London: Leicester University Press.

Canterbury, D. C. (2005). *Neoliberal Democratization and New Authoritarianism*, Burlington, VT: Ashgate.

Carney, T. (1989) "The unexpected victory," in K. D. Jackson (ed.) *Cambodia 1975–1978: Rendezvous with Death*, Princeton, NJ: Princeton University Press, pp. 13–36.

Carr, S., M. Francis, L. G. Rivlin, and A. M. Stone. (1992) *Public Space*, Cambridge, UK: Cambridge University Press.

Carroll, W. K., and C. Carson. (2006) "Neoliberalism, capitalist class formation and the global network of corporations and policy groups," in D. Plehwe, B. Walpen, and G. Neunhoffer (eds.) *Neoliberal Hegemony: A Global Critique*, New York: Routledge, pp. 51–69.

Casey, M. (2004) "De-dyking queer space(s): Heterosexual female visibility in gay and lesbian spaces," *Sexualities*, 7: 446–62.

Chandler, D. P. (1991) *The Tragedy of Cambodian History: Politics, War, and Revolution Since 1945*, New Haven, CT: Yale University Press.

—— (1996) *A History of Cambodia*, Boulder, CO: Westview Press.

—— (1998a) "Cambodia's historical legacy," in D. Hendrickson (ed.) *Safeguarding Peace: Cambodia's Constitutional Challenge*, Accord: An international review of peace initiatives, London: Conciliation Resources, pp. 12–20.

—— (1998b) "The burden of Cambodia's past," in F. Z. Brown and D. G. Timberman (eds.) *Cambodia and the International Community: The Quest for Peace, Development, and Democracy*, New York, NY: Asia Society, pp. 33–48.

—— (1999) *Voices from S-21: Terror and History in Pol Pot's Secret Prison*, Berkley, CA: University of California Press.

Chanthou Boua. (1993) "Development aid and democracy in Cambodia," in B. Kiernan (ed.) *Genocide and Democracy in Cambodia: The Khmer Rouge, the United Nations and the International Community*, New Haven, CT: Yale Southeast Asia Studies, pp. 273–83.

Chea Sotheacheath, and J. Eckardt. (1998) "Activist monks dare to defy authorities," *Phnom Penh Post*, Special Edition (12–17 September): 2.

Cheang Sokha. (2007) "Rights groups echo PM's fear of farmer revolution," *Phnom Penh Post* (9–22 February): 4.

Chhay Channyda. (2009) "Sidewalk vendors face eviction," *Phnom Penh Post*

(25 August): Available HTTP: <http://www.phnompenhpost.com> (accessed 4 November 2009).

Chomsky, N. (1991) *Necessary Illusions: Thought Control in Democratic Societies*, Don Mills, Ontario: Anansi.

Chopra, J. (1994) *United Nations Authority in Cambodia*, Occasional Paper 15. Providence, RI: The Thomas J. Watson Jr. Institute for International Studies.

Chossudovsky, M. (1997) *The Globalization of Poverty: Impacts of IMF and World Bank Reforms*, London: Zed Books.

Church, P. (ed.) (1997) *Focus on Southeast Asia*, St. Leonards, Australia: Allen and Unwin.

Clifford, J. (1988) *The Predicament of Culture: Twentieth-Century Ethnography, Literature, and Art*, Cambridge, MA: Harvard University Press.

Cochrane, L., and Cheang Sokha. (2004) "Vichea murder: 2 arrests," *Phnom Penh Post* (30 January–12 February). Available HTTP: <http://www.phnompenhpost.com> (accessed 04 November 2009).

Cochrane, L., L. Hunt, and Vong Sokheng. (2004) "Rainsy disputes 'bloody street-fight' story," *Phnom Penh Post* (27 August–9 September): 1, 3.

Cochrane, L., S. Rith, and Vong Sokheng. (2004) "Rainsy summoned by court," *Phnom Penh Post* (5–18 November). Available HTTP: <http://www.phnompenhpost.com> (accessed 4 November 2009).

Cohen, J. L., and Arato, A. (1992) *Civil Society and Political Theory*, Cambridge, MA: MIT Press.

Coleman, L. (2007) "The gendered violence of development: Imaginative geographies of exclusion in the imposition of neo-liberal capitalism," *The British Journal of Politics and International Relations*, 9: 204–19.

Colhoun, J. (1990) "On the side of Pol Pot: U.S. supports Khmer Rouge," *Covert Action Quarterly*, 34 (Summer): 37–40.

Cooper, M. (2004) "Insecure times, tough decisions: The *nomos* of neoliberalism," *Alternatives*, 29: 515–33.

Cope, M. (1996) "Weaving the everyday: Identity, space, and power in Lawrence, Massachusetts, 1920–39," *Urban Geography*, 17: 179–204.

Corfield, J., and L. Summers. (2003) *Historical Dictionary of Cambodia*, Oxford: The Scarecrow Press, Inc.

Cowen, M., and R. Shenton. (1995) "The invention of development," in J. Crush (ed.) *Power of Development*, New York, NY: Routledge, pp. 27–43.

Crang, M. (2000) "Public space, urban space and electronic space: Would the real city please stand up?" *Urban Studies*, 37: 307–17.

Crawford, M. (1992) "The world in a shopping mall," in M. Sorkin (ed.) *Variations on a Theme Park: The New American City*, New York, NY: Hill and Wang, pp. 3–30.

Crush, J. (1995) "Introduction: Imagining development," in J. Crush (ed.) *Power of Development*, New York, NY: Routledge, pp. 1–23.

Curtis, G. (1993) *Transition to What? Cambodia, UNTAC and the Peace Process*, United Nations Research Institute for Social Development Discussion Paper (November), Geneva: UNRISD.

—— (1998) *Cambodia Reborn? The Transition to Development and Democracy*, Washington, DC: Brookings Institution Press.

Cybriwsky, R. (1999) "Changing patterns of urban public space: Observations and assessments from the Tokyo and New York metropolitan areas," *Cities*, 16: 223–31.

Dahl, R. A. (1971) *Polyarchy: Participation and Opposition*, New Haven, CT: Yale University Press.

Daly, G. (1998) "Homelessness and the street: Observations from Britain, Canada and the United States," in N. R. Fyfe (ed.) *Images of the Street: Planning, Identity and Control in Public Space*, London: Routledge, pp. 111–28.

Dasgupta, B. (1998) *Structural Adjustment, Global Trade, and the New Political Economy of Development*, New York, NY: Zed Books.

Dasgupta, P. (1993) *An Inquiry into Well-Being and Destitution*, New York, NY: Oxford University Press.

Davies, J. C. (1973) "Political violence: The domination-submission nexus," in H. Hirsch, and D. C. Perry (eds.) *Violence as Politics: A Series of Original Essays*, New York: Harper and Row Publishers, pp. 52–71.

Davis, M. (1992) "Fortress Los Angeles: The militarization of urban space," in M. Sorkin (ed.) *Variations on a Theme Park: The New American City*, New York, NY: Hill and Wang, pp. 154–80.

Day, K. (2001) "Constructing masculinity and women's fear in public space in Irvine, California," *Gender, Place and Culture*, 8: 109–27.

Dean, J. (2003) "Why the Net is not a public sphere," *Constellations*, 10: 95–112.

Diamond, L. (1989) "Introduction: Persistence, erosion, breakdown," in. L. Diamond, J. J. Linz, and S. M. Lipset (eds.) *Democracy in Developing Countries, Volume Three: Asia*, Boulder, CO: Lynne Rienner Publishers, Inc., pp. 1–52.

—— (1992). "Introduction: Civil society and the struggle for democracy," in L. Diamond (ed.) *The Democratic Revolution: Struggles for Freedom and Pluralism in the Developing World*, New York: Freedom House, pp. 1–27

—— (1993). "Introduction: Political culture and democracy," in L. Diamond (ed.) *Political Culture and Democracy in Developing Countries*, Boulder: Lynne Rienner Publishers, pp. 1–33.

—— (1994). "Rethinking civil society: Toward democratic consolidation," *Journal of Democracy* 5: 4–17.

—— (1999) *Developing Democracy: Towards Consolidation*, Baltimore, MD: Johns Hopkins University Press.

Diamond, L., J. J. Linz, and S. M. Lipset. (1989) Preface, in L. Diamond, J. J. Linz, and S. M. Lipset (eds.) *Democracy in Developing Countries, Volume Three: Asia*, Boulder: Lynne Rienner Publishers, pp. ix–xxvii.

Diamond, L., and M. F. Plattner. (1993) "Introduction," in L. Diamond, and M. F. Plattner (eds.) *The Global Resurgence of Democracy*, Baltimore: The Johns Hopkins University Press, pp. ix–xxvi.

Dollar, D., and A. Kraay. (2002) "Growth is good for the poor," *Journal of Economic Growth*, 7: 195–225.

Dommen, A. J. (2001) *The Indochinese Experience of the French and the Americans: Nationalism and Communism in Cambodia, Laos, and Vietnam*, Indianapolis, IN: Indiana University Press.

Donnelly, J. (1999) "Human rights and Asian values: A defense of 'Western' universalism'," in J. R. Bauer, and D. A. Bell (eds.) *The East Asian Challenge for Human Rights*, New York: Cambridge University Press, pp. 60–87.

Downie, S. (2000) "Cambodia's 1998 election: Understanding why it was not the 'miracle on the Mekong'," *Australian Journal of International Affairs*, 54: 43–61.

Doyle, K. (2005) "The revenue fields: A scandal erupts over the privatization of Cambodia's genocide memorial," *Time Asia Magazine* (11 April). Available HTTP:

<http://www.time.com/time/magazine/article/0,9171,1047552,00.html>   (accessed 4 November 2009).

Doyle, M. W. (1995) *UN Peacekeeping in Cambodia: UNTAC's Civil Mandate*, Boulder, CO: Lynne Rienner Publishers Inc.

—— (1997) "Authority and elections in Cambodia," in M. W. Doyle, I. Johnstone, and R. C. Orr (eds.) *Keeping the Peace: Multidimensional UN Operations in Cambodia and El Salvador,* New York: Cambridge University Press, pp. 134–64.

—— (1998) "Peacebuilding in Cambodia: The continuing quest for power and legitimacy," in F. Z. Brown, and D. G. Timberman (eds.) *Cambodia and the International Community: The Quest for Peace, Development, and Democracy*, New York: Asia Society, pp. 79–100.

Drummond, L. (2000) "Street scenes: Practices of public and private space in urban Vietnam," *Urban Studies*, 37: 2377–91.

Duffy, T. (1994) "Toward a culture of human rights in Cambodia," *Human Rights Quarterly*, 16: 82–104.

Duménil, G., and Lévy, D. (2004) *Capital Resurgent: Roots of the Neoliberal Revolution*, Cambridge, MA: Harvard University Press.

Duncan, N. (1996) "Renegotiating gender and sexuality in public and private spaces," in N. Duncan (ed.) *Bodyspace*, London: Routledge, pp. 127–45.

Ear, S. (1997) "Cambodia and the 'Washington consensus'," *Crossroads: An Interdisciplinary Journal of Southeast Asian Studies*, 11: 73–97.

—— (2006). "The political economy of aid, governance, and policy-making: Cambodia in global, national, and sectoral perspectives," unpublished thesis, Berkeley: University of California, Berkeley.

Eckardt, J. (1998) "Voter registration tops 97%," *Phnom Penh Post* (19 June–2 July): 3.

Eckardt, J., and Chea Sotheacheath. (1998) "Diary of a demonstration," *Phnom Penh Post* (4–17 September): 4.

Economist. (1997a) "Demo of death," *Economist* (5 April): 35–36.

—— (1997b) "Victims of Cambodia's coup," *Economist* (13 September): 42.

Economist Intelligence Unit. (2009) *Political Stability Index 2009*. Report (25 March). Available HTTP: <http://viewswire.eiu.com/site_info.asp?info_name=social_unrest_table&page = noads&rf = 0> (accessed 4 November 2009).

Edensor, T. (1998) "The culture of the Indian street," in N. R. Fyfe (ed.) *Images of the Street: Planning, Identity and Control in Public Space*, London: Routledge, pp. 205–23.

Edmonton Journal. (1996) "Eco briefs," *Edmonton Journal* (25 February): E7.

Edwards, M. (2004) *Civil society*, Malden, MA: Polity Press.

Elsley, S. (2004) "Children's experience of public space," *Children & Society*, 18: 155–65.

Embree, A. T. (2002) "Religion in public space: Two centuries of a problem in governance in modern India," *India Review*, 1: 52–76.

Emerson, D. K. (1984) " 'Southeast Asia': What's in a name?," *Journal of Southeast Asian Studies*, 15: 1–21.

Eng, P. (1998) "Cambodian democracy: In a bleak landscape, strong signs of hope," *The Washington Quarterly*, 21: 71–91.

Entrikin, J. N. (2002) "Perfectibility and democratic place-making," in R. D. Sack (ed.) *Progress: Geographical Essays*, Baltimore, MA: Johns Hopkins University Press, pp. 97–112.

Escobar, A. (1995) *Encountering Development: The Making and Unmaking of the Third World*, Princeton, NJ: Princeton University Press.

—— (2004) "Development, violence and the new imperial order," *Development*, 47: 15–21.

Etounga-Manguelle, D. (2000) "Does Africa need a cultural adjustment program?" in L. E. Harrison, and S. P. Huntington (eds.) *Culture Matters: How Human Values Shape Human Progress*, New York: Basic Books, pp. 65–77.

European Union Election Observation Mission. (2008) *Kingdom of Cambodia Final Report: National Assembly Elections, 27 July 2008*, Report (13 October). Available HTTP: <http://www.eueomcambodia.org/English/Final_Report.html> (accessed 4 November 2009).

Evans, T. (2001) "If democracy, then human rights?," *Third World Quarterly*, 22: 623–42.

Farmer, P. (2004) "An anthropology of structural violence," *Current Anthropology*, 45: 305–25.

Faulder, D. (2000) "A state of injustice: Violence and impunity are alive and well", *Asiaweek* (3 March), np.

Feierabend, I. K., R. L. Feierabend, and T. R. Gurr. (1972) "Theories of revolution," in I. K. Feierabend, R. L. Feierabend, and T. R. Gurr (eds.) *Anger, Violence, and Politics: Theories and Research*, Englewood Cliffs, NJ: Prentice Hall Inc., pp. 1–7.

Fertl, D. (2005) "Ecuador: People drive out president," *Z Net* (25 April). Available HTTP: <http://www.zcommunications.org/znet/viewArticle/6399> (accessed 4 November 2009).

Findlay, T. (1995) *Cambodia: The Legacy and Lessons of UNTAC*, New York, NY: Oxford University Press.

Fraser, N. (1990) "Rethinking the public sphere: A contribution to the critique of actually existing democracy," *Social Texts*, 25/26: 56–80.

French, L. (2002) "From politics to economics at the Thai-Cambodian border: Plus Ca change . . .," *International Journal of Politics, Culture and Society*, 15: 427–70.

Frieson, K. (1993) "Revolution and rural response in Cambodia, 1970–75," in B. Kiernan (ed.) *Genocide and Democracy in Cambodia: The Khmer Rouge, the United Nations and the International Community*, New Haven, CT: Yale University Southeast Asian Studies, pp. 33–50.

—— (1996a) "The Cambodian elections of 1993: A case of power to the people?," in R. H. Taylor (ed.) *The Politics of Elections in Southeast Asia*, New York, NY: Woodrow Wilson Center Press, pp. 224–42.

—— (1996b) "The politics of getting the vote in Cambodia," in S. Heder, and J. Ledgerwood (eds.) *Propaganda, Politics, and Violence in Cambodia: Democratic Transition Under United Nations Peace-Keeping*, Armonk, NY: M.E. Sharpe, Inc., pp. 183–207.

—— (1997) "Cambodia in crisis," *Asia Pacific News*, 11: np.

Fukuyama, F. (1992) *The End of History and the Last Man*, New York, NY: The Free Press.

Fyfe, N. R. (1998) "Introduction: Reading the street," in N. R. Fyfe (ed.) *Images of the Street: Planning, Identity and Control in Public Space*, London: Routledge, pp. 1–10.

Gallup, J. C. (2002) "Cambodia: A shaky start for democracy," in J. F. Hsieh, and D. Newman (eds.) *How Asia Votes*, New York, NY: Chatham House Publishers of Seven Bridges Press, LLC., pp. 165–85.

Ganesan, N. (1997) "Cultural pluralism and the unifying potential of democracy in Southeast Asia," in M. Schmiegelow (ed.) *Democracy in Asia*, New York, NY: St. Martin's Press, pp. 195–214.

Geertz, C. (1988) *Works and Lives: The Anthropologist as Author*, Stanford, CA: Stanford University Press.

George, S. (1987) *A Fate Worse Than Debt*, New York, NY: Grove Weidenfeld.

—— (1992) *The Debt Boomerang*, Boulder, CO: Westview.

Gillespie, W. (2006) "Capitalist world-economy, globalization, and violence: implications for criminology and social justice," *International Criminal Justice Review*, 16: 24–44.

Giorgi, L., J. Crowley, and S. Ney. (2001) "Surveying the European public space: A political and research agenda," *Innovation*, 14: 73–83.

Giroux, H. A. (2004) *The Terror of Neoliberalism: Authoritarianism and the Eclipse of Democracy*, Boulder, CO: Paradigm Publishers.

Glassman, J. (1999) "State power beyond the 'territorial trap': The internationalization of the state," *Political Geography*, 18: 669–96.

—— (2005) "On the borders of Southeast Asia: Cold War geography and the construction of the other," *Political Geography*, 24: 784–807.

Glassman, J., and Samatar, A. I. (1997) "Development geography and the global south state," *Progress in Human Geography*, 21: 164–98.

Global Witness. (1997) *Just Deserts for Cambodia: Deforestation and the Co-Prime Ministers' Legacy to the Country*, Report (June), London: Global Witness.

Godfrey, M., Chan Sophal, T. Kato, Long Vou Piseth, Pon Dorina, Tep Saravy, Tia Savora, and Soso Vannarith. (2002) "Technical assistance and capacity development in an aid-dependent economy: The experience of Cambodia," *World Development*, 30: 355–73.

Goheen, P. G. (1994) "Negotiating access to public space in mid-nineteenth century Toronto," *Journal of Historical Geography*, 20: 430–49.

—— (1998) "Public space and the geography of the modern city," *Progress in Human Geography*, 22: 479–96.

—— (2003) "The assertion of middle-class claims to public space in late Victorian Toronto," *Journal of Historical Geography*, 29: 73–92.

Goldstein, D. (2005) "Flexible justice: Neoliberal violence and 'self-help' security in Bolivia," *Critique of Anthropology*, 25: 389–411.

Gollogly, L. (2002) "The dilemmas of aid: Cambodia 1992–2002," *The Lancet* 360: 793–98.

Goss, J. (1996) "Disquiet on the waterfront: Reflections on nostalgia and utopia in the urban archetypes of festival marketplaces," *Urban Geography*, 17: 221–47.

Grainger, M. (1998a) "Campaign 'hunting season' begins," *Phnom Penh Post* (3–16 July): 1, 3.

—— (1998b) "UN blasts CPP's domination of state run media," *Phnom Penh Post* (3–16 July): 4.

—— (1998c) "UNTAC officials speak out on election," *Phnom Penh Post* (4–17 September): 2, 15.

Grainger, M., and C. Chaumeau. (1998) "Old enemies of Hun Sen pulling strings?," *Phnom Penh Post*, Special Edition (12–17 September): Available HTTP: <http://www.phnompenhpost.com> (accessed 4 November 2009).

Gray, J. (1998) *False Dawn: The Delusions of Global Capitalism*, London: Granta Books.

Green, C. (2002) "Rise in mob killings worries UN," *Phnom Penh Post* (21 June–4 July): Available HTTP: <http://www.phnompenhpost.com> (accessed 4 November 2009).

—— (2003) "$35m up for grabs as PM orders privatization," *Phnom Penh Post* (31 January–13 February). Available HTTP: <http://www.phnompenhpost.com> (accessed 4 November 2009).

Grugel, J. (2002) *Democratization: A Critical Introduction*, New York, NY: Palgrave.

Gupta, A., and J. Ferguson. (1997) "Culture, power, place: Ethnography at the end of an era," in A. Gupta, and J. Ferguson (eds.) *Culture, Power, Place: Explorations in Critical Anthropology*, Durham, NC: Duke University Press, pp. 1–32.

Gupta, D. (1990) *The Economics of Political Violence: The Effect of Political Instability on Economic Growth*, New York, NY: Praeger Publishers.

Haas, M. (1991) *Cambodia, Pol Pot, and the United States: The Faustian Pact*, New York, NY: Praeger Publishers.

Habermas, J. (1989) *The Structural Transformation of the Public Sphere*, Cambridge, MA: The MIT Press.

Hadenius, A., and F. Uggla. (1996) "Making civil society work, promoting demo-cratic development: what can states and donors do?," *World Development*, 24: 1621–39.

Halbert, D. J. (2002) "Citizenship, pluralism, and modern public space," *Innovation*, 15: 33–42.

Hammarberg, T. (2000) *Situation of Human Rights in Cambodia*, Report of the Special Representative of the Secretary-General of human rights in Cambodia (13 January), New York, NY: United Nations Economic and Social Council.

Harrison, L. E., and S. P. Huntington (eds.) (2000) *Culture Matters: How Human Values Shape Human Progress*, New York: Basic Books.

Harvey, D. (1992) "Social justice, postmodernism and the city," *International Journal of Urban and Regional Research*, 16: 558–601.

—— (2000) *Spaces of Hope*, Edinburgh: Edinburgh University Press.

—— (2001) *Spaces of Capital: Towards a Critical Geography*, New York, NY: Routledge.

—— (2005) *A Brief History of Neoliberalism*, New York, NY: Oxford University Press.

Hayes, M. (1998) "Another chapter opens as Hun Sen gives Ranariddh the deal," *Phnom Penh Post*, (27 November–December): 1, 3.

Haynes, J. (1997) *Democracy and Civil Society in the Third World: Politics and New Political Movements*, Malden, MA: Polity Press.

Heder, S. (1995) "Cambodia's democratic transition to neoauthoritarianism," *Current History*, 94: 425–29.

—— (1996) "The resumption of armed struggle by the Party of Democratic Kampuchea: Evidence from National Army of Democratic Kampuchea 'self-demobilizers'," in S. Heder, and J. Ledgerwood (eds.) *Propaganda, Politics, and Violence in Cambodia: Democratic Transition Under United Nations Peace-Keeping*, Armonk, NY: M.E. Sharpe, Inc., pp. 73–113.

Heder, S., and J. Ledgerwood. (1996) "Politics of violence: An introduction," in S. Heder, and J. Ledgerwood (eds.) *Propaganda, Politics, and Violence in Cambodia: Democratic Transition Under United Nations Peace-Keeping*, Armonk, NY: M.E. Sharpe, Inc., pp. 3–49.

Hee, L., and G. L. Ooi. (2003) "The politics of public space planning in Singapore," *Planning Perspectives*, 18: 79–103.

Heininger, J. E. (1994) *Peacekeeping in Transition: The United Nations in Cambodia*, New York, NY: The Twentieth Century Fund Press.

Henaff, M., and T. B. Strong. (2001a) "Conclusion: Public space, virtual space, and democracy," in M. Henaff, and T. B. Strong (eds.) *Public Space and Democracy*, Minneapolis, MN: University of Minnesota Press, pp. 221–31

—— (2001b) "The conditions of public space: Vision, speech and theatricality," in M. Henaff, and T. B. Strong (eds.) *Public Space and Democracy,* Minneapolis, MN: University of Minnesota Press, pp. 1–31

Hendrickson, D. (1998) "Full text of the Paris agreements with commentary," in D. Hendrickson (ed.) *Safeguarding Peace: Cambodia's Constitutional Challenge*, Accord: An international review of peace initiatives, London: Conciliation Resources, pp. 43–70.

—— (2001) "Globalization, insecurity and post-war reconstruction: Cambodia's precarious transition," *IDS Bulletin*, 32: 98–105.

Herbert, S. (1998) "Policing contested space: On patrol at Smiley and Sauser," in N. R. Fyfe (ed.) *Images of the Street: Planning, Identity and Control in Public Space*, London: Routledge, pp. 225–35.

Herman, E. S. (1997) "Pol Pot and Kissinger: On war criminality and impunity," *Z Magazine* (September). Available HTTP: <http://www.zmag.org/zmag/view Article/12966> (4 November 2009).

Hershkovitz, L. (1993) "Tiananmen Square and the politics of place," *Political Geography*, 12: 395–420.

Heuveline, P. (2001) "Approaches to measuring genocide: Excess mortality during the Khmer Rouge period," in D. Chirot, and M. E. P. Selgman (eds.) *Ethnopolitical Warfare: Causes, Consequences, and Possible Solutions*, Washington, DC: American Psychological Association, pp. 93–108.

Hewison, K., G. Rodan, and R. Robison. (1993) "Introduction: Changing forms of state power in Southeast Asia," in K. Hewison, G. Rodan, and R. Robison (eds.) *Southeast Asia in the 1990s: Authoritarianism, Democracy and Capitalism*, St. Leonards, Australia: Allen and Unwin, pp. 2–8.

Hewitt, C. (1993) *Consequences of Political Violence*, Aldershot: Dartmouth.

Hibbs, D. (1973) *Mass Political Violence: A Cross-National Causal Analysis*, Toronto: John Wiley and Sons, Inc.

Hinton, A. (2006) "Khmerness and the Thai 'Other': Violence, discourse and symbolism in the 2003 anti-Thai riots in Cambodia," *Journal of Southeast Asian Studies*, 37: 445–68.

Hippler, J. (1995) "The democratization of the Third World after the end of the Cold War," in J. Hippler (ed.) *The Democratization of Disempowerment: The Problem of Democracy in the Third World*, London: Pluto Press, pp. 1–31.

Hirsch, H., and D. C. Perry. (1973) "Introduction," in H. Hirsch, and D. C. Perry (eds.) *Violence as Politics: A Series of Original Essays*, New York, NY: Harper and Row Publishers, pp. xi–xv.

Honderich, T. (1980) *Violence for Equality: Inquiries in Political Philosophy*, Markham, ON: Penguin Books Canada Ltd.

Hood, M., and D. A. Ablin. (1990) "The path to Cambodia's present," in D. A. Ablin, and M. Hood (eds.) *The Cambodian Agony*, Armonk, NY: M.E. Sharpe, Inc., pp. xv–lxi.

Howell, P. (1993) "Public space and the public sphere: Political theory and the historical geography of modernity," *Environment and Planning D: Society and Space*, 11: 303–22.

Hubbard, P. (2001) "Sex zones: Intimacy, citizenship and public space," *Sexualities*, 4: 51–72.

Hughes, C. (1996) *UNTAC in Cambodia: The Impact on Human Rights*, Singapore: Institute of Southeast Asian Studies.

—— (1999) "Surveillance and resistance in the Cambodian elections: The prisoner's dilemma?" *Southeast Asian Affairs*: 92–109.

—— (2001a) "Cambodia: Democracy or dictatorship?" *Southeast Asian Affairs*: 113–29.

—— (2001b) "Khmer land, Khmer soul: Sam Rainsy, populism, and the problem of seeing Cambodia," *South East Asia Research*, 9: 45–71.

—— (2001c) "Transforming oppositions in Cambodia," *Global Society*, 15: 295–318.

—— (2002a) "International intervention and the people's will: The demoralization of democracy in Cambodia," *Critical Asian Studies*, 34: 539–62.

—— (2002b) "Parties, protest and pluralism in Cambodia," *Democratization*, 9: 165–86.

—— (2003a) "Phnom Penh: Beautification and corruption," *IIAS Bulletin*, 31 (July): 13.

—— (2003b) *The Political Economy of Cambodia's Transition, 1991–2001*, New York: RoutledgeCurzon.

—— (2009a) "Cambodia in 2008: Consolidation in the midst of crisis," *Asian Survey*, 49: 206–12.

—— (2009b) *Dependent Communities: Aid and Politics in Cambodia and East Timor*, Ithaca, NY: Cornell Southeast Asia Program.

Human Rights Watch. (1997) *Aftermath of the coup*, Report 9.8 (August). Available HTTP: <http://www.hrw.org/reports/1997/cambodia/> (accessed 4 November 2009).

—— (1998a) *Cambodia: Fair Elections Not Possible*, Report 10.4 (June). Available HTTP: <http://www.hrw.org/en/reports/1998/06/01/cambodia-fair-elections-not-possible> (accessed 4 November 2009).

—— (1998b) *Statement by Human Rights Watch, Asia Division to the Senate Foreign Relations Committee Subcommittee on East Asia and the Pacific. Press*, Oral Statement (2 October). Available HTTP: <http://www.hrw.org/en/news/1998/10/01/statement-human-rights-watch-asia-division> (accessed 4 November 2009).

—— (1999) *Impunity in Cambodia: How Human Rights Offenders Escape Justice*, Report 11.3 (June). Available HTTP: <http://www.hrw.org/legacy/reports/1999/cambo2/> (accessed 4 November 2009).

—— (2002a) *Cambodia's Commune Council Elections*, Backgrounder (January). Available HTTP: <http://www.hrw.org/legacy/backgrounder/asia/cambodia_elections.htm> (4 November 2009).

—— (2002b) *Cambodia's Commune Elections: Setting the Stage for National Elections*, Report 14.4 (April). Available HTTP: <http://www.hrw.org/legacy/reports/2002/cambo0402/> (accessed 4 November 2009).

—— (2003a) *Don't Bite the Hand that Feeds You: Coercion, Threats, and Vote-Buying in Cambodia's National Elections*, Briefing Paper (July). Available HTTP: <http://www.hrw.org/legacy/backgrounder/asia/cambodia/elections.htm> (accessed 4 November 2009).

—— (2003b) *The Run Up to Cambodia's National Assembly Election: Political*

Expression and Freedom of Assembly Under Assault, Briefing Paper (June). Available HTTP: <http://www.hrw.org/legacy/backgrounder/asia/cambodia/> (accessed 4 November 2009).

—— (2008) *Cambodia: Murder of Journalist Jolts Run-Up to Election*, News Brief (July): Available HTTP: <http://www.hrw.org/en/news/2008/07/15/cambodia-murder-journalist-jolts-run-election> (4 November 2009)

—— (2009) *Cambodia: End Assault on Opposition, Critics*, News Brief (July). Available HTTP: <http://www.hrw.org/en/news/2009/07/14/cambodia-end-assault-opposition-critics> (4 November 2009).

Huntington, S. P. (1991) "Democracy's third wave," *Journal of Democracy*, 2: 12–34.

—— (1993) "The clash of civilizations," *Foreign Affairs*, 72: 22–49.

Iadicola, P., and A. Shupe. (2003) *Violence, Inequality and Human Freedom*, Toronto: Rowman and Littlefield Publishers, Inc.

Ingram, G. B., A. Bouthillette, and Y. Retter (eds.) (1997) *Queers in Space: Communities, Public Places, Sites of Resistance*, Seattle: Bay Press.

International Crisis Group. (2000) *Cambodia: The Elusive Peace Dividend*. ICG Asia, Report 8 (11 August). Available HTTP: <http://www.crisisgroup.org/home/index.cfm?id = 1425&l = 1> (accessed 4 November 2009).

International Monetary Fund. (2007) *Cambodia: Financial Position in the Fund* (October 22). Available HTTP: <http://www.imf.org/external/country/KHM/index.htm> (accessed 4 November 2009).

International Textile, Garment and Leather Workers' Federation. (2005) *WTO Inaction May Condemn Cambodian Garment Workers to Prostitution*, Press Release (20 January). Available HTTP: <http://www.itglwf.org/DisplayDocument.aspx?idarticle = 939&langue = 2> (accessed 4 November 2009).

Irvin, G. (1993) "Cambodia: Why recovery is unlikely in the short term," *The European Journal of Development Research*, 5: 123–41.

Jackson, K. D. (1989) "Introduction: The Khmer Rouge in context," in K. D. Jackson (ed.) *Cambodia 1975–1978: Rendezvous with Death*, Princeton, NJ: Princeton University Press, pp. 3–12.

Jackson, P. (1998) "Domesticating the street: The contested spaces of the high street and the mall," in N. R. Fyfe (ed.) *Images of the Street: Planning, Identity and Control in Public Space*, London: Routledge, pp. 176–91.

Jeldres, J. A. (1996) "Cambodia's fading hopes," *Journal of Democracy*, 7: 148–57.

Jenks Clarke, H. (2001) "Research for empowerment in a divided Cambodia," in M. Smyth, and G. Robinson (eds.) *Researching Violently Divided Societies*, New York, NY: United Nations University Press, pp. 92–105.

Jennar, R. M. (ed.) (1995) *The Cambodian Constitutions (1953–1993)*, Bangkok: White Lotus.

Jones, D. M., K. Jayasuriya, D. A. Bell, and D. Brown. (1995) "Towards a model of illiberal democracy," in D. A. Bell, D. Brown, K. Jayasuriya, and D. M. Jones (eds.) *Towards Illiberal Democracy in Pacific Asia*, New York, NY: St. Martin's Press, pp. 163–67.

Jones, S., and D. PoKempner. (1993) "Human rights in Cambodia: Past, present, and future," in D. A. Donovan, S. Jones, D. PoKempner, and R. J. Muscat (eds.) *Rebuilding Cambodia: Human Resources, Human Rights, and Law*, Washington DC: Johns Hopkins Foreign Policy Institute, pp. 43–68.

Kamm, H. (1998) *Cambodia: Report from a Stricken Land*, New York, NY: Arcade Publishing.

Kao Kim Hourn. (1998) "Cambodia and the international community: The road ahead," in F. Z. Brown, and D. G. Timberman (eds.) *Cambodia and the International Community: The Quest for Peace, Development, and Democracy*, New York, NY: Asia Society, pp. 187–202.

—— (1999) *Grassroots Democracy in Cambodia: Opportunities, Challenges and Prospects*, Phnom Penh: Cambodian Institute for Cooperation and Peace.

Kay Kimsong. (2004) "Route 4 tolls to begin charging all vehicles," *The Cambodia Daily*, (23 December): 16.

Kay Kimsong, and E. Wasson. (2005) "Postal, telephone services to be privatized," *The Cambodia Daily* (11 March): 20.

Keane, J. (ed.) (1988) *Civil Society and the State: New European Perspectives*, New York, NY: Verso.

Kevin, T. (2000a) "Cambodia and Southeast Asia," *Australian Journal of International Affairs*, 54: 33–41.

—— (2000b) "Cambodia's international rehabilitation, 1997–2000," *Contemporary Southeast Asia*, 22: 594–612.

Keyes, C. F. (2002) "The case of the Purloined Lintel: The politics of a Khmer shrine as a Thai national treasure," in C. J. Reynolds (ed.) *National Identity and its Defenders: Thailand Today*, Chiang-Mai: Silkworm Books, pp. 212–37.

Khy Sovuthy. (2009) "After 7 days, 525 penal code articles approved," *The Cambodia Daily: Weekly Review* (9–16 October): 14.

Kiernan, B. (1985) *How Pol Pot Came to Power: A History of Communism in Kampuchea, 1930–1975*, London: Verso.

—— (1992) "The Cambodian crisis, 1990–92: The UN plan, the Khmer Rouge, and the State of Cambodia," *Bulletin of Concerned Asian Scholars*, 24: 3–23.

—— (1993a) "The impact on Cambodia of the U.S. intervention in Vietnam," in J. S. Werner, and L. D. Huynh (eds.) *The Vietnam War: Vietnamese and American Perspectives*, Armonk, NY: M.E. Sharpe, pp. 216–29.

—— (1993b) "The inclusion of the Khmer Rouge in the Cambodian peace process: Causes and consequences," in B. Kiernan (ed.) *Genocide and Democracy in Cambodia: The Khmer Rouge, the United Nations and the International Community*, New Haven, CT: Yale Southeast Asia Studies, pp. 191–272.

—— (1996) *The Pol Pot Regime: Race, Power, and Genocide in Cambodia under the Khmer Rouge, 1975–79*, New Haven, CT: Yale University Press.

—— (2001) "Myth, nationalism and genocide," *Journal of Genocide Research*, 3: 187–206.

Kiljunen, K. (ed.) (1984) *Kampuchea: Decade of the Genocide: Report of a Finnish Inquiry Commission*, London: Zed Books Ltd.

Killick, T. (1995) *IMF Programmes in Developing Countries: Design and Impact*, New York: Routledge.

Kirby, M. (1995) "Human rights, the United Nations and Cambodia," *Australia Quarterly*, 67: 26–39.

Kobayashi, A. (1994) "Coloring the field: Gender, 'race', and the politics of fieldwork," *Professional Geographer*, 14: 73–80.

Koh Santepheap (2008) "Hun Sen: Nobody can topple Hun Sen." *Koh Santepheap* (March 24), trans. Vong Socheata. Available HTTP: <http://ki-media.blogspot.com/2008/03/hun-sens-speech-points-to-internal.html> (4 November 2009).

Korner, P., G. Maass, T. Siebold, and R. Tetzlaff. (1986) *The IMF and the Debt Crisis: A Guide to the Third World's Dilemma*, trans. P. Knight, London: Zed Books.

Ku, A. S. (2000) "Revisiting the notion of 'public' in Habermas's theory: Toward a theory of politics of public credibility," *Sociological Theory*, 18: 216–40.

Kuch Naren. (2005a) "Japan asked to comment on Choeung Ek lease," *The Cambodia Daily* (13 April): 12.

—— (2005b) "PM warns land-grabbers of a 'farmer revolution'," *The Cambodia Daily* (9 December): 17.

Kuch Naren, and Solana Pyne. (2004a) "Spiriting away the homeless," *The Cambodia Daily* (7–8 August): 4–5.

—— (2004b) "Villagers say Pheapimex still clearing," *The Cambodia Daily* (23 November): 1, 16.

Kurlantzick, J. (2000) "Letter from the killing fields: Cambodia now," *The Washington Quarterly*, 23: 21–26.

Lao Mong Hay. (1998a) "Building democracy in Cambodia: Problems and prospects," in F. Z. Brown, and D. G. Timberman (eds.) *Cambodia and the International Community: The Quest for Peace, Development, and Democracy*, New York, NY: Asia Society, pp. 169–86.

—— (1998b) "Cambodia's agonising quest: Political progress amidst institutional backwardness," in D. Hendrickson (ed.) *Safeguarding Peace: Cambodia's Constitutional Challenge*, Accord: An international review of peace initiative, London: Conciliation Resources, pp. 36–42.

Langran, I. V. (2001) "Cambodia in 2000: New hopes are challenged," *Asian Survey*, 41: 156–63.

Law, L. (2002) "Defying disappearance: Cosmopolitan public spaces in Hong Kong," *Urban Studies*, 39: 1625–45.

Le Billon, P. (2000) "The political ecology of transition in Cambodia, 1989–99: War, peace and forest exploitation," *Development and Change*, 31: 785–805.

—— (2002) "Logging in muddy waters: The politics of forest exploitation in Cambodia," *Critical Asian Studies*, 34: 563–86.

Le Billon, P., and S. Springer. (2007) "Between war and peace: violence and accommodation in the Cambodian logging sector," in W. de Jong, D. Donovan, and K. Abe (eds.) *Extreme Conflict and Tropical Forests*, New York, NY: Springer, pp. 17–36.

Le Vine, V. T. (2001) "Violence and the paradox of democratic renewal: A preliminary assessment," in D. C. Rapoport, and L. Weinberg (eds.) *The Democratic Experience and Political Violence*, Portland, OR: Frank Cass Publishers, pp. 261–92.

Leap, W. (ed.) (1999) *Pubic Sex / Gay Space*, New York, NY: Columbia University Press.

Lees, L. (1998) "Urban renaissance and the street: Spaces of control and contestation," in N. R. Fyfe (ed.) *Images of the Street: Planning, Identity and Control in Public Space*, London: Routledge, pp. 236–53.

Lees, L. H. (1994) "Urban public space and imagined communities in the 1980s and 1990s," *Journal of Urban History*, 20: 443–65.

Lefebvre, H. (1991) *The Production of Space*, trans. D. Nicholson-Smith, Oxford: Blackwell Publishers.

—— (1996) *Writings on Cities*, trans. E. Kofman, and E. Lebas, Cambridge, MA: Blackwell Publishers.

Ledgerwood, J. (nd) "The July 5–6 1997 'events': When is a coup not a coup?," *Cambodian Recent History and Contemporary Society: An Introductory Course*,

DeKalb, IL: Department of Anthropology and Center for Southeast Asian Studies, Northern Illinois University. Available HTTP: <http://www.seasite.niu.edu/khmer/Ledgerwood/july_56_1997_events.htm> (accessed 4 November 2009).

—— (1996) "Patterns of CPP political repression and violence during the UNTAC period," in S. Heder, and J. Ledgerwood (eds.) *Propaganda, Politics, and Violence in Cambodia: Democratic Transition Under United Nations Peace-Keeping*, Armonk, NY: M.E. Sharpe, Inc., pp. 114–33.

Ledgerwood, J., and J. Vijghen. (2002) "Decision-making in rural Khmer villages," in J. Ledgerwood (ed.) *Cambodia Emerges From the Past: Eight Essays*, DeKalb, IL: Southeast Asia Publications, Center for Southeast Asian Studies, Northern Illinois University, pp. 109–50.

Lempert, D. (2006) "Foreign aid: Creating conditions for the next civil war," *Phnom Penh Post*, Commentary (29 December 2006–11 January 2007): 14–15.

Levine, C. (2002) "The paradox of public art: Democratic space, the avant-garde and Richard Serra's 'Tilted Arc'," *Philosophy and Geography*, 5: 51–68.

Lewis, D. (2002) "Civil society in African contexts: reflections on the usefulness of a concept," *Development and Change*, 33: 569–86.

Leys, C. (1996) *The Rise and Fall of Development Theory*, Indianapolis, IN: Indiana University Press.

Lizée, P. (1993) "The challenge of conflict resolution in Cambodia," *Canadian Defence Quarterly*, 23: 35–38, 40, 42, 44.

—— (1994) "Peacekeeping, peace-building and the challenge of conflict resolution in Cambodia," in D. A. Charters (ed.) *Peacekeeping and the Challenge of Civil Conflict Resolution*, Proceedings of the sixth annual conflict studies conference, University of New Brunswick, September 1992, Fredericton: Centre for Conflict Studies, University of New Brunswick, pp. 135–48.

—— (1996) "Cambodia in 1995: From hope to despair," *Asian Survey*, 36: 83–88.

—— (1997) "Cambodia in 1996: Of crocodiles, tigers, and doves," *Asian Survey* 37: 65–71.

—— (2000) *Peace, Power and Resistance in Cambodia: Global Governance and the Failure of International Conflict Resolution*, New York: St. Martin's Press.

Llosa, M. V. (1993) "The culture of liberty," in L. Diamond, and M. F. Plattner (eds.) *The Global Resurgence of Democracy*, Baltimore, MD: The Johns Hopkins University Press, pp. 83–91.

Lor Chandara. (2004) "Summit security tightened after Jakarta blast," *The Cambodia Daily* (11 September): 3.

Lor Chandara, and Phann Ana. (2005) "NA to question ministers on land swaps," *The Cambodia Daily* (26–27 February): 3.

Low, S. M. (1996) "Spatializing culture: The social production and social construction of public space in Costa Rica," *American Ethnologist*, 23: 861–79.

Lummis, C. D. (1996) *Radical Democracy*, Ithaca: Cornell University Press.

Mabbett, I., and D. P. Chandler. (1995) *The Khmers*, Cambridge, MA: Blackwell Publishers.

MacEwan, A. (1999) *Neoliberalism or Democracy? Economic Strategy, Markets, and Alternatives for the 21st Century*, New York, NY: Zed Books.

Mah, H. (2000) "Phantasies of the public sphere: Rethinking the Habermas of historians," *Journal of Modern History*, 72: 153–82.

Manalansan, M. F. (2005) "Race, violence, and neoliberal spatial politics in the global city," *Social Text*, 23: 141–55.

Manzo, K. (1991) "Modernist discourse and the crisis of development theory," *Studies in Comparative International Development*, 26: 3–36.

Marchand, M. H. (2004) "Neo-liberal disciplining, violence and transnational organizing: the struggle for women's rights in Ciudad Juárez," *Development*, 47: 88–93.

Marks, S. P. (1994) "The new Cambodian constitution: From civil war to a fragile democracy," *Columbia Human Rights Law Review*, 26: 45–110.

Markussen, T. (2008) "Property rights, productivity, and common property resources: insights from rural Cambodia," *World Development*, 36: 2277–96.

Marston, J. (1994) "Metaphors of the Khmer Rouge," in M. M. Ebihara, C. A. Mortland, and J. Ledgerwood (eds.) *Cambodian Culture Since 1975: Homeland and Exile*, Ithaca, NY: Cornell University Press, pp. 105–18.

—— (2002) "Cambodia: Transnational pressures and local agendas," *Southeast Asian Affairs*: 95–108.

Martin, M. A. (1994) *Cambodia: A Shattered Society*, Berkley, CA: University of California Press.

Massey, D. (1994) *Space, Place and Gender*, Minneapolis, MN: University of Minnesota Press.

—— (2005) *For Space*, London, Sage.

Mattson, K. (1999) "Reclaiming and remaking public space: Toward an architecture for American democracy," *National Civic Review*, 88: 133–44.

McCann, E. (1999) "Race, protest and public space: Contextualizing Lefebvre in the U.S. city," *Antipode*, 32: 163–84.

McDowell, L. (1999) *Gender, Identity, and Place: Understanding Feminist Geographies*, Cambridge, MA: Polity Press.

McIlwaine, C. (1999) "Geography and development: violence and crime as development issues," *Progress In Human Geography*, 23: 453–63.

—— (2007) "From local to global to transnational civil society: re-framing development perspectives on the non-state sector," *Geography Compass*, 1: 1252–81.

McInroy, N. (2000) "Urban regeneration and public space: The story of an urban park," *Space and Polity*, 4: 23–40.

McLaren, E. (2006) "Foreign debts must be rescheduled to get IMF loan," *Phnom Penh Post*, (10 May–1 June): 4.

Meas Sokchea. (2009a) "Assembly passes demonstration law," *Phnom Penh Post* (22 October). Available HTTP: <http://www.phnompenhpost.com> (accessed 4 November 2009).

—— (2009b) "PM warns opponents away from lawsuits," *Phnom Penh Post* (13 August). Available HTTP: <http://www.phnompenhpost.com> (accessed 4 November 2009).

Mercer, C. (2002) "NGOs, civil society and democratization: A critical review of the literature," *Progress in Development Studies*, 2: 5–22.

Meyer, C. (1971) *Derrière Le Sourire Khmer*, Paris: Plon

Migdal, J.S. (1988) *Strong Societies and Weak States: State-Society Relations and State Capabilities in the Third World*, Princeton, NJ: Princeton University Press.

Miles, M. (2002) "After the public realm: Spaces of representation, transition and plurality," *International Journal of Art Design Education*, 19: 253–61

Milward, B. (2000) "What is structural adjustment?," in G. Mohan, E. Brown, B. Milward, and A. B. Zack-Williams (eds.) *Structural Adjustment: Theory, Practice, and Impacts*, New York, NY: Routledge, pp. 24–38.

Mitchell, D. (1995) "The end of public space? People's park, definitions of the

public, and democracy," *Annals of the Association of American Geographers*, 85: 108–33.
—— (1996a) "Introduction: Public space and the city," *Urban Geography*, 17: 127–31.
—— (1996b) "Political violence: Order, and the legal construction of public space: Power and the public forum doctrine," *Urban Geography*, 17: 152–78.
—— (1997a) "State restructuring and the importance of rights talk," in L. Staeheli, J. Kodras, and C. Flint (eds.) *State Devolution in America: Implications for a Diverse Society*, Thousand Oaks, CA: Sage Publications, pp. 7–38.
—— (1997b) "The annihilation of space by law: The roots and implications of anti-homeless laws in the United States," *Antipode*, 29: 303–35.
—— (2001) "Postmodern geographical praxis? The postmodern impulse in the war against the homeless in the post-justice city," in C. Minca (ed.) *Postmodern Geography: Theory and Praxis*, Oxford: Blackwell Publishers Inc., pp. 57–92.
—— (2003a) "The liberalization of free speech: Or, how protest in public space is silenced," *Stanford Agora: An Online Journal of Legal Perspectives*, 4: 1–45.
—— (2003b) *The Right to the City: Social Justice and the Fight for Public Space*, New York, NY: The Guilford Press.
Mockenhaupt, B. (2001) "Cambodia: Try again," *Far Eastern Economic Review*, (5 July): 27.
Moghadam, V. M. (2002) "Patriarchy, the Taleban and politics of public space in Afghanistan," *Women's Studies International Forum*, 25: 19–31.
Mohan, G. (2000) "Contested sovereignty and democratic contradictions: The political impacts of adjustment," in G. Mohan, E. Brown, B. Milward, and A. B. Zack-Williams (eds.) *Structural Adjustment: Theory, Practice, and Impacts*, New York, NY: Routledge, pp. 75–95.
—— (2002) "The disappointments of civil society: the politics of NGO intervention in Northern Ghana," *Progress in Human Geography*, 21: 125–54.
Mohan, G., E. Brown, B. Milward, and A. B. Zack-Williams (eds.) (2000) *Structural Adjustment: Theory, Practice, and Impacts*, New York, NY: Routledge.
Moorthy, B., and Samreth Sopha. (1998) "Grenade attack lights fuse of crackdown," *Phnom Penh Post*, Special Edition (12–17 September): 3, 7.
Moreau, R. (1998) "The culture of violence: can anyone destroy the legacy of Pol Pot?," *Newsweek* (4 May). Available HTTP: <http://www.newsweek.com/id/92323> (accessed 4 November 2009).
Multinational Monitor. (1997) "Malaysia's Samling vs. the world's saplings," *Multinational Monitor*, 18.9 (September): 17.
Munck, G. L., and C. Kumar. (1995) "Civil conflicts and the conditions for successful international intervention: A comparative study of Cambodia and El Salvador," *Review of International Studies*, 21: 159–81.
Mysliwiec, E. (1988) *Punishing the Poor: The International Isolation of Kampuchea*, Oxford: Oxfam.
National Election Committee (NEC). (2008) *Election Results*. Available HTTP: <http://www.necelect.org.kh/English/elecResults.htm> (11 February 2010).
Nautiyal, A. (1992) "Cambodia: A problem of peace and stability," *India Quarterly*, 48: 43–50.
Neher, C. D., and R. Marlay. (1995) *Democracy and Development in Southeast Asia*, Boulder, CO: Westview Press, Inc.
Neou, K. and J. C. Gallup. (1997) "Teaching human rights in Cambodia," *Journal of Democracy*, 8: 154–64.

—— (1999) "Conducting Cambodia's elections," *Journal of Democracy*, 10: 152–64.

Neubauer, I., and Pin Sisovann. (2005) "Police bulldoze tents of evicted S'ville families," *The Cambodia Daily* (14 March): 17.

Neumann, A. L. (2002) "Cambodia's newspapers emerge from a repressive era," *Nieman Reports*, 56: 71–73.

Nolin, C., and F. Shankar. (2000) "Gendered spaces of terror and assault: The testimonio of REMIII and the Commission for Historical Clarification in Guatemala," *Gender, Place and Culture*, 7: 265–86.

O'Connell, S., and Bou Saroeun. (2000) "Stupa standoff simmers after fourth round," *Phnom Penh Post* (26 May–8 June): 5.

O'Neil, M. L. (2002) "Youth curfews in the United States: The creation of public spheres for some young people," *Journal of Youth Studies*, 5: 49–68.

Ojendal, J. (1996) "Democracy lost? The fate of the U.N.-implanted democracy in Cambodia," *Contemporary Southeast Asia*, 18: 193–218.

Olsen, M. (1993) "Dictatorship, democracy and development," *American Political Science Review*, 87: 567–76.

Orwell, G. (1993) *A Collection of Essays*, San Diego, CA: Harcourt.

Osborne, B. S. (2001) "Landscapes, memory, monuments, and commemoration: Putting identity in its place," *Canadian Ethnic Studies*, 33: 39–77.

Osborne, M. (2000) "Cambodia," *Southeast Asian Affairs*: 101–12.

Ovesen, J., I.-B. Trankell, and J. Ojendall. (1996) *When Every Household is an Island: Social Organization and Power Structures in Rural Cambodia*, Uppsala: Uppsala Research Reports in Cultural Anthropology.

Owen, T., and B. Kiernan. (2006) "Bombs over Cambodia," *The Walrus* (October): 62–69.

Pape, E. (1998) "Will voters agree to bite the bullet," *Phnom Penh Post*, 7 (22 May–4 June): 8.

Parekh, B. (1981) *Hannah Arendt and the Search for a New Political Philosophy*, London: Macmillan Press.

Pateman, C. (1970) *Participation and Democratic Theory*, Cambridge, UK: Cambridge University Press.

Peang-Meth, A. (1991) "Understanding the Khmer: Sociological-cultural observations," *Asian Survey*, 31: 442–55.

—— (1997) "Understanding Cambodia's political developments," *Contemporary Southeast Asia*, 19: 286–308.

Peck, J. (2001) "Neoliberalizing states: thin policies/hard outcomes," *Progress in Human Geography*, 25: 445–55.

Peck, J., and A. Tickell. (2002) "Neoliberalizing space," *Antipode*, 34: 380–404.

Pen Khon. (2000) *Phnom Penh before and after 1997*, Phnom Penh: Raksmey Kampuchea.

Peou, S. (1997) *Conflict Neutralization in the Cambodia War: From Battlefield to Ballot-box*, New York, NY: Oxford University Press.

—— (1998a) "Cambodia in 1997: Back to square one?," *Asian Survey*, 38: 69–74.

—— (1998b) "Diplomatic pragmatism: ASEAN's response to the July 1997 coup," in D. Hendrickson (ed.) *Safeguarding Peace: Cambodia's Constitutional Challenge*, Accord: An international review of peace initiatives, London: Conciliation Resources, pp. 30–35.

—— (1998c) "Hun Sen's pre-emptive coup: Causes and consequences," *Southeast Asian Affairs*: 86–102.

—— (1999) "Cambodia in 1998: From hope to despair," *Asian Survey*, 39: 20–26.

—— (2000) *Intervention and Change in Cambodia: Towards Democracy?* New York, NY: St. Martin's Press.

Pile, S. (1997) "Introduction: Opposition, political identities and spaces of resistance," in S. Pile, and M. Keith (eds.) *Geographies of Resistance*, New York, NY: Routledge, pp. 1–32.

Pilger, J. (1997) "The long secret alliance: Uncle Sam and Pol Pot," *Covert Action Quarterly*, 62: 5–9.

—— (1998) "Friends of Pol Pot," *The Nation* (11 May): 4–5.

Pin Sisovann. (2005) "Gov't defends ban on public demonstrations," *The Cambodia Daily* (14 April): 12.

Pinkney, R. (1994) *Democracy in the Third World*, Boulder, CO: Lynne Rienner Publishers, Inc.

Pok Sokundara, and B. Moorthy. (1998) "Monks walk tight rope between peace and politics," *Phnom Penh Post* (2–15 October): 4.

Post Staff. (1998) "Democracy Square flattened, but protests live on," *Phnom Penh Post*, Special Edition (12–17 September): 7, 8.

—— (2003) "Mobs go berserk in anti-Thai frenzy: Thai embassy torched; businesses gutted," *Phnom Penh Post* (31 January–13 February). Available HTTP: <http://www.phnompenhpost.com> (accessed 4 November 2009).

—— (2004) 'Chea Vichea: The shooting and its aftermath,' *Phnom Penh Post* (30 January – 12 February). Available HTTP: <http://www.phnompenhpost.com> (accessed 4 November 2009).

—— (2009) 'Criticism of eviction mounts,' *Phnom Penh Post* (20 July). Available HTTP: <http://www.phnompenhpost.com> (accessed 4 November 2009).

Prak Chan Thul. (2009) 'City governor bans hanging laundry outside,' *The Cambodia Daily: Weekly Review* (4–10 April): 12.

Prak Chan Thul, and Eang Mengleng. (2009) 'Four people charged in anti-government case,' *The Cambodia Daily: Weekly Review* (12–16 January): 14.

Prasso, S. (1994) 'Cambodia: A heritage of violence,' *World Policy Journal*, 11: 71–77.

Preston, P. W. (1996) *Development Theory: An Introduction*, Malden, MA: Blackwell Publishers Ltd.

Przeworski, A. (1999) 'Minimalist conception of democracy: A defense,' in I. Shapiro, and C. Hacker-Cordón (eds.) *Democracy's Value*. New York, NY: Cambridge University Press, pp. 23–55.

Przeworski, A., J. A. Cheibub, and F. Limongi. (2003) 'Culture and democracy,' in R. A. Dahl, I. Shapiro, and J. A. Cheibub (eds.) *The Democracy Sourcebook*, Cambridge, MA: The MIT Press, pp. 181–90.

Purcell, M. (2005) 'Globalization, urban enfranchisement and the right to the city: Towards and urban politics of the inhabitant,' in D. Wastl-Walter, L. Staeheli, and L. Dowler (eds.) *Rights to the City*, IGU – Home of Geography, Publication Series, Volume III, Società Geografica Italiana, Rome.

Purtill, C. (2004) 'Route 1 expansion may displace 4000 families,' *The Cambodia Daily* (27 December): 1, 17.

Quinn, K. M. (1989) 'The pattern and scope of violence,' in K. D. Jackson (ed.) *Cambodia 1975–1979: Rendezvous with Death*, Princeton, NJ: Princeton University Press, pp. 179–208.

Rapley, J. (2002) *Understanding Development: Theory and Practice in the Third World*, Boulder, CO: Lynne Rienner Publishers, Inc.

—— (2004) *Globalization and Inequality: Neoliberalism's Downward Spiral*, Boulder, CO: Lynne Rienner.

Rapoport, D. C., and L. Weinberg. (2001) 'Introduction,' in D. C. Rapoport and L. Weinberg (eds.) *The Democratic Experience and Political Violence*, Portland: Frank Cass Publishers, pp. 1–14.

Rappa, A. L. (2002) 'Modernity and the politics of public space: An introduction,' *Innovation*, 15: 5–10

Ratner, S. R. (1995) *The New UN Peacekeeping: Building Peace in Lands of Conflict After the Cold War*, New York, NY: St. Martin's Press.

Reddi, V. M. (1970) *A History of the Cambodian Independence Movement, 1863–1955*, Tirupati: Sri Venkateswara University Press.

Rendell, J. (1998) 'Displaying sexuality: Gendered identities and the early nineteenth-century street,' in N. R. Fyfe (ed.) *Images of the Street: Planning, Identity and Control in Public Space*, London: Routledge, pp. 75–91.

Reno, W. (1995) *Corruption and State Politics in Sierra Leone*, New York, NY: Cambridge University Press.

Reynolds, L., and Yun Samean. (2004a) 'Gov't says begging villagers should go home,' *The Cambodia Daily* (29 November): 12.

—— (2004b) 'Ranariddh, Hun Sen sign coalition deal,' *The Cambodia Daily* (1 July): 1, 12.

Richmond, O. P., and J. Franks. (2007) 'Liberal hubris? Virtual peace in Cambodia,' *Security Dialogue*, 38: 27–49.

Riddell, B. (1992) 'Things fall apart again: Structural Adjustment Programmes in Sub-Saharan Africa,' *Journal of Modern African Studies*, 30: 115–28.

—— (2003a) 'A tale of contestation, disciples, and damned: The lessons of the spread of globalization into Trinidad and Tobago,' *Environment and Planning A*, 35: 659–78.

—— (2003b) 'The face of neo-liberalism in the Third World: Landscapes of coping in Trinidad and Tobago,' *Canadian Journal of Development Studies*, 24: 593–615.

Rist, G. (1997) *The History of Development: From Western Origins to Global Faith*, New York, NY: Zed Books.

Roberts, D. (1997) 'From bombs to ballots: US intervention in Cambodia,' *Covert Action Quarterly*, 62: 10–14.

—— (2001) *Political Transition in Cambodia 1991–99: Power, Elitism and Democracy*, Richmond, Surrey: Curzon Press.

Ruddick, S. (1996) 'Constructing difference in public spaces: Race, class, and gender as interlocking systems,' *Urban Geography*, 17: 132–51.

Rumdoul, H. (1997) 'Urban poverty: Evictions and housing rights,' in E. Mysliwiec, and C. Morris (eds.) *Dispute Resolution in Cambodia: A Road to Peace and Reconciliation*, Proceedings of a conference held in Phnom Penh Cambodia, 28–30 November 1995, Victoria: Institute for Dispute Resolution, University of Victoria, pp. 53–68.

Said, E. W. (2003) *Orientalism*, 25th Anniversary edn, New York, NY: Vintage Books.

Saing Soenthrith. (2004) 'Police bulldoze homes to enforce court order,' *The Cambodia Daily*, (1 September): 1, 13.

—— (2009) '5th suspect arrested, charged in link to Tiger Head Group,' *The Cambodia Daily: Weekly Review* (31 January – 6 February): 17.

Saing Soenthrith and Yun Samean. (2004) 'Hun Sen says opposition plans revolt,' *The Cambodia Daily* (19 July): 1–2.

Sainsbury, P. (1998) 'Burned like old rubbish,' *Phnom Penh Post* (24 April – 7 May): 1–2.

Samreth Sopha, and E. Moorthy. (1998) 'Media access one of the flashpoints of poll boycott threat,' *Phnom Penh Post* (22 May – 4 June): 8.

Sánchez-Prado, I. M. (2006) 'Amores perros: exotic violence and neoliberal fear,' *Journal of Latin American Cultural Studies*, 15: 39–57.

Sanderson, J. (2001) 'The Cambodian experience: A success story still?,' in R. Thakur, and A. Schnabel (eds.) *United Nations Peacekeeping Operations: Ad Hoc Missions, Permanent Engagement*, New York, NY: United Nations University Press, pp. 155–66.

Sanderson, J., and M. Maley. (1998) 'Elections and liberal democracy in Cambodia,' *Australian Journal of International Affairs*, 52: 241–53.

SarDesai, D. R. (1994) *Southeast Asia: Past and Present*, 3rd edn, Boulder, CO: Westview Press.

Sartori, G. (1995) 'How far can free government travel?,' *Journal of Democracy*, 6: 101–11.

Sato, S. (1997) 'Asia and Democracy,' in M. Schmiegelow (ed.) *Democracy in Asia*, New York, NY: St. Martin's Press, pp. 81–91.

Schmiegelow, M. (1997a) 'Democracy in Asia: Cultures, power economics and civilization,' in M. Schmiegelow (ed.) *Democracy in Asia*, New York, NY: St. Martin's Press, pp. 533–49.

—— (1997b) 'The meaning of democracy in Asia,' in M. Schmiegelow (ed.) *Democracy in Asia*, New York, NY: St. Martin's Press, pp. 21–59.

Schmitter, P. C., and T. L. Karl. (1993) 'What democracy is . . . and is not,' in L. Diamond, and M. F. Plattner (eds.) *The Global Resurgence of Democracy*, Baltimore, MD: The Johns Hopkins University Press, pp. 39–52.

Schutz, A. (1999) 'Creating local "public spaces" in schools: Insights from Hannah Arendt and Maxine Greene,' *Curriculum Inquiry*, 29: 77–98.

Schumpeter, J. A. (1975) *Capitalism, Socialism, and Democracy*, New York, NY: Harper Torchbooks.

Scott, J. C. (1972) 'Erosion of patron-client bonds and social change in rural Southeast Asia,' *Journal of Asian Studies*, 32: 5–37.

—— (1985) *Weapons of the Weak: Everyday Forms of Peasant Resistance*, New Haven, CT: Yale University Press.

—— (1990) *Domination and the Arts of Resistance: Hidden Transcripts*, New Haven, CT: Yale University Press.

Scott, J. C., and B. J. Kerkvliet. (1977) 'How traditional rural patrons lose legitimacy: A theory with special reference to Southeast Asia,' in S. Schmidt, L. Guasti, C. H. Lande, and J. C. Scott (eds.) *Friends, Followers, and Factions*, Berkeley, CA: University of California Press, pp. 439–58.

Seidman, S. (ed.) (1989) *Jurgen Habermas on Society and Politics: A Reader*, Boston, MA: Beacon Press.

Sen, A. (1999a) *Development as Freedom*, Toronto: Random House of Canada Ltd.

—— (1999b) 'Human rights and economic achievements,' in J. R. Bauer, and D. A. Bell (eds.) *The East Asian Challenge for Human Rights*, New York, NY: Cambridge University Press, pp. 88–99.

Sennett, R. (1970) *The Uses of Disorder: Personal Identity and City Life*, New York, NY: Knopf.

—— (1978) *The Fall of Public Man*, New York, NY: Vintage Books.

Shaw, W. (2005) 'Survey finds Cambodian youth losing hope,' *The Cambodia Daily* (1 January): 3.

Shawcross, W. (1979) *Sideshow: Kissinger, Nixon and the Destruction of Cambodia*, New York, NY: Simon and Schuster.

—— (1994) *Cambodia's New Deal*, Washington, DC: Carnegie Endowment for International Peace.

—— (2002) 'Cambodia and the perils of humanitarian intervention,' *Dissent*, (Spring): 47–53.

Simon, D. (2002) 'Neo-liberalism, structural adjustment and poverty reduction strategies,' in V. Desai, and R. B. Potter (eds.) *The Companion to Development Studies*, London: Arnold, pp. 86–92.

Slater, D. (1989) *Territory and State Power in Latin America: The Peruvian Case*, New York, NY: St Martin's Press.

Slocomb, M. (2004) 'Commune elections in Cambodia: 1981 foundations and 2002 Reformations,' *Modern Asian Studies*, 38: 447–67.

Slyomovics, S. (1995) ' "Hassiba Ben Bouali, if you could see our Algeria": Women and public space in Algeria,' *Middle East Report*, 192: 8–13.

Smith, G. (1997) 'The chainsaw billionaires,' *Earth Island Journal*, 12: 28.

Smyth, M. (2001) 'Introduction,' in M. Smyth, and G. Robinson (eds.) *Researching Violently Divided Societies: Ethical and Methodological Issues*, New York, NY: United Nations University Press, pp. 1–11.

Sneddon, C. (2007) 'Nature's materiality and the circuitous paths of accumulation: Dispossession of freshwater fisheries in Cambodia,' *Antipode*, 39: 167–93.

Sodhy, P. (2004) 'Modernization and Cambodia,' *Journal of Third World Studies*, 21: 153–74.

Soja, E. W. (1989) *Postmodern Geographies: The Reassertion of Space in Critical Social Theory*, New York, NY: Verso.

Sorkin, M. (1992) 'Introduction: Variations on a theme park,' in M. Sorkin (ed.) *Variations on a Theme Park: The New American City*, New York, NY: Hill and Wang, pp. xi–xv.

Soros, G. (1998) *The Crisis of Global Capitalism: Open Society Endangered*, New York, NY: Public Affairs.

Springer, S. (2008) 'The nonillusory effects of neoliberalization: Linking geographies of poverty, inequality, and violence,' *Geoforum*, 39: 1520–25.

St. John, R. B. (1995) 'The political economy of the Royal Government of Cambodia,' *Contemporary Southeast Asia*, 17: 265–81.

—— (1997) 'End of the beginning: Economic reform in Cambodia, Laos, and Vietnam,' *Contemporary Southeast Asia*, 19: 172–89.

Staeheli, L. A., and V. A. Lawson. (1994) 'A discussion of "Women in the Field": The politics of feminist fieldwork,' *The Professional Geographer*, 46: 96–102.

Staeheli, L. A., and A. Thompson. (1997) 'Citizenship, community, and struggles for public space,' *Professional Geographer*, 49: 28–38.

Stanko, E. A., and R. M. Lee. (2003) 'Introduction: Methodological reflections,' in R. M. Lee, and E. A. Stanko (eds.) *Researching Violence: Essays on Methodology and Measurement*, New York, NY: Routledge, pp. 1–11.

Steinberger, P. (1999) 'Public and private,' *Political Studies*, 47: 292–313.

Stepan, A. (1988) 'Rethinking Military Politics: Brazil and the Southern Cone,' Princeton, NJ: Princeton University Press.

—— (1993) 'On the tasks of a democratic opposition,' in L. Diamond, and M. F.

Plattner (eds.) *The Global Resurgence of Democracy*, Baltimore, MD: The Johns Hopkins University Press, pp. 61–69.

Stöhr, W. B. (1981) 'Development from below: The bottom-up and periphery-inward development paradigm,' in W. B. Stöhr, and D. R. F. Taylor (eds.) *Development from Above or Below? The Dialectics of Regional Planning in Developing Countries*, New York, NY: John Wiley and Sons Ltd., pp. 39–72.

Stöhr, W. B., and D. R. F. Taylor. (eds.) (1981) *Development from Above or Below? The Dialectics of Regional Planning in Developing Countries*, New York, NY: John Wiley and Sons Ltd.

Stormann, W. F. (2000) 'The death of the Olmstedian vision of public space,' *Journal of Leisure Research*, 31: 166–70.

Sullivan, M. (2005) 'The parliamentary election in Cambodia, July 2003,' *Electoral Studies*, 24: 129–36.

Suntharalingam, N. (1997) 'The Cambodia settlement agreements,' in M. W. Doyle, I. Johnstone, and R. C. Orr (eds.) *Keeping the Peace: Multidimensional UN Operations in Cambodia and El Salvador*, New York, NY: Cambridge University Press, pp. 82–106.

Takei, M. (1998) 'Collective memory as the key to national and ethnic identity: The case of Cambodia,' *Nationalism and Ethnic Politics*, 4: 59–78.

Talbott, K. (1998) 'Logging in Cambodia: Politics and plunder,' in F. Z. Brown, and D. G. Timberman (eds.) *Cambodia and the International Community: The Quest for Peace, Development, and Democracy*, New York, NY: Asia Society, pp. 149–68.

Talentino, A. K. (2003) 'Evaluating success and failure: conflict prevention in Cambodia and Bosnia,' in D. Carment, and A. Schnabel (eds.) *Conflict Prevention: Path to Peace or Grand Illusion?* New York, NY: United Nations University Press, pp. 70–87.

Tambiah, S. J. (1977) 'The galactic polity: The structure of traditional kingdoms in Southeast Asia,' *Annals of the New York Academy of Sciences*, 293: 69–97.

Tan, S. (2002) 'Is public space suited to co-operative inquiry?,' *Innovation*, 15: 23–31.

Tatsuo, I. (1999) 'Liberal democracy and Asian Orientalism,' in J. R. Bauer, and D. A. Bell (eds.) *The East Asian Challenge for Human Rights*, New York, NY: Cambridge University Press, pp. 27–59.

Taylor, D. R. F. (1992) 'Development from within and survival in rural Africa: A synthesis of theory and practice,' in D. R. F. Taylor, and F. Mackenzie (eds.) *Development from Within: Survival in Rural Africa*, New York, NY: Routledge, pp. 214–58.

Taylor, D. R. F., and F. Mackenzie (eds.) (1992) *Development from Within: Survival in Rural Africa*, New York, NY: Routledge.

Taylor, M. (1991) *The Fanatics: A Behavioural Approach to Political Violence*, London: Brassey's.

Thayer, N. (1998) 'The resurrected: The Khmer Rouge haven't disappeared, they're in power,' *Far Eastern Economic Review* (April 16), np.

Thet Sambath. (2004) 'Police remove beggars from Siem Reap streets,' *The Cambodia Daily* (20 September): 12.

Thet Sambath, and W. Shaw. (2005) 'Poipet violence raises concerns about future evictions,' *The Cambodia Daily* (24 March): 17.

Thion, S. (1993) *Watching Cambodia: Ten Paths to Enter the Cambodian Tangle*, Bangkok: White Lotus Co., Ltd.

Thittara and Shay (2009) 'Group 78 evicted,' *Phnom Penh Post* (17 July). Available HTTP: <http://www.phnompenhpost.com> (accessed 4 November 2009).

Thomas, M. (2001) 'Public spaces/public disgraces: Crowds and the state in contemporary Vietnam,' *Sojourn*, 16: 306–30.

Tilly, C. (2003) *The Politics of Collective Violence*, New York, NY: Cambridge University Press.

Tin Maung Maung Than. (2004) 'Cambodia: Strongman, terrible man, invisible man, and politics of power sharing,' *Southeast Asian Affairs*: 73–86.

Tith, N. (1998) 'The challenge of sustainable economic growth and development in Cambodia,' in F. Z. Brown, and D. G. Timberman (eds.) *Cambodia and the International Community: The Quest for Peace, Development, and Democracy*, New York, NY: Asia Society, pp. 101–26.

Tombes, J. (1994) 'Cambodia lessons for UN peacekeepers,' *American Enterprise*, 5: 46–58.

Tyner, J. (2002) 'Narrating interracial relations and the negotiation of public spaces,' *Environment & Planning D: Society & Space*, 20: 441–59.

Um, K. (1990) 'Cambodia in 1989: Still talking but no settlement,' *Asian Survey*, 30: 96–104.

—— (1994) 'Cambodia in 1993: Year Zero plus one,' *Asian Survey*, 34: 72–81.

Un, K. (2006) 'State, society and democratic consolidation: the case of Cambodia,' *Pacific Affairs*, 79: 225–45.

Un, K., and J. Ledgerwood. (2002) 'Cambodia in 2001: Toward democratic consolidation?,' *Asian Survey*, 42: 100–106.

—— (2003) 'Cambodia in 2002: Decentralization and its effects on party politics,' *Asian Survey*, 43: 113–19.

UNDP. (2002) *Human development report: Deepening democracy in a fragmented world*, New York, NY: Oxford University Press.

Ungar, M. (2002) 'State violence and LGBT rights,' in K. Worcester, S. A. Bermanzohn, and M. Ungar (eds.) *Violence and Politics: Globalization's Paradox*. New York, NY: Routledge, pp. 48–66.

Ungar, M., S. A. Bermanzohn, and K. Worcester. (2002) 'Introduction: Violence and politics,' in K. Worcester, S. A. Bermanzohn, and M. Ungar (eds.) *Violence and Politics: Globalization's Paradox*, New York, NY: Routledge, pp. 1–12.

U.S. Department of State. (2000) *Cambodia: 2000 Country Report on Human Rights Practices*, Report (23 February). Available HTTP: <http://www.state.gov/g/drl/rls/hrrpt/2000/eap/681.htm> (4 November 2009).

—— (2001) *Cambodia: 2001 Country Report on Human Rights Practices*, Report (4 March). Available HTTP: <http://www.state.gov/g/drl/rls/hrrpt/2001/eap/8283.htm> (4 November 2009).

Uvin, P. (2003) 'Global dreams and local anger: from structural to acute violence in a globalizing world,' in M. A. Tetreault, R. A. Denemark, K. P. Thomas, and K. Burch (eds.) *Rethinking Global Political Economy: Emerging Issues, Unfolding Odysseys*, New York, NY: Routledge, pp. 147–61.

Valentine, G. (1993) '(Hetero)sexing space: Lesbian perceptions of everyday spaces,' *Environment and Planning D: Society and Space*, 11: 395–413.

—— (1996) 'Children should be seen and not heard: The production and transgression of adults' public space,' *Urban Geography*, 17: 205–20.

—— (1997) ' "Oh yes I can." "Oh no you can't": Children and parents' understandings of kids' competence to negotiate public space safely,' *Antipode*, 29: 65–89.

—— (2001) *Social Geographies: Spaces and Society*, Toronto: Prentice Hall.

van der Kroef, J. M. (1991) 'Cambodia in 1990: The elusive peace,' *Asian Survey*, 31: 94–102.

Vanderschueren, F. (1996) 'From violence to justice and security in cities,' *Environment and Urbanization*, 8: 93–112.

Vashee, B. (1995) 'Democracy and development in the 1990s,' in J. Hippler (ed.) *The Democratization of Disempowerment: The Problem of Democracy in the Third World*, London: Pluto Press, pp. 1–31.

Vatikiotis, M. R. J. (1996) *Political Change in Southeast Asia: Trimming the Banyan Tree*, New York, NY: Routledge.

Verkoren, W. (2005) 'Bringing it all together: a case study of Cambodia,' in G. Junne, and W. Verkoren (eds.) *Postconflict Development: Meeting New Challenges*, London: Lynne Rienner, pp. 289–306.

Villa, D. R. (2001) 'Theatricality in the public realm of Hanna Arendt,' in M. Henaff, and T. B. Strong (eds.) *Public Space and Democracy*, Minneapolis, MN: University of Minnesota Press, pp. 144–71.

Vickery, M. (1986) *Kampuchea: Politics, Economics and Society*, Boulder, CO: Lynne Rienner Publishers, Inc.

—— (1995) ' "Whither Cambodia? Beyond the Election", and "Cambodia: The Legacy and Lessons of UNTAC",' Book reviews, *Journal of Southeast Asian Studies*, 26: 439–44.

Vong Sokheng. (2003a) 'Police crackdown on opposition activists condemned,' *Phnom Penh Post* (12–25 September). Available HTTP: <http://www.phnompenhpost.com> (accessed 4 November 2009).

—— (2003b) 'Radsady killing raises political tensions,' *Phnom Penh Post* (28 February – 13 March). Available HTTP: <http://www.phnompenhpost.com> (accessed 4 November 2009).

—— (2005) 'Stop land theft, warns Hun Sen: PM sees danger of farmers' revolt,' *Phnom Penh Post* (16 December). Available HTTP: <http://www.phnompenhpost.com> (accessed 4 November 2009).

Vong Sokheng, and L. Cochrane. (2004) 'Gov't halts land clearing after grenade attack,' *Phnom Penh Post* (19 November – 2 December): 4.

Vong Sokheng, and C. McDermid. (2005) 'Rainsy thunders against "fascist" state,' *Phnom Penh Post* (30 December). Available HTTP: <http://www.phnompenhpost.com> (accessed 4 November 2009).

Vong Sokheng, and R. Wood. (2004) 'Jumbo cabinet ends stalemate,' *Phnom Penh Post* (2–15 July): 1–2.

Wacquant, L. (2001) 'The penalisation of poverty and the rise of neo-liberalism,' *European Journal on Criminal Policy and Research*, 9: 401–12.

Wade, R. (2004) 'Is globalization reducing poverty and inequality?' *World Development* 32: 567–89

Warner, M. (2002) *Publics and Counterpublics*, New York, NY: Zone Books.

Wasson, E., and Pin Sisovann. (2005) 'PM defends toll, land grabbing on Route 4,' *The Cambodia Daily* (22 March): 12.

Wayden, P. (2000) 'Parliamentary elections in Cambodia 1998,' *Electoral Studies*, 19: 615–46.

Weber, S. (2001) 'Replacing the body: An approach to the question of digital democracy,' in M. Henaff, and T. B. Strong (eds.) *Public Space and Democracy*, Minneapolis, MN: University of Minnesota Press, pp. 172–88.

Weinberger, E. (2003) 'Government steps up committee for privatization,' *Phnom*

Penh Post (6–19 June). Available HTTP: <http://www.phnompenhpost.com> (accessed 4 November 2009).

Weintraub, J. (1995) 'Varieties and vicissitudes of public space,' in P. Kasinitz (ed.) *Metropolis: Center and Symbol of Our Times*, London: Macmillan Press Ltd, pp. 280–319.

Weitz, E. D. (2003) *A Century of Genocide: Utopias of Race and Nation*, Princeton, NJ: Princeton University Press.

Welsh, B. (2002) 'Globalization, weak states, and the death toll in East Asia,' in K. Worcester, S. A. Bermanzohn, and M. Ungar (eds.) *Violence and Politics: Globalization's Paradox*, New York, NY: Routledge, pp. 67–89.

Wesley, M. (1995) 'The Cambodian waltz: The Khmer Rouge and United Nations Intervention,' *Terrorism and Political Violence*, 7: 60–81.

Wiarda, H. J. (2003) *Civil Society: The American Model and Third World Development*, Boulder, CO: Westview Press.

Will, G. (1993) 'The elections in Cambodia: Taking stock of a UN mission,' *Aussenpolitik*, 44: 393–402.

Williamson, J. (1990) 'What Washington means by policy reform,' in J. Williamson (ed.) *Latin American Adjustment: How Much Has Happened?* Washington, DC: Institute for International Economics, pp. 7–20.

Willner, A. R. (1972) 'Public protests in Indonesia,' in I. K. Feierabend, R. L. Feierabend, and T. R. Gurr (eds.) *Anger, Violence, and Politics: Theories and Research*, Englewood Cliffs, NJ: Prentice-Hall Inc., pp. 352–58.

Wood, L. J. (2004) 'Breaking the Bank and taking to the streets: How protesters target Neoliberalism,' *Journal of World Systems Research*, 10: 68–89.

Woods, L. S. (1997) 'The myth of Cambodia's recovery,' *Contemporary Southeast Asia*, 20: 279–97.

World Bank. (2004) *Steering a Steady Course – Special Focus: Strengthening the Investment Climate in East Asia*, East Asia Update (November), Washington, DC, World Bank. Available HTTP: <http://www.worldbank.org/reference/> (4 November 2009).

—— (2006) *Cambodia: Halving Poverty by 2015? Poverty Assessment 2006*, Phnom Penh: World Bank. Available HTTP: <http://www.worldbank.org/kh> (accessed 4 November 2009).

—— (2008) *Cambodia: Projects and Programs*, (23 January). Available HTTP: <http://www.worldbank.org/kh> (accessed 4 November 2009).

Yacobi, H. (2007) 'The NGOization of space: dilemmas of social change, planning policy, and the Israeli public sphere,' *Environment and Planning D: Society and Space*, 25: 745–58.

Yeoh, B. S. A., and S. Huang. (1998) 'Negotiating public space: Strategies and styles of migrant female domestic workers in Singapore,' *Urban Studies*, 35: 583–602.

Yeung, H. W. (1998) 'Capital, state and space: contesting the borderless world,' *Transactions of the Institute of British Geographers*, 23: 291–309.

Young, I. M. (2000) *Inclusion and Democracy*, New York, NY: Oxford University Press, Inc.

Yun Samean. (2004a) 'Gas protests scheduled,' *The Cambodia Daily* (14 September): 13.

—— (2004b) 'Mob kills 2 men who tried to rob woman,' *The Cambodia Daily* (23 November): 15.

—— (2004c) 'New police tactics seen as threat to protesters,' *The Cambodia Daily* (21 September): 1, 13.

—— (2004d) 'Police use force to prevent demonstration,' *The Cambodia Daily* (20 September): 1, 13.

—— (2004e) 'Sam Rainsy returns, unperturbed by threats,' *The Cambodia Daily* (29 October): 12.

—— (2005a) 'Hun Sen: NGOs, media abusing privileges,' *The Cambodia Daily* (9 February): 16.

—— (2005b) 'Life in isolation', *The Cambodia Daily* (22 January): 2.

—— (2007) 'This is war, Hun Sen tells land-grabbers,' *The Cambodia Daily* (6 March): 1–2.

Yun Samean, and Neou Vannarin. (2009) 'No signs of crisis in Cambodia, Hun Sen says,' *The Cambodia Daily: Weekly Review* (21–27 March): 3.

Yun Samean, and L. Reynolds. (2004) 'Grenade blast injures 8 land demonstrators,' *The Cambodia Daily* (15 November): 1, 12.

Yun Samean, and Pin Sisovann. (2005) 'Sam Rainsy's immunity stripped,' *The Cambodia Daily* (4 February): 1–2.

Yun Samean, and Wency Leung. (2005a) 'Fear within the ranks,' *The Cambodia Daily* (22 January): 4.

—— (2005b) 'Remembering a fallen leader,' *The Cambodia Daily* (22 January): 13.

Yun Samean, and W. Kvasager. (2006) 'King pardons Sam Rainsy at PM's request,' *The Cambodia Daily* (6 February): 1, 2.

Zasloff, J. J. (2002) 'Emerging stability in Cambodia,' *Asian Affairs, an American Review*, 28: 187–200.

Zepp, R. (2004) 'Political Transition in Cambodia, 1991–99: Power, Elitism and Democracy,' Book review, *Journal of Cambodian Studies*, 1: 59–62.

Zimmerman, E. (1983) *Political Violence, Crises and Revolutions: Theories and Research*, Boston, MA: Schenkman Publishing Co.

Zukin, S. (1995) *The Cultures of Cities*, Cambridge, MA: Blackwell Publishers Inc.

Index

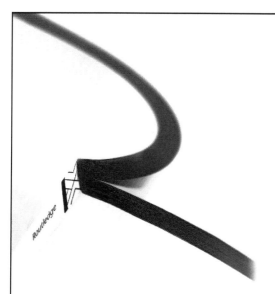

ROUTLEDGE
Revivals

Are there some elusive titles you've been searching for but thought you'd never be able to find?

Well this may be the end of your quest. We now offer a fantastic opportunity to discover past brilliance and purchase previously out of print and unavailable titles by some of the greatest academic scholars of the last 120 years.

Routledge Revivals is an exciting new programme whereby key titles from the distinguished and extensive backlists of the many acclaimed imprints associated with Routledge are re-issued.

The programme draws upon the backlists of Kegan Paul, Trench & Trubner, Routledge & Kegan Paul, Methuen, Allen & Unwin and Routledge itself.

Routledge Revivals spans the whole of the Humanities and Social Sciences, and includes works by scholars such as Emile Durkheim, Max Weber, Simone Weil and Martin Buber.

FOR MORE INFORMATION

Please email us at **reference@routledge.com** or visit:
www.routledge.com/books/series/Routledge_Revivals

www.routledge.com